From Metternich
to Hitler

Essays by

H. W. V. TEMPERLEY

C. K. WEBSTER

IRENE COLLINS

ASA BRIGGS

D. C. SOMERVELL

H. MOYSE-BARTLETT

RICHARD W. VAN ALSTYNE

R. A. HUMPHREYS

ERICH EYCK

BERNADOTTE E. SCHMITT

A. J. RYDER

W. N. MEDLICOTT

From Metternich to Hitler

Aspects of British and Foreign History

1814—1939

HISTORICAL ASSOCIATION ESSAYS
EDITED BY

W. N. Medlicott

GREENWOOD PRESS, PUBLISHERS
WESTPORT, CONNECTICUT

Library of Congress Cataloging in Publication Data

Main entry under title:

From Metternich to Hitler.

    Reprint. Originally published: London : Routledge
and Kegan Paul, 1963.
    Bibliography: p.
    Includes index.
    1. History, Modern--19th century--Addresses, essays,
lectures. 2. History, Modern--20th century--Addresses,
essays, lectures. I. Medlicott, W. N. (William Norton),
1900-   . II. Historical Association (Great Britain)
D358.F76 1983   909.8   83-10688
ISBN 0-313-24085-X (lib. bdg.)

© Historical Association 1963

Reprinted with the permisson of Routledge & Kegan Paul, Ltd., London

Reprinted in 1983 by Greenwood Press
A division of Congressional Information Service
88 Post Road West, Westport, Connecticut 06881

Printed in the United States of America

10 9 8 7 6 5 4 3 2 1

Contents

Introduction

In his introduction to the volume of essays on *Social Life in Early England*, published in 1960, Professor Barraclough explained that the collection was selected from the long list of individual pamphlets issued by the Historical Association over the previous fifty years, and that it was hoped to put out further volumes if the first were as successful as there was every reason to hope. This has indeed proved to be the case, and I have gladly undertaken the editorship of the present volume, which covers the field of nineteenth and twentieth-century history.

The essays collected here reflect the continued interest of students and teachers and the reading public generally in three aspects of recent history: the Victorian age in England, the German problem, and the rôle of the Americas in world affairs. Thus they have a rather wide range and in some cases illustrate in an interesting way the changing moods and outlook of our own lifetime. The first, which was also the first to be written, was printed in 1923 and reveals the cautious optimism about the League of Nations experiment of our two greatest authorities on the 1815 peace settlement. The last, which was also the last to be written, explains in part the failure of their hopes. In between we have nine essays by British and American historians which can all perhaps be said to have been written to satisfy the uneasy or nostalgic interest of our generation in the historical background of present-day problems. All are based on a wide and scholarly grasp of their subjects, and usually embody important historical revisions. Professor Briggs and Mrs. Irene Collins illustrate the continuing interest in the Victorians which led to Mr. D. C. Somervell's delightful essay on the Victorian Age in 1937, the centenary of the queen's accession; the essay on Bismarck by Dr. Erich Eyck is a statement, which first appeared on the fiftieth anniversary of Bismarck's death in 1948, of the more critical assessment of Bismarck's achievement which Eyck had inaugurated among European scholars. It is followed by Dr. Bernadotte Schmitt's reflexions on the problem of 1914 war origins, written some thirty years after the first appearance of his own authoritative study of that subject. Mr. Moyse-Bartlett provides a link with the overseas world by discussing a neglected subject of major importance—the nineteenth-century revolution in shipping. In turn the two essays by Professor Humphreys and Professor Van Alstyne reflect an awareness of transatlantic history which it took the Second World War really to establish in this country.

For the most part my task as editor has been a light one, for the authors of all these essays except the first have themselves been able to make any revision necessary to bring them up to date. Owing to the deaths of H. W. V. Temperley and Sir Charles Webster I have made such revision as was necessary to their contribution, which remains however substantially as it was when they read it as two papers to the International Congress of Historical Sciences at Brussels in 1923. At that moment they had completed the substance of their research on the Metternich era and the post-1815 settlement and both had vivid first-hand recollections of the peace conference of 1919. The comparisons which they make are still interesting and it is difficult to think of a more succinct summary. The same is true of Professor Humphreys' essay on Latin American history, which must have opened up the subject for the first time to many members of the Historical Association when it appeared in 1943. The text has not been substantially altered, but the author has supplemented it with a very full range of notes. The only essay which called for thorough revision was my own on the origins of the Second World War. This was originally published in 1940, and has now been entirely rewritten in the light of recent knowledge.

It is a great pleasure to me to be able to bring together within the covers of this small volume the work of a number of distinguished and established scholars and to add to these some able contributions by younger historians. The long series of Historical Association pamphlets, which have been appearing continuously since before 1914, has included many on recent history of a somewhat ephemeral character. The essays in the present collection are those of more permanent interest and value which seemed worthy of reissue, and it is hoped that their appearance will be welcomed in this more durable form.

W. N. MEDLICOTT

H. W. V. TEMPERLEY and C. K. WEBSTER

The Congress of Vienna 1814–15 and the Conference of Paris 1919[1]

---

1. A COMPARISON OF THEIR ORGANIZATION AND RESULTS

by C. K. WEBSTER

THE comparative method is exceedingly valuable to historians and above all to those concerned with the difficult task of surveying impartially contemporary history. Whatever view is held of the value of history as a means of understanding the present, it at least enables us to obtain a standpoint and a perspective which can be obtained in no other way. In this strange and momentous age when new and unknown sources of energy are moulding a new world before our eyes so violently that civilization is threatened with destruction, it may be that we can find in the past some fixed points on which to take our bearings. If we are careful to remember continually the immense changes between our own day and that of a hundred years ago, and to avoid the hypnotic influence which the history of great events, in which their own country has shared, exercises on some individuals, we can, I think, obtain some help in the solution of the immense problems with which we are today confronted.

In endeavouring therefore to appreciate the methods and results

[1] These two essays are based on papers read to the Fifth International Historical Congress at Brussels in March 1923.

of the present settlement our thoughts turn naturally to that of 1814–15, which centred on the Congress of Vienna and the two treaties with France that preceded and followed it. Even Gentz, while he had little good to say of the Congress itself, hoped that it might at least serve as a preliminary to another reunion with a more complete programme. However puny its problems appear in comparison with those of today, it is the only settlement in any way to be compared in scope and importance with that recently made. The boundaries of almost every state in Europe were remodelled; a barrier was erected against and reparations were inflicted upon the dominant military power; colonial territories were redistributed; new international organizations were erected, and even schemes for the perpetuation of world peace considered. The world was not yet one, but Europe had become one in the course of the Napoleonic wars, and she was the centre of the world. A vast complex of problems was, therefore, settled at the conference table in the years 1814–15.

So clear was this fact that, during the 1914–18 War, diplomatists turned naturally to the Congress of Vienna as a precedent for that greater Congress which must sometime be summoned. Strangely enough it had not yet found its historian, or rather that historian had not yet completed his work—and he died, indeed, leaving it still incomplete. Yet when men talked of a 'Congress', it was the model of Vienna which was in their minds. The diplomacy of Talleyrand, whose success had been much exaggerated, and the dissensions of the victorious Alliance were regarded as a special warning, and perhaps influenced events to some degree. The actual organization of the Congress of Vienna had, however, been little studied, and the exact process by which it had arrived at its decisions was largely unknown. I endeavoured to write some account of these for the British government in 1918, but I cannot say that much effect was produced by them. In some details the organization of the British delegation may have been affected—in the personnel of its domestics and the character of its waste-paper baskets, for example—but as will be seen, the Conference of Paris developed in such a manner as to make plans for its organization of little importance. Nor in the discussions at Paris did the precedent often appear. For M. Clemenceau history began in 1871, Mr. Lloyd George knew little history, and President Wilson, in one of the early meetings of the Council of Ten, expressed a hope that no reference would be made to the doings of the statesmen of Vienna.[1]

[1] 'The present enterprise was very different from that undertaken at Vienna a century ago, and he [the President] hoped that even by reference no odour of Vienna would again be brought into their proceedings.' Minutes of 28 January 1919.

It was true, indeed, that the Conference of Paris met in very different circumstances. In 1814 peace was made with the enemy before the Congress began. His boundaries were defined, his colonial territories were appropriated or restored, and he was released from all penal indemnities. Moreover, since a new government had been received by the French people, which had been suggested by the Allied Powers, and, in turn, accepted their principles of political life, France was immediately received into the community of nations and invited to take part in the coming Congress. The four great powers whose armies had entered France did not, indeed, intend to give to their defeated enemy an equal voice in the settlement of Central Europe. By a secret clause France was bound to accept the decisions which they intended to impose on the other states. But France in all else was placed on an equality with the Alliance which had overcome her, and was able to send her most distinguished diplomatist to defend her interests in a capital which her troops had twice occupied.

Not so was it in 1919. Though the Allied and Associated Powers through President Wilson insisted on a change in the form of government of the principal enemy state in a far more definite fashion than their predecessors in 1814, and though this condition had been accepted by the enemy people far more completely than the Bourbons were ever accepted in France, this fact was not allowed to influence the negotiations in the slightest degree. The feelings of the Allied peoples no less than those of their leaders prevented any intercourse with the principal enemy until the moment came to impose peace upon him, and his case was left without an advocate until the Allies had completed their discussions. Moreover, while in 1814 the Allies had already made peace with their enemy before they proceeded to dispose of his empire, the meeting at Paris was summoned to make a treaty of peace. It was, therefore, a 'Conference' amongst the Allies, though presumably it became a 'Congress' when the enemy was admitted to the barbed-wire enclosures at Versailles.

Both in 1814 and 1918 victory came in a swifter and more triumphant manner than had been anticipated until shortly before the final overthrow of the enemy, and on neither occasion was there ready any common agreement as to the plan of procedure to be followed. In each case the men who were in power in the final stages of the war met to arrange the treaty of peace and most of them had been far too occupied with the co-ordination and direction of the immense efforts, which had made victory possible, to devote much attention to the methods by which the foundations of the new world were to be laid.

When Castlereagh went on the continent in 1814, he intended to get his Allies to draw up a complete scheme of European recon-

3

struction before an armistice was made, and the subsidies were to be used as a means to force them to come to an agreement. But he found that he risked division in the face of a still unbeaten enemy, if he persisted in this course, and had therefore reluctantly to agree to postpone the settlement. Only one or two points of especial interest to his own country was he able to secure before the armistice was signed.

By 1919 the Allies had an agreed programme. It had been made at a time when victory had still seemed far distant, but President Wilson had established it in the public opinion of the world. He had disdained all bargains with his Associates, and of their secret agreements among themselves he was officially ignorant. Yet since many of the Fourteen Points were drawn up in a very general manner, the exact methods by which they were to be realized in practice were left vague. In France, the United States, and England there had, indeed, been in existence since 1917 organizations to study and prepare the terms of peace. They included amongst them some of the most distinguished *savants* of these countries—and notably historians. But they did not meet to prepare a joint scheme for the approval of their governments. There was no organization corresponding to the other Inter-Allied Committees which by the end of 1919 were controlling so much of the world's energies. Nor in the two months that elapsed between the Armistice and the Conference was agreement brought closer. In 1814 it was hoped that by discussions in London the Four Powers would arrive at decisions ready to be presented to the Congress. These hopes were vain, and such discussions as ensued only revealed the differences whose solution was postponed once more to a preliminary meeting at Vienna. Any similar hopes that may have existed in 1919 were also doomed to disappointment. A French scheme for the organization of the Conference was indeed presented to the Allies at the end of November, but it was not accepted and never discussed. Both Mr. Lloyd George and President Wilson had much to do in the interval. Those preparing for the peace therefore still went on working without control or direction until the moment at last came for them to transfer the results of their labours to Paris.

In 1814 it was generally supposed that the Congress would be over in two months; it lasted nine months, prolonged, it is true, by the return of Napoleon. None of those who went to it had imagined or prepared for so long a duration or such grave difficulties as arose. In 1919 there was on the whole the same expectation of quick and easy results both among the statesmen and amongst their peoples. When at the end of March no results were forthcoming there was everywhere an indignant protest, and in 1919, as in 1814, the value of results of the Congress were seriously affected by the imperative necessity of terminating an impossible situation, which had not been foreseen.

The difficulties in 1919 were indeed much greater owing to the greater number of problems to be settled and their far greater complexity. The Congress of Vienna had to confine its attention almost entirely to Europe. The colonial problems were settled at the first Peace of Paris at the dictation of Britain, whose navy was supreme in every sea. Both Germany and Italy were at that time, it is true, split up into a number of small states whose frontiers had been submerged in the Napoleonic Empire and had now to be redrawn. But a frontier could be drawn far more easily in 1814 than in 1919. There was no such complicated network of economic connexions to be adjusted. Strategic advantages, numbers of population, and dynastic claims had alone to be considered. The wishes of the inhabitants were not thought to be of importance and, indeed, in many cases could not be ascertained. A transference of 'souls' by the thousand from one government to another could therefore be easily arranged. In 1919 four empires had been destroyed and many new states had arisen from their débris, while the British Empire changed its character in the course of the war. Some of the new states had only existed in a long distant past, others were to be increased to so great an extent as to make them practically new creations. In all there was a mixture of nationalities who were now self-conscious and who had been promised consideration. The economic connexions of the nineteenth century had followed the imperial power and these had now to be violently disrupted. Communications both by land and river had also to be adjusted, and as Europe could not live without the rest of the world, access to the sea assumed a new significance. The same factors made it necessary for the conference to include Asia, Africa, and the Pacific under its purview. Even the cables that united the continents were affected. The world has even yet scarcely realized the immensity of the problems that were brought to Paris, and scant justice has been done to the immense amount of disinterested, scientific, and laborious service that was brought to their solution. The advice of the experts was indeed often rejected or distorted by the politicians, but it could not be ignored; and much of the greatest permanent value was thus secured. Where men of learning and science were allowed by their governments to co-operate together without interference even the thorniest problems were successfully solved.

It must also be remembered that the Conference of Paris had a vast quantity of executive work thrust upon it which finds no parallel at Vienna. A large portion of its energy was devoted not to the permanent settlement, but to the solution of temporary but urgent problems which pressed continually upon its attention. During the Congress of Vienna, until the return of Napoleon, Europe remained quiescent and could at least feed itself. In 1919 it appeared at one time to be on the verge of dissolution, and over it hung the unknown menace of Bolshevism. The Allied statesmen and delegates had constantly to intervene in every part of Europe, and to Paris came an unending succession of appeals for help and sustenance. The map of Europe was changing while the Conference deliberated. New armies appeared as old ones disintegrated. Starvation and disease assumed the most formidable dimensions. These difficulties were perhaps too tardily dealt with, but they were solved in some degree by statesmen who were at the same time confronted with the overwhelming difficulties of the permanent settlement.

Such a vast complex of problems necessitated naturally the services of a much larger number of people than were needed at Vienna. There the work was concentrated in the hands of a comparatively few persons. The British delegation to Vienna was composed of fourteen persons. At Paris it had two hundred and as many clerks and secretaries. Moreover, a large number of others paid visits to bring it information, advice, or exhortation. Of other delegations I have no precise information, since the official lists are not complete, but they were on a similar scale. In all of them there were doubtless a large number whose presence was more ornamental than useful. But the great majority had plenty of work to do, once the Conference machinery had really begun to function, while many had more duties thrust upon them than could be successfully accomplished. Only a small minority were professional diplomatists. The Congress of Vienna was notable for the great advance which was made in dispensing with diplomatic formalities. At Paris these formalities ceased to exist. The Conference was for the most part managed by men who knew scarcely anything of the niceties of diplomatic intercourse. The French delegates, indeed, sometimes attempted to recall a forgotten art, but without success; and though they controlled to a certain extent the operation and agenda of the Conference, yet in the end it was Sir Maurice Hankey and not M. Dutasta who was its Gentz. Even the full-powers of the delegates were only examined as an afterthought. Moreover, for the first time in Europe for two hundred years French was not the main language of intercourse. Three of the great powers used English normally, and though French was the more natural mode of expression for the majority of the states interested, many of the Anglo-Saxon delegates were unable or unwilling to learn it. This duality of language had undoubtedly a great effect on the discussions. In spite of the amazing powers of translation displayed by the official interpreter and his assistants, it cannot be doubted that barriers were often erected between minds that might otherwise have understood one another. Fortunately for France her chief negotiators could use English almost as well as French. Yet when their interests were most clearly at stake and their emotions most deeply stirred it was noticed that they reverted instinctively to their native language.

Neither at Vienna nor at Paris were the statesmen free to discuss frankly the problems of the settlement. Alliances are built up on bargaining, and during the great wars each power is concerned to obtain as soon as possible a guarantee from its Allies of what it considers to be its own special interests. Its success depends upon the urgency of its needs, the value of its assistance, and the diplomatic skill of its statesmen. Both in the Napoleonic and in the 1914–18 War this process was carried out on a large scale, and thus when victory came there was in each case a number of treaties, agreements, and understandings which could not be ignored. Thus in 1812 Bernadotte obtained the promise of Norway, in 1813 Prussia and Austria the guarantee of their reconstruction before they joined Russia. It was round Poland, however, that the intricate diplomacy of that year mainly centred. By two treaties of Reichenbach and Toeplitz Russia had promised partition. Alexander was determined, however, to make the Poles once more a nation under his own rule. To win Prussia's consent he was prepared to offer the whole of Saxony. Austria had perforce to follow suit, and Metternich gave in 1814 a verbal promise to the same effect to Hardenberg. Castlereagh, who was deeply concerned at the expansion of Russian power and influence in Europe, attempted to liquidate this situation when he arrived on the continent. But he failed, and when the statesmen met at Vienna their discussions were dominated by the interpretation of these secret agreements. Russia claimed that the overwhelming success of the Allies had freed her from all obligations to them as regards Poland. Castlereagh and Metternich attempted to hold her to her bond as they interpreted it. Hardenberg pleaded the secret understanding with regard to Saxony. The result was a diplomatic explosion which nearly resulted in another European war. Only the introduction of the defeated enemy into an equal position to her conquerors restored the peace of Europe.

The greater size and scope of the 1914–18 War meant an extension of the secret treaties to every quarter of the globe. The co-operation of Italy, Japan, and Rumania was obtained by offering better terms than the enemy could give. Britain, Russia, and France, moreover, attempted to ensure their special interests before the terms of peace were discussed, by promises of mutual support. The real claim of the United States to inaugurate a new diplomacy lies in the fact that she refused all such bargaining. Her constitution, indeed, made it almost impossible, she had no territory to obtain, and her economic interests were easily safeguarded without recourse to such a defence. The Bolshevik Revolution which revealed most of these agreements diverted the Alliance to the more successful device of open programmes. The position of the secret treaties was thus jeopardized; they remained, however, a continual embarrassment to those who had made them, since in some cases they were obviously mutually contradictory, while only a subtle casuistry could bring them into harmony with the Fourteen Points which the Allies had openly accepted. Nevertheless at Paris the statesmen of the Alliance still professed themselves to be bound by them. The collapse of Russia had removed some of the most formidable difficulties, but Italy and Japan still claimed their bond from their Allies, and France and Britain had obligations towards one another. For President Wilson, it is true, these treaties were non-existent, but at no time did he get his associates to take that point of view. That could only have been done while the issue hung in the balance, and at that time President Wilson was officially ignorant of the treaties. The Paris Conference no less than the Congress of Vienna both demonstrated the elementary fact that the issues of Congresses are largely decided before the powers meet at the council table, unless they are prepared to fight once more. In both cases there was compromise and adjustment, but in both cases the main lines of the territorial settlement had been settled before the last shot had been fired.

At Paris there was, however, an addition of overwhelming importance for which there is no equivalent at Vienna. The Allied sovereigns and statesmen in 1813–14 had issued proclamations and appeals to the European peoples, but they were mainly concerned with the expulsion of foreign invaders and made no reference to the future. There had been vague hints of a united Germany and Poland, but no more, and the references to an Italian Italy had been made only by subordinates and been disavowed. For the rest merely such vague phrases as the 're-establishment of public law' and the 'security of the world against fresh attacks' had been used. But in 1919 there was in existence a public document which summed up in explicit if general language the professed aims of the ultimate victors. This document and the additional interpretations which followed it, had played an immense part in the winning of the final victory, and since it was the only agreed programme in existence it became in law the basis of the Peace Conference. By it were bound not only the vanquished but the victors. In November, 1918, it appeared as if the public opinion of Europe had rallied unitedly round this declaration in such a way as to make it unassailable. Not only the statesmen but

8

their peoples were pledged to support it. In the final adjustments, which were made in the Armistice negotiations, some modifications were, indeed, introduced. Britain refused to accept the 'Freedom of the Seas'. She did not refuse all discussion of the subject as she had done in 1813, when the question of 'Maritime Rights' was expressly excluded at her peremptory demand from the negotiations; in 1918 she merely insisted that she should go to the Conference free to place her own interpretation on the phrase. It was the subsequent plans for a League of Nations that relegated the President's point to a complete obscurity. The reparations point was redefined but accepted; Italy's refusal to accept Point Nine as to her own frontiers was unfortunately not revealed at the time, a blunder in diplomatic technique which was to have serious consequences. Substantially, therefore, the Fourteen Points remained intact as the basis of the Paris Conference, and President Wilson had thus accomplished in theory more than Castlereagh had succeeded in doing in 1814. He had done this by new diplomatic methods. His discussions had been with peoples rather than with the statesmen of his Associates, and it was confidently expected both in America and in Europe, that he would continue throughout the Congress this method which had produced such striking results.

At Vienna secret diplomacy was natural and inevitable. Its efficacy was never questioned, and no other method was possible. The main work of the Vienna Congress was done in a small secret committee of the five powers or by informal conversations between the principal statesmen. The committee kept *procès-verbaux*, which, however, merely recorded decisions, with occasional notes of argument and protest added as appendices. Even this procedure was only adopted at a late stage, and of the momentous discussions of the first three months few records exist except the reports of the principal statesmen to their sovereigns or the accounts given in their diaries and personal correspondence.

But at Paris there was a real issue between secret and open diplomacy. The press of the world had made unexampled preparation for the Conference, and from the first they demanded 'full publicity to the Peace Negotiations'. The question was hotly debated in the early sessions of the Council of Ten, but the main issue went practically by default. President Wilson made no sustained effort to induce his colleagues to concede anything like real publicity of proceedings. In spite, therefore, of the protests of the Anglo-American press, a system of almost complete secrecy was instituted. The President accepted the position that the Conference was a Cabinet and not a Parliament. The *communiqués* were bald and no record of dissensions was allowed to appear. This was in a sense the most important decision of the Paris Conference; there is much to be said for it, but it re-established the old diplomacy. Henceforward public opinion was at the mercy of the sensational journalist and the controlled press; for it could not follow accurately the course of events. Secret diplomacy, however, is never complete. There are always leakages both accidental and calculated. Both Metternich and Talleyrand revealed to the journalists secret discussions when they wished to rally public opinion to their side, and even the Czar made an effort to get support in British newspapers. But news moved too slowly in 1814 for much to be accomplished by those methods. In 1919, however, an indiscretion could find its way round the world in a few hours, and during the first part of the Paris Conference, at any rate, leakages were frequent and provoked the most violent recriminations amongst the plenipotentiaries. The public was thus told a succession of half-truths which confused it still more. This was one of the reasons for the institution of the Council of Four, and the intensified secrecy of that body was perhaps preferable to the diplomatic manœuvres of the earlier period.

One last unpalatable truth must be referred to in this connexion. At the Congress of Vienna there was instituted one of the most scientific systems of espionage ever established, and the secrets of almost all the delegations were disclosed by it. Yet it cannot be said that much progress in this form of international morality had been made by 1919. During the war the Allied governments developed a wonderful system for discovering the secrets of the enemy. No cipher was so elaborate but that it would not be eventually solved. I suppose it was only inevitable that they should apply the same methods to one another, but there is something exceedingly repugnant in the thought that governments whose dead soldiers lay side by side in France and Flanders should be spying upon one another's confidential communications.

This similarity in diplomatic atmosphere is reflected in the machinery which was set up at Vienna and Paris. The actual problem of Paris was of course infinitely bigger and more complicated, but it was solved substantially in the same way. The Paris Conference was in effect a committee of the great powers just as that at Vienna. There were, however, important differences of development. At Vienna the statesmen were confronted with a situation without precedent. They had summoned to a Congress all the powers, great and small, who had taken part in the 1914–18 War, not to make a treaty of peace, but to redistribute and reorganize the territory that had been freed from the domination of Napoleon. But the four great powers, whose united efforts had at last overthrown their great enemy, had no intention of allowing the other powers a voice in the settlement. They had intended to be able to present to them at Vienna an agreed scheme, and the Congress was only summoned as the most convenient method of making their wishes known and arranging the necessary legal formalities. But in spite of all their efforts agreement was still far off when the twice postponed Congress at last met. The statesmen of the Four Powers were thus faced with a situation, when they met at Vienna in the early days of September, 1814, such as they had never contemplated, and the problem of how to keep to themselves legally all the power of the Congress defied all their efforts at solution. The Prussians alone submitted a systematic scheme of procedure which had been drawn up by Humboldt. It contained an elaborate agenda of all the topics which her statesmen wished to be brought before the Congress, and it proposed to announce bluntly that the great powers intended to dispose of all the available territory before the other powers were consulted. Castlereagh, while in substance he desired the same procedure, was shocked at the Prussian's lack of susceptibility. He suggested that instead of an ultimatum the consent of the other powers might be obtained by those methods which great powers know so well how to apply. These manœuvres were, however, dramatically frustrated by Talleyrand. By championing the equality of states he was able to overthrow all the schemes of the Four.

Nevertheless, his victory was in reality a very barren one. For, denied a legal basis, the Four Powers simply continued their private discussions and allowed the Congress to look after itself. During the years 1813–14, the Allied Powers had become accustomed to sit round a table as the Supreme War Council of the Alliance. They had even on occasion kept a protocol and appointed a secretary. Now these conversations were resumed, and in them all the important affairs of the Congress were debated. It was only when the dissensions of the Four grew so bitter that war was threatened that Austria and Britain insisted on the admission of Talleyrand and the 'Four' became the 'Committee of Five', which was the real Congress of Vienna. More general questions such as the abolition of the slave trade or the navigation of international rivers were indeed discussed in a 'Committee of Eight'—the eight powers which had signed the Paris treaties. But in these discussions no exchanges of territory were involved. No meeting of all the powers, great and small, was ever summoned. Once Talleyrand had taken his place beside the Four, the small powers had no longer a champion.

In 1919 there was a situation in some ways extraordinarily similar to that of 1814, and it was solved in substance though not in form in very much the same way. When the statesmen of the great powers met at Paris on 12 January 1919, they also had no agreed plan of

procedure. M. Tardieu, like Humboldt in 1814, had ready an elaborate plan, the substance of which had been communicated to the
Allies in November, 1918. But as he points out in his book 'l'instinc-
tive répugnance des Anglo-Saxons pour les constructions syste-
matisées de l'esprit latin', prevented his plan from having any more
success than Humboldt's. There was, however, no Talleyrand to
embarrass the Great Powers of the Alliance, nor were these latter so
concerned in 1919 to find an exact legal basis for their procedure.
They continued, therefore, without much discussion the organization
which had served them so well during the war. The Council of Ten,
which kept in its hands the principal decisions during the earlier
stages of the Conference, was simply the Supreme War Council
under another name—a name indeed which was hard to find. But the
great powers were able to do what their predecessors in 1814 found
impossible. They constituted a Plenary Conference of all the Powers,
Great and Small, which had taken part in the war, and promised it
the final ratification of their decisions. It met seven times, and it had
the satisfaction of approving the Treaty of Peace with Germany the
day before the Germans themselves received it.

While, however, in 1814 the early Committee was completely informal, and was only made into a formal organization when it had
become the Committee of Five, in 1919 the reverse process took
place. The Committee of Ten had an elaborate procedure—so elaborate indeed that its secrets could not be preserved and the principal
statesmen felt that they had an audience rather than a secretariat. The
'Council of Four', which was really a 'Council of Three', was, therefore, instituted, and it is this body which corresponds to the 'Council
of Five' at the Congress of Vienna. In these two bodies the main
work of the Conference was concluded and all other subsidiary
organizations were controlled by them. There is in 1919, however,
one great and fundamental exception to this rule. For the Covenant
of the League of Nations was not only drawn up by a Committee
appointed by the Plenary Conference, but this Committee reported
direct to it without interference by any other body, and was substantially affected by its discussions. For this purpose alone was the
Paris Conference really a reunion of the Allied nations.[1]

The number of subsidiary Committees and Commissions set up at
Paris was of course very much greater than at Vienna. They may be
variously estimated, but M. Tardieu has reckoned them as fifty-eight.
Ten sufficed at Vienna, and their records have now practically all
been published. Most of the Committees at Paris kept very full

---

[1] The procedure by which the International Labour Organization was made
was the same.

minutes of their discussions, and the total volume is a little formidable.

I have but little time to compare the results of these two meetings. Perhaps the time has not yet come when much can be said. But I may point out that statesmen are invariably behind the main currents of their age. They can only apply to the problems of their times ideas that have already become outworn. Looking back on the Congress of Vienna, we can see that the statesmen went to the eighteenth century for their main principle of action, and endeavoured to apply the Balance of Power to an entirely changed condition of things. Only Alexander made any effort to recognize the force of Nationality which we now know was to be the strongest force in the nineteenth century. In the same way the statesmen at Paris recognized to the full the great dictum of the nineteenth century, but they attempted to ignore the elementary economic truths which will control our destinies in the twentieth century—with results which we can already appreciate. But at Vienna the statesmen had to deal with a world which was still only sluggishly alive. The great mass of mankind was only partially conscious of its interest in politics, and autocrats and oligarchies still ruled the world. In the decisions of the Paris Conference there are, therefore, clearly apparent new elements which have no analogues in the older age. The statesmen of Vienna scarcely hoped to avoid war for long, yet they claimed also to make a final settlement of the problems of the world. But in Paris, by the Covenant of the League of Nations, the interdependence of all nations was recognized, and for the first time in history an organization was set up which admitted that society is dynamic and not static. We may hope, therefore, that the good points of the various treaties may be preserved and the bad ones altered. The world now knows at least that unless war can be avoided civilization will be completely overthrown. But I must leave the development of these problems to my learned colleague who follows me (*v. No.* 2).

2. ATTEMPTS AT INTERNATIONAL GOVERNMENT IN EUROPE: 1814–25; 1919–22

by H. W. V. TEMPERLEY

I. THE OBLIGATIONS OF 1814–15

Professor Webster, in the companion paper to this, has explained and compared the organization of the Congress of Vienna (1814–15) and the Congress (or Conference) of Paris (1919). My aim is to contrast and compare certain other aspects of these two great international meetings for regulating the peace of the world. Each aimed at determining the settlement of the world not only by an ordinary treaty instrument for the moment, but by setting up machinery for regulating future international disputes at any rate for a time. The experience of the past is often a guide to the tendencies of the present, and it has been shown recently in an interesting manner by a great authority that, in fact, the methods employed at Vienna in 1814–15 were not wholly different from those in use in Paris in 1919.[1] While this statement is, as regards methods, unquestionably true, it has not been asserted that the ends and the objects are the same. And it is with this aspect, therefore, that the present paper is concerned.

The bonds uniting the Allies in 1814–15 were first the Treaty of Chaumont (9 March[2] 1814), an alliance between Russia, Austria, and Great Britain, with the object of overturning Napoleon and of assuring a peace for Europe on the definite territorial basis and comprising a France somewhat exceeding the boundaries of 1792 (i.e., excluding the Rhine frontier and Belgium, but assuring Alsace and Lorraine to France). After the return of Napoleon from Elba these arrangements were deliberately stiffened. France had now to accept the frontiers of 1790, and had to pay a war indemnity, but, apart from this, the territorial settlement was not materially altered. It was strengthened in the first Treaty of Paris (30 May 1814) and in the Treaty of Vienna (9 June 1815), and finally all these arrangements were comprised in the Second Treaty of Paris of 20 November 1815. One important article (vi) was added by the British Minister, Castlereagh, arranging for the periodic reunion of the states concerned for discussing the situation in Europe. The British interpretation of these arrangements was that England bound herself, along with the other powers, to repel by force of arms any attempts to violate the territorial arrangements of Vienna for a period extending to twenty years, and to exclude, also by force of arms, the Napoleonic dynasty from France. In the case of internal revolution in France, England agreed to meet and discuss the situation with her Allies, but bound herself to no other action. Later on both Russia, under Alexander, and Austria, under Metternich, tried to contend that England had bound herself to action as well as to discussion under this last head. But this interpretation was always denied by Castlereagh, and apparently with justice.

What contributed, however, to misunderstanding was that the Czar Alexander, on 26 September 1815, issued an extraordinary document known as 'The Holy Alliance', which was signed ultimately by almost all the sovereigns of Europe. This vague and

---

[1] v. Sir Ernest Satow, 'Peace-making Old and New', *Cambridge Historical Journal*, October, 1923, pp. 23-60.

[2] A fictitious date, 1 March, is given on the document.

sentimental paper was conceived in very general terms and expressed the desire of the kings of Europe to have relations with their subjects and with one another on the basis of Christian charity, peace, and love. It was a document addressed to and signed by sovereigns alone. This fact was very important because, as England was a parliamentary state, the Prince Regent (afterwards George IV) was unable to sign it, as the royal assent required a counter-signature. He did send a private letter to Alexander, expressing his sympathy with the pious and sublime sentiments contained in the Holy Alliance document, but Castlereagh always denied (and with justice) that England was bound in any way by this instrument. The 'Holy Alliance', in the form assumed in 1815, was merely a vague and romantic piece of sentiment. Alexander certainly attached importance to it. But neither Metternich nor Castlereagh considered that it had any juridical value, or bound anyone to anything more than a vague belief in charity and love and Christianity, for these are subjects not usually defined with precision in diplomatic documents.

II. THE OBLIGATIONS OF 1919

Such, in bald outline, were the obligations of 1814–15. What were those of 1919? They included first a guaranteed territorial settlement, which rearranged the map of Europe, lopping different areas from Germany, e.g. part of Silesia, Eupen and Malmedy, and Alsace and Lorraine, and (in conjunction with the treaties of St. Germain, Trianon, Neuilly, etc.) breaking up Austria-Hungary and diminishing the territory of Bulgaria, etc. Besides this there were very important provisions enforcing disarmament upon enemy powers (Germany, Austria, Hungary, and Bulgaria), abolishing conscription, imposing a long period voluntary service army upon these states, destroying their fortifications and munitions, and permanently limiting their armed forces and armaments. This provision was very important, for it arranged for a permanent supervision and control, first by the Entente over the enemy powers, then by the League, and cannot be ultimately successful unless the Entente Powers also limit their armaments. As a result, at the present time the army of Belgium is larger than the army of Germany. That situation clearly cannot go on for ever, and the best hope of peace would be in voluntary limitations of armaments by Entente Powers, which would cause the Enemy Powers to acquiesce in the compulsory limitations of their armaments. No similar attempt was made in 1815, and a half-hearted proposal put forward in 1816 by Alexander was a failure.[1] Here, then,

[1] *Contemporary Review*, November 1922, article by Professor Webster on 'Disarmament Proposals in 1816'.

is a provision of the peace treaties of 1919 which implies permanent and perpetual negotiation between the entente and enemy powers.

The territorial settlements, as guaranteed in 1919–20, are first secured by the disarmament clauses above indicated, and next by the written guarantee of the Signatory Powers to defend them by force of arms. They are guaranteed also by the Covenant of the League of Nations (Article X), and can only be abrogated by consent of the Committee of the League.

For, in addition also to the Treaty of Versailles (1919) and its subsidiary instruments, there was signed a document known as 'The Covenant of the League of Nations'.

III. CONTRAST BETWEEN THE COVENANT AND THE 'HOLY ALLIANCE'

The Covenant has often been compared to the 'Holy Alliance', but the comparison is, in fact, very misleading. Like that document it owed its existence largely to the efforts of a single man. The Holy Alliance was due to the Russian Czar Alexander; the Covenant to the American President Wilson. Everyone must be struck by the superficial resemblances. In each case the ruler of a state, with more autocratic powers than those exercised by any other plenipotentiary, carried his project. Neither could, in fact, be resisted. For Alexander possessed supreme military power in 1815, Wilson very great military and supreme financial power in 1919. Both men possessed also a temperament that was imaginative and sincere. Alexander, indeed, had territorial designs on Poland and other places, while Wilson disclaimed any such desire. But, while Wilson had no selfish ends to serve, it would be wrong to deny that Alexander had considerable loftiness of thought and of purpose.

Perhaps the most striking difference in the two ages and the two men is that Alexander addressed himself wholly to the heads of governments (i.e., to actual ruling monarchs), though he included the Swiss President and later approached the United States. Wilson based his scheme wholly on the consent and support of peoples of all countries, and showed resolute opposition to despotic rulers in all lands. This distinction was very far-reaching, for even in 1815 despotic monarchy was a vanishing factor in modern history, whereas constitutional or democratic government seemed to be an increasing one in 1919. The Czar was as certainly trying to dam the waters, as the President was seeking to open the sluice-gates, of a new age.

Thus, though both documents abounded in generous and not always dissimilar sentiments, their practical effect was very different. As has already been indicated, the Holy Alliance was not binding upon the signatories of Vienna, and (even more important) the treaty could be, and was, worked independently of it. The Covenant is not only binding on the signatories of Versailles, but it cannot be separated from the working of the treaties connected therewith. Hence, the Holy Alliance was neither a workable instrument, nor a permanent bond, while the Covenant appears to be both. For good or for evil, the Covenant is part of the treaties, and of the public law of Europe. And not only is it part of the texture and tissue of the treaties, but it has an existence quite independent of them. For it provided for, and has now set up, three important international and permanent agencies, the Secretariat of the League, the International Labour Secretariat and Conference, and the Permanent Court of International Justice. These agencies include neutral as well as Entente states, and in some cases also enemy ones, and provide for arrangements independent of the treaties. They cannot wither or be destroyed except by the general consent of the family of nations. They are not dependent on the goodwill of the powers victorious in the war, but on all the powers, both enemy and neutral, who are members of the League as a whole, or of the other international organs which are its outgrowths.

IV. THE BREAKDOWN OF CONGRESSIONAL GOVERNMENT, 1815–25

Immediately after a war the powers which have been victorious in it naturally remain closely associated, for they are afraid of their old enemies and wish to enforce their execution of the peace. After 1815 the Allied armies remained in occupation of parts of France until 1818. At that time France was considered to have fulfilled her obligations, and her territory was accordingly evacuated. During the years 1919–21 the Allies effectively disarmed Germany, Austria, Hungary, and Bulgaria. Hence in the respective years 1818 and 1921, the Allies realized that any immediate danger from their old enemies was over. The fear of danger and the necessity of co-operation being thus removed, the fact that different members of the Alliance had totally different views in certain important matters was at once revealed, and these differences tended to increase as time went on.

(a) *The Neo-Holy Alliance. Aix-la-Chapelle* (1818), *Troppau and Laybach* (1820–1)

Let us take first the differences revealed in 1818. They were really fundamental. Castlereagh was the minister of England, that is of a state based on a revolution (that of 1688), and was responsible for his actions and utterances to a parliament. Alexander was a Czar, at first a liberal, but by 1820 at any rate an enemy of revolutions, always and

17

everywhere, and responsible to no one. Hence Castlereagh held to a narrow interpretation of the obligations of 1814–15 in the sense that it had been explained to Parliament; Alexander sought to commit him to action against internal revolution in all countries. In 1818, at the Congress of Aix-la-Chapelle, and still more during 1820–1 at the Congresses of Troppau and Laybach, Alexander sought to commit his Allies to action against revolution. In 1820 democratic constitutions were proclaimed at Madrid and at Naples, and in 1821 in Piedmont. In each case the King was forced to accept one, and in each case the Czar Alexander worked to suppress the constitution by the force of the Alliance and by means of an international army. Ultimately an Austrian army invaded Naples, suppressed the constitutions and restored the absolute Kings in Naples and Piedmont (1821). Austria was supported by the moral force of the Alliance as a whole. Alexander invoked the 'Holy Alliance' as the bond by which the Allies were united, and proclaimed the common object of the Alliance to be the suppression of internal or democratic revolution in all countries. This was clearly a very dangerous and almost unlimited extension of the obligations of 1814–15. It was met by Castlereagh with a resolute and determined denial of all such interpretations (5 May 1820).[1] This was not published at the time. Then, at the Congress of Troppau, the Allies (Austria, Russia, and Prussia) announced in a circular (November 1820) that they would only recognize governments not produced by revolution. Castlereagh openly dissented from this view, and in a published despatch of 20 January 1821, he laid the foundations of future British foreign policy. He denied that England was bound by the doctrines of the 'Holy Alliance' at all. Alexander, he said, was now proposing a new bond entailing fresh obligations. I venture to suggest that we might call this new bond (in which Austria and Prussia, and to some extent, France, concurred) the 'Neo-Holy Alliance'. Castlereagh analysed their clauses and declared that they were advancing novel pretensions, and claiming, in fact, to be a sovereign international tribunal with the right of interfering in the internal affairs of all countries whose institutions or political experiments displeased them. He declined definitely to commit England to any such courses, and declared the claims of the 'Neo-Holy Alliance' to be an unauthorized and improper extension of the guarantees of 1814–15. At the Congresses of Troppau and Laybach the British representatives were restricted to the part of spectators, and refused to concur in their decisions. Castlereagh maintained this attitude of separation from the Neo-Holy Alliance until his death (12 August 1822).

[1] Full text is given in *Cambridge History of British Foreign Policy*, Vol. II, App. 1

(b) *Verona* (1822) *and Canning's destruction of the Congress System,* 1823-5

Immediately after his death another Congress met at Verona, which was ultimately concerned with Spain and its democratic constitution. Castlereagh had been succeeded by Canning, and that vigorous minister refused to be a party to the policy of the Neo-Holy Alliance, which presented a collective note to Spain and withdrew their diplomatic representatives from Madrid, in order to force Spain to abandon her constitution. This action broke up the Congress of Verona, and openly separated the action of England from that of the Neo-Holy Alliance. The breach, indicated by Castlereagh, had become wide and definite. But, though England had broken up this Congress of European powers, she might conceivably have attended another one in accordance with the policy of periodic reunions laid down in the Second Treaty of Paris, 20 November 1815. But, under the influence of Canning, she refused to do anything of the sort. In December 1823, Spain, now again a despotic monarchy, invited the various powers to attend a congress to discuss the question of the Spanish American colonies, then in revolt. Canning, on 31 January 1824, formally refused to attend. England, he said, would take her own course regardless of other European powers. On 31 December 1824, Canning took measures which amounted to the recognition of the independence of three Spanish American colonies —Mexico, Buenos Ayres, and Colombia—thus recognizing three states which owed their existence to revolution. In thus acting separately, he announced to the world that the period of congressional or collective government was over. For he had recognized these colonies without consulting or regarding the views of the Neo-Holy Alliance, which declined to recognize states based on revolution. Other steps were taken at the same time which rendered the breach irreparable. In December 1824, when a congress was proposed on the affairs of Turkey, Canning, in effect, declined to attend. Alexander held a Congress without him at which Russian, Austrian, French, and Prussian representatives were present. But in May 1825, this Congress broke up in confusion because Austria would not support Russia in the use of force against Turkey. Now Alexander had been the chief promoter of Congresses, and his wrath at the failure of this one was great. His death at the end of 1825 made way for Nicholas, who looked at things with the eye of Russia rather than of the Neo-Holy Alliance. Congresses ceased to meet, and with their cessation there came a definite end to the system of world-organization and congressional government which had prevailed, in one form or another, between 1815 and 1825.

Thus the policy of a collective international control or of world-organization had been definitely ended by 1825. The views of the three chief European personages were as follows: Metternich had refused in 1815 to recognize the Holy Alliance, but he consented in 1820 to the Neo-Holy Alliance, an extension of the treaty obligations of 1814–15, which permitted interference in the internal affairs of independent states. Alexander, on the other hand, held that the old Holy Alliance was the chief bond uniting the powers and, in virtue of it, he approved Metternich's armed repression of the constitutional movement in Naples and Piedmont (1821), and the French armed suppression of the Spanish constitution in 1823. In 1825, the Czar summoned a conference at St. Petersburg to sanction the use of armed force by Russia against Turkey. When he found that Metternich refused to do this, he broke off the conference in anger, stating that the doctrine of the 'European Police' and of a superior controlling international force was dead.

Canning had followed Castlereagh in denouncing the sanctioning by a European congress of armed interference with the rights or independence of states. He declined to commit his country either to abstract principles or enforcement of general principles by collective menace or by arms. In the case of the Spanish American colonies, he definitely refused to attend a congress (1) because the United States were not to be invited, (2) because such congress would decide on matters of commerce and navigation which hardly affected any of the Powers concerned and were peculiarly of the domain of England, and (3) because England's vital interests were concerned.

Canning's attitude was much strengthened by that of France which, as a parliamentary state, could not sanction all the pretensions of the Neo-Holy Alliance, and was in reality opposed to them.

Thus in 1825 England had openly separated herself from the European Concert. France was endeavouring to do so, Prussia followed Austria, and Austria had quarrelled with Russia as to the meaning of their obligations. It is clear that a stage of fundamental difference of view had been reached in which collective action or control or even agreement had become a mockery. And this was the dismal end of this great international experiment. Its fall was welcomed by liberals in all countries, and particularly by the smaller states. For states such as Saxony, Würtemburg, Sweden, and the Netherlands had suffered much from collective intimidation, and the Neo-Holy Alliance policy, in its later form, had been simply a monarchical trades union, in which the despotic ruler of one country sent his own troops to aid his brother despot in another country if he wished to oppress his subjects. To that conception, smaller states were generally, parliamentary states and liberal opinions invariably, opposed. The world was not then governed on a uniform system either of despotism or of constitutionalism, and hence the split was inevitable.

V. ATTEMPTS AT INTERNATIONAL ORGANIZATION, 1919–22

It is clear that the congressional system of Vienna ultimately broke down because some of its members tried to commit others to obligations which were not implied in the original treaty bonds. The Neo-Holy Alliance tried to support a despotic system throughout Europe, and to maintain it by the use of armed force or of intimidation. Very different is the idea of the Covenant. States which are admitted as members of the League can have any system of government, kingly or republican, provided it is constitutional and free. They must also show a reasonable limitation of armaments and evidence of having observed international obligations. The League itself is, in no sense, a super-state, as is proved by the fact that it cannot conclude treaties. It is a method, rather than an institution, for advising, conferring, recommending, and discussing. Of its ten members of the Council, four only represent the great powers (England, France, Japan, and Italy); the other six members are elected from the smaller powers. In the Assembly all states members of the League are represented, and freedom of discussion on international objects is open to all. The Secretariats of both League and International Labour Organization are genuinely international in composition, and include a number of American representatives as well as nearly all the nationalities who are members of the League. Hence it is impossible, or at least improbable, that in the preparation of business the interests of one or other power will be unduly favoured or unduly neglected. This is a great contrast to the period 1815–25. During the congressional period the international conferences were overpowered by the influence of Austria, whose Secretariat in effect controlled and prepared the subjects for discussion.

The same strictly international character was preserved in the International Court of Justice, of which the eleven judges included an Englishman, a Frenchman, a Japanese, an Italian, an American, a Switzer, two Latin-Americans, a Spaniard, a Dane, and a Dutchman. Assistant judges included a Serb-Croat-Slovene, a Rumanian, a Chinaman, and a Norwegian.

Further, the Covenant imposes, in the last resort, but one obligation on its members. Each of its members agrees to allow a stated period of peaceful discussion to elapse before going to war with any other member.[1] This is the only compelling obligation, for the League disclaims the use of force. It is true that Article X guarantees the maintenance of the territorial integrity of all member states. But this integrity is to be enforced, if necessary, by the economic blockade. The Council recommends and advises as to the application of that measure, but each individual state remains the judge as to whether it will, for its own part, apply the measure. State sovereignty is therefore fully preserved and methods of cowing and intimidating smaller states, such as were pursued by the Neo-Holy Alliance, cannot be employed by the Council of the League, and are not easily applied by a single great power or by groups of great powers.

In one direction, indeed, it has already been made clear that the smaller powers possess and can exercise a moral coercion over the great. The admission of a state as a new member of the League is, in the last resort, decided by a majority of two-thirds of the Assembly. This provision means that, in practice, the small states can have their way independent of the great. In one case, at least, they have actually exercised this right. The discussions on the admission of Albania to the League (December 1920) prove that it was opposed by one great power (Great Britain) and possibly also by another. None the less it was decided, and Great Britain finally withdrew her opposition and then new circumstances arose. The great powers had been obliged to admit Albania as a member of the League. But they could themselves refuse to recognize her as an independent state, and they did so. None the less the debates at the Council and in the Assembly exercised considerable moral pressure and, within a year from her admission to the League, Albania had been recognized by every great power, including Great Britain, which had started by opposing her admission. While, therefore, even in this matter, the individual sovereignty of each state has been preserved, the moral coercion exercised by the League is evident. It is in this way that the League may acquire new powers and control in the future.

During the period 1920–2 the activities of the League extended along the lines laid down in the treaties. In striking contrast with the developments after 1815, these activities extended with the general consent of the signatories of the treaties, and with the general admission that they were legitimate or authorized interpretations or extensions of actual treaty obligations. Such activities included, among many others, the settlement of the status and international frontiers

[1] The obligation is 'not to go to war suddenly and secretly'. It has been claimed that this *may* mean that a state can occupy part of the territory of another state temporarily, as Mussolini did at Corfu. It means, at any rate, that a state undertakes not permanently to deprive a member-state of territory, unless with consent of the League.

of Albania, the division as to the partition of Upper Silesia, and the economic reconstruction and control of Austria. In each case the views of opposed or dissentient states were reconciled, and in each case the League is admitted to have acted within the limits assigned to it by general consent.

VI. CONCLUSION

The result of this survey and comparison seems clear. The Congressional System (1815–25) failed because it attempted too much. It sought to develop and extend obligations beyond their legitimate sphere, it was too exclusively despotic in political principle, and it considered too little the rights and sovereignty of smaller states. As the system developed, its members, France and England, hung back or openly dissented from its measures.

It ended by becoming a mere union of three great despotic and military powers (Austria, Russia, and Prussia), basing its doctrines and its decisions on force. The League started by numbering thirty-eight states and has, within four years, risen to include fifty-three. It includes all sorts of states—monarchical and republican, pacific and militaristic. Its activities and doctrines are based wholly on peace, on conference, persuasion, and discussion. It has already attained a facility in adjusting international points of view and in preparing business for international discussion such as no other similar organization has ever possessed. The limits of international obligation in 1815 were so indefinite and ambiguous as to cause alarm and compel caution in 1821, but these of 1919 were so much more reasonable and precise that any contemplated extension of them, though viewed as a subject for consideration, is regarded by no one as reason for suspicion and panic.

The moral seems to be that too much should not be attempted in the first instance, as was the case in 1815, and more notably in 1821. The Neo-Holy Alliance was a 'strait-waistcoat'; the League is elastic and flexible, and will expand with greater activities or contract with lesser ones. That is as it should be. For no one would wish the League to survive if it does not fit into the facts of the period and respect the beliefs of its members. It is not without significance that even in 1820, barely half a dozen years from its foundation, the system of congressional government was already seen to be an artificial union and in serious danger of collapse. There are in 1923 no such signs of dissolution in the international structure set up in 1919, and even if there were, its collapse would be slow.

For institutions which grow like the League can only perish by decay or by direct strangulation. Historical comparisons with the only other essay in international government of similar magnitude certainly suggest that the League has a good chance of survival. Perhaps even a historian may be allowed to express the enthusiastic hope that this may be the case.

IRENE COLLINS

Liberalism in Nineteenth-Century Europe

I

THE term 'liberal', meaning a type of political opinion, was new in the nineteenth century. The word itself was not new, but hitherto it had been used to describe a type of education, or to describe a man of generous inclinations—a liberal, open-handed fellow. The political term 'liberal' was coined in Spain and was first widely used with reference to the Spanish rebels of 1820. This was an unfortunate beginning for it, since the Spanish rebels were looked down upon by respectable people in Europe; and the term 'liberal' consequently came to be regarded as a term of abuse. It was used as such by the French royalists of the Restoration period, who referred to their opponents on the Left of the Chamber as 'liberal' in order to imply that they were a disreputable lot. In England the term was at first usually used in its French or in its Spanish form, and we hear from the 1820s scathing references to 'English *libéraux*' or 'English *liberales*'. It was not until the middle of the century that the term was really accepted in England as English and respectable; but once it had been accepted it got itself thoroughly well dug in, and from the 'sixties onwards it took on a very specialized meaning. 'Liberal' in England came to mean purely and simply a member of Mr. Gladstone's party.

On the continent of Europe the term never had such a specialized meaning, except perhaps in Belgium. In most other countries of Europe it was never applied solely to the members of one particular party. Indeed, it was often used to describe at one and the same time men who were vigorously opposing each other on political platforms. When Englishmen wanted to refer to a French liberal they usually chose M. Guizot, who seemed a fairly near approach to their own Mr. Gladstone; but the French not only gave the name liberal to Guizot and the members of his group, they gave it also to Thiers, who was the bitterest opponent of Guizot, and they gave it at the same time to Odilon Barrot, who led a political party in opposition to both Guizot and Thiers. In Italy the name liberal was given in the 1840s to writers who advocated a federation of Italian states under the presidency of the Pope, and to writers who urged that Italy should fall into step behind the King of Piedmont.

What was there in common between the motley group of students, merchants, and soldiers who made the liberal revolution in Spain in 1820, and an experienced French politician like Guizot? Or between the sophisticated liberal aristocrats of Naples who despised the brutal rule of King Ferdinand I, and the German professors and lawyers who sat in the Frankfurt Assembly in 1848 and tried to make a united Germany? That they had something in common was realized at least by the opponents of liberalism. Metternich knew a liberal when he met with one, whatever guise the man appeared under. To embrace all the variations of liberalism throughout the century a complicated definition would be required, yet liberals themselves, certainly up to 1860 or 1870, saw nothing complicated in their creed. Whatever twists and turns were demanded of them by circumstances, they held at heart a simple faith: a belief that progress, leading to final perfection, could be achieved by means of free institutions. The liberals of nineteenth-century Europe were not exclusively dreamers and theorists. Liberalism drew its staunchest supporters from business men, technicians, and men of the hard-working professions; competent men of sound common sense who applied themselves in a businesslike fashion to the tasks which came to hand. But in liberalism even in its most prosaic forms there was always an idealistic element. The inspiration behind liberalism was not a sense of duty, or a feeling for the inevitable, or a love of tidiness and efficiency, though all were present to some degree, but the vision of an ideal society. The vision was not strictly speaking a Utopia, an unattainable dream world: it was a vision which liberals believed could be translated into reality, and by a known method. Perfection was to be reached by means of free institutions.

Liberals in practice often betrayed their ideal and often behaved in a manner unworthy of men pursuing an ideal. The French liberals who had talked so much of an ideal society in the 1820s, when they got into power in the 1840s spent much of their time speculating in railway shares for their own financial profit and filling government offices with their own relatives and friends. This kind of behaviour made it easy for Karl Marx to condemn most liberals as insincere and to present their talk of an ideal society as a cloak for selfish ambition. More recently the liberals of the Frankfurt Assembly of 1848 have been singled out for especial condemnation by historians because, after all their talk of freedom, they displayed their greatest energy in an attempt to bring Posen and Bohemia into United Germany by force and against the wishes of the people living there. But it is possible to believe sincerely in an ideal and yet to fall short of that ideal in one's behaviour, and neither Karl Marx nor sceptical historians of a later date have put forward conclusive reasons for condemning liberals as hypocrites when they proclaimed that free institutions could and would result in progress; progress in all spheres, material and spiritual; progress leading to a perfect society to be enjoyed by all men, of all classes, creeds, and nations. When liberals lost sight of this vision, as many did in the closing years of the century, they lost the spirit with which liberals in former days had battled joyously against outnumbering enemies.

Liberals from time to time and from place to place differed as to what they meant by 'free institutions'. The young liberal advisers of Alexander I of Russia, with little hope of making headway against the diehard Russian aristocracy, were content that the Czar should begin with a reformed Council of State and leave the idea of a constitution to be considered in the far-distant future. Guizot in France in the 1840s thought that the Revolution of 1830 had established all the free institutions that Frenchmen could possibly require for their progress towards perfection. Cavour in Italy in the 1850s worked to establish a form of government very much like that to be found in England at the time of Sir Robert Peel, though he was prepared to envisage the lower classes playing more part in politics as their education advanced. Many liberals, particularly in the early years of the century, had only vague notions concerning the form which free institutions ought to take; hence the adoption, by both Spanish and Neapolitan liberals in 1820, of the abortive Spanish Constitution of 1812, a concoction produced from the many French constitutions of the revolutionary period and hardly applicable to the circumstances prevailing in southern Europe. None of the liberals believed that the free institutions which they advocated in themselves constituted a perfect state. They were merely the framework within which men would have the best opportunity to advance towards perfection. When Guizot in 1847 insisted that no further reform was needed in France he was not trying to say that France was already perfect, but merely that the essential framework had been established. He was no doubt over-sanguine in his hopes, but his opponents were wrong when they accused him of being completely blind to the suffering going on around him.

Often liberals had to concentrate on achieving some immediate object which they regarded as the first step on the road to freedom. Thus the liberals in Vienna in 1848 agitated for the dismissal of the chancellor Metternich; the Belgian liberals after 1815 worked for the separation of Belgium from the Dutch crown; the Italian and German liberals worked for national unity. But it must not be forgotten that their further aim was to set up free institutions. It was this higher aim which distinguished the nationalism of the German liberals of 1848 from the nationalism of Bismarck, who did not fulfil the aims of 1848, as he is sometimes credited with doing, so much as denature and destroy them. It was this higher aim, too, which distinguished the making of United Italy by Cavour from the making of United Germany by Bismarck. If Cavour's methods were sometimes regrettably like those of Bismarck, his final aim was fundamentally different; he worked for a freedom which Bismarck never understood.

After 1815, liberals in Europe tended to look to France for a shining example of freedom, and for support in their own struggles. After 1830 they ceased to do so. The result of the 1830 Revolution in France profoundly disappointed liberals elsewhere in Europe. The aim of the new French king, Louis-Philippe, seemed to be solely to kick down the revolutionary ladder by which he had risen, and to dissociate himself and France from revolutionary movements anywhere in Europe. In their disappointment, liberals elsewhere in Europe learnt in time to turn away from France and to look rather to their own efforts. Oddly enough, they learnt to do this from men whom we cannot count as belonging to the liberal cause. German liberals learnt from the works of Hegel to think that Germany was destined to play the leading role in Europe, and in 1848 we find them urging that Germany, not France, should give the shining example to Europe. Italian liberals learnt to stand on their own feet from Mazzini, the democrat. That Italy must help herself, and that each nation must fulfil its own destiny, was the most potent part of Mazzini's teaching; it was the message which caused Metternich to describe Mazzini as the most dangerous man in Europe. Only after 1848 did Italian liberals unlearn the lesson and turn again to France, under Louis Napoleon, for active help. Louis Napoleon restored some of France's prestige among European liberals by his two earliest exploits in foreign policy—his intervention in the Crimean War, which discredited Russian autocracy by revealing its military weakness, and his help to Cavour in driving the Austrians out of

Lombardy. His incentive in European politics was romantic rather than liberal, however, and at home he sapped the strength of liberalism by giving the French people more material benefits than they had ever received from the freer governments of earlier years.

It is nevertheless to France that we usually look for expositions of liberal theory. French liberals had some experience of government at their command; they were not silenced, except for brief intervals, by censorship laws; they did not have to concentrate their energies in a nationalistic movement; they were in a better position than most for theorizing. In the early years of the nineteenth century we find many French liberals urgently stressing the point that liberalism was a new creed. They could not deny that men in former times had worked for liberty, but they contended that the liberty which had been seen in ancient Greece and Rome, and even the liberty understood in the French Revolution, was entirely different from the liberty which would appear in the modern world. This anxiety to show that a break had been made with the past arose from an anxiety to deny all connexion with the excesses of the French Revolution. Most people in France and indeed in Europe dreaded a recurrence of the turmoil and bloodshed of the Revolution, and most liberals felt obliged to fight these memories of the Revolution as their worst enemies. When Benjamin Constant, in a speech before a learned society in Paris in 1819, condemned the liberty of the ancient world as subjecting the individual to the community, he was clearly thinking of the Jacobins, and his elaborate argument on this occasion was really in the same category as the impassioned claim which he made to the French voters in the next election: 'We do not want any revolutions!'

This denial of the past put French liberals in sharp contrast to English liberals, who liked to trace their descent in unbroken line as far back as Magna Carta. The English liberals' fondness for the past was to French liberals a sign that the English, successful though they were in the practice of parliamentary government, did not really understand the nature of liberty. What the Englishman wanted, said the French, was not liberty, but a collection of liberties; not freedom for everybody, but privileges for everybody. Yet the French owed a great deal to the past which some of them denied so vigorously; especially to the recent past. The real origin of their creed lay in the philosophy of the eighteenth century, known as the Enlightenment. From the Enlightenment, and especially from Rousseau, came the belief that man can on earth and by his own efforts achieve perfection; because man is born good, and given the right surroundings, he will grow in goodness. From the Enlightenment, too, came the belief that the right surroundings consist of free institutions. From the Enlightenment, the belief that the fight for a perfect state of happiness on earth must be waged, cannot be neglected, because it is the whole object of man's life on earth. Man has been born with intelligence and talents so that he can advance at least a few steps in the right direction and benefit others who come after him. All these older ideas were to be found at the heart of the so-called 'new' liberalism; but they had to be stated in a new form. For one thing, they had to be extricated from all talk of 'reason'. There was a popular assumption in the nineteenth century, wrong but no less powerful, that the 'reason' of the eighteenth century had been cold and hard and heartless, allowing no room for faith and feeling, and the early nineteenth century, which was an emotional age, would have nothing to do with it. The old idea of liberty had also to be dissociated from 'equality'. 'Liberty, equality, fraternity' had been the motto of 1789, but the Revolution had shown that talk of equality led to demands which lovers of liberty were not always ready to concede.

For restating the old beliefs in a new form, Europe was indebted to a group of French liberals called the *doctrinaires*. The group deserves to be better known by historians than it has been hitherto. The politicians of the group sat on the Left-centre of the French Chamber in the 'teens and 'twenties of the century; amongst them was the philosopher Royer-Collard, whose long dissertations upon the *juste milieu* taught liberals how to re-interpret the French Revolution. The chief publicists of the group were Guizot and Charles de Rémusat, and the members met socially in the salon of the Duchesse de Broglie. From their writings and speeches we can formulate a statement which might well have come from any liberal in Europe at any time later in the century. The individual can best achieve his own welfare through the welfare of all. No individual can know what is the welfare of all, so some political system must be devised which allows the voice of each individual to be heard. Essential features of such a political system are: a freely elected parliament to deliberate upon the laws; a ministry dependent on that parliament, to carry out the laws; a judicature entirely independent of other branches of government, to deal with offenders against the laws; freedom of speech, freedom of religion, freedom from arbitrary arrest, freedom for the individual to enter any trade or profession according to his ability, freedom for the individual to accumulate property and to possess it in safety. In this way the individual can find his fullest expression and will be able to grow in that essential goodness which leads to perfection.

An important difference between this conception of liberty and those of the eighteenth century lies in the origin which it attributes to individual freedom. Most eighteenth-century philosophers had favoured the idea that the individual possessed natural rights which were quite independent of the State and which the State was obliged to recognize. This idea, expressed in the American Bill of Rights of 1776 and the Declaration of the Rights of Man preceding the first French Constitution of 1791, had been a powerful weapon in the destruction of the personal privileges so well known to the ancient régime; but it had also contained the seeds of endless revolution. If freedom belongs to nature and not to the State, government institutions must be reduced to a minimum so that natural law can flourish: an anarchical idea which seemed to the liberals of the nineteenth century more conducive to chaos than to liberty. They favoured, rather, Rousseau's conception of civil liberty. The individual has no rights in nature; he merely has claims, which might in nature be thwarted by the claims of other individuals. These claims become rights only when they are recognized by society, and when the State guarantees to each individual the liberty which does not conflict with the liberty of others. The belief in natural rights was to have some lingerings in the nineteenth century. From it came the belief, prevalent in the many disturbances of the 1820s, that the mere publication of a 'paper' constitution guaranteeing men's rights would suffice to achieve liberty, regardless of tradition and social background; from it, too, came the tendency among many liberals to regard the State as the inevitable enemy of the individual. But the clearest thinkers discarded it from the beginning.

Another difference is the emphasis on the individual rather than on the people. It is in the individual rather than in the people that the goodness which will lead to perfection is to be found. The French Revolution had shown that 'the people' is something different from a sum total of individuals, and in the nineteenth century, references to 'the people' came from democrats rather than from liberals. The idea of 'the sovereignty of the people' could not be discarded altogether, because it was needed as a guarantee against assumptions of sovereignty by the monarch, but henceforth sovereignty of the people was to be recognized as limited by liberty of the individual. Royer-Collard's invocation of 'the sovereignty of reason', which he believed resided in a sphere above the conflicting interests of individuals, was rejected by most liberals as leading back to Rousseau's doctrine of the general will. Respectability was a craving by no means confined to Victorian England, and it was with a creed shorn of all elements that had come to be regarded as disreputable that European liberals made their attack upon the old order.

II

If liberalism had been only an attack upon the old order, its task would have been difficult enough. The old order was by no means as decrepit as liberals liked to pretend, for the absolute monarchs controlled the armed forces of their realms, and they had learnt, from Napoleon, to extend their bureaucracies and to equip themselves with police forces and spy services. Many people had a vested interest in the maintenance of the old régime—a factor whose importance was demonstrated very clearly in the collapse of the 1848 revolutions in Austria. The theory of legitimacy, with which Metternich tried to bolster up absolute monarchy in western Europe, was not very impressive, but Russian Czars continued to derive strength and zeal from their belief in the divine right of kings, and their sense of a mission to Europe led Alexander I in the 1820s and Nicholas I in 1849 to offer their services in defence of the old order in western Europe. This was not the whole of the problem, however. Despotism was sometimes of a new order, as in the case of Napoleon III and Bismarck. Napoleon III's 'cæsarian democracy' had a wide appeal in France, whilst Bismarck's stand against the Prussian parliament in the early 'sixties seemed justified by the ever-growing success of his nationalist campaign.

Moreover, liberals felt obliged all along to take action against another new creed: democracy. Democracy, like liberalism, had had its origin in the philosophy of the eighteenth century, and the two had developed side by side for a time, but they had parted company during the French Revolution. The democratic ideal—that all political power should belong to the people—seemed to the liberals to spell tyranny rather than liberty. They believed that it would lead to the tyranny of the mass over the individual and of the majority over the minority, and as proof they pointed to the example of Jacobinism during the French Revolution. Jacobinism was hardly a fair trial of democracy, but nineteenth-century liberals were too near to it to admit that, or perhaps even to see it. Jacobinism had shown them all the worst features of democracy, and consequently they not only hated democracy but feared it, with a fear that could very easily turn to sheer panic, as it did in France after the rising of the workers in June 1848. The fear of democracy brought with it other fears; amongst them the fear of revolution. Liberals always remembered that Jacobinism had come to the fore as the result of a revolution prolonged beyond its original aims; and though the liberals made many revolutions during the nineteenth century, they always tried to stop their revolutions after the initial stages. This was one of the most noticeable features of the revolutions of 1848. As soon as free institutions had been established, and sometimes when they had merely been promised, the liberals began forming National Guards and taking other security measures, lest the populace should begin to make demands which had not been included in the original programme.

The fear of democracy also brought with it the fear of republicanism. A republic, in which not only the parliament but the president was elected by the people, would encourage too much mass intervention in politics, and the president would be too much under the influence of the majority opinion which had carried him into office. The liberals wished to destroy absolute monarchy in Europe, but most of them dared not go the whole way and destroy monarchy entirely. They recognized the value of kings as centres of loyalty, as permanent heads of society, as defenders of government institutions against popular attack. What they really wanted to do was to persuade the old absolute monarchs of Europe to grant parliaments and other free institutions and then help in defending them. This was a much more difficult task than an attack on monarchy, because it meant trying to co-operate with kings who were never enthusiastic about the cause and who could seldom be relied upon to stick to it even if they were driven to join it in moments of weakness. Liberals were again and again let down by the monarchs with whom they were trying to co-operate, but most of them persevered, even when the monarch in question was as stupid as Victor Emmanuel II of Piedmont. Austrian liberals, in spite of their betrayal by the Emperor Ferdinand in 1848, threw in their lot with the new Emperor Francis Joseph and imagined, in the 1860s, that they could bribe him into granting free institutions by supporting the claims of his dynasty to rule Greater Germany. French liberals between 1814 and 1870 tried three kings and an emperor in the attempt to achieve the permanent head which they thought so necessary to a constitutional régime, and when they were finally driven in the 1870s, by the obstinacy of the Bourbon Pretender, to accept a republic, they consoled themselves by making it as little like a republic as an unmonarchical state could be.

An obvious move in the struggle against democracy was for liberals to cling to a limited franchise. The Italian Moderates of the 1840s and 1850s could easily defend such a policy in a country where large numbers of the population were illiterate, but the task was more difficult for Guizot in France, where radical orators claimed that the electoral law of 1831 excluded from the franchise many millions of bourgeois who had all the education necessary to understand the use of a vote. To all attacks Guizot replied that freedom could not be improved upon merely by increasing the number of voters—an argument which gained some support from the events of a later age, when extensions of the franchise brought with them methods of electioneering little in keeping with liberal ideas of the supremacy of the individual. Unfortunately, Guizot and his supporters used weapons even less justifiable than a limited franchise: they curtailed two of their own dearest freedoms, liberty of the press and liberty of association, so anxious were they to prevent democratic leaders from appealing to the public. It is more to the credit of German liberals in the post-1870 period that they refused to pass penal legislation against the Social Democrats, although this refusal worked towards their own downfall. In Italy the struggle between liberalism and democracy crystallized, in the middle years of the century, into the struggle between Cavour on the one hand and Mazzini and Garibaldi on the other. Cavour saw Mazzini as a demagogue and dictator combined, a man who would stir the masses to action and then dominate them in their ignorance; whilst Garibaldi, with his irresponsible guerilla activities and his extraordinary sympathy for the depressed peasantry of southern Italy, could hardly fail to jeopardize the parliamentary state which Cavour was patiently founding on the middle-class society of the north. In the dramatic year of 1860, which afterwards ranked as the pinnacle of Cavour's liberal achievement, Mazzini remained under sentence of death from the Piedmontese government, and Cavour did all he could to prevent Garibaldi's expedition to Sicily.

Liberals always spoke of democracy as a disreputable force, springing from all the worst passions of mankind. In French middle-class homes in the early nineteenth century the words democracy and republic were not considered suitable for use before the children. Democrats, on the other hand, presented liberalism as a selfish creed, shrouded in a lot of talk about freedom for everybody, but in actual fact designed to put power and privileges into the hands of the middle classes. This was a powerful argument because it could be supported by fact. French liberal governments during the July Monarchy failed in eighteen years to pass a single measure of social reform. They claimed that social legislation demanded too much activity from the state; and French liberalism never produced a group like the English Benthamites whose ideas on the duties of the state could act as a corrective to exaggerated notions of laissez-faire. When Guizot refused to introduce so much as a poor law, democrats hastened to the conclusion that here was liberalism in its true colours. One French liberal, Alexis de Tocqueville, believed that this was not liberalism in its true colours, but liberalism in the hands of unimaginative men, and in 1848 he urged the deputies to mend their ways before it was too late; but he entirely failed to convince them of the urgency of the situation. At this point matters were complicated by the events of the 1848 revolution in France. The demands put forward by the workers during the months from February to June 1848 were so excessive that property-owners began to fear for the safety of private property. Shopkeepers could not sell anything because people preferred to keep their property in cash lest they should have to flee the country; and as late as 1851 farmers were cutting down their corn before it was ripe lest at any moment their fields should be seized and divided into strips amongst the workers. After this panic, any political party which wanted to keep middle-class votes had to promise the protection of property and had to keep off any social reform which might in the smallest way strike at the interests of property owners. Social reform on the continent became almost exclusively the property of the democrats, and socialism and democracy allied against liberalism increasingly as the century proceeded. Consequently liberalism was regarded by many people as a conservative creed, even as an outworn creed, long before it had finished its attack on the old order in Europe.

Meanwhile liberals had had other enemies to face. The most insidious enemy, in the early years of the century, was romanticism. Amongst the origins of romanticism lay a desire to free the individual mind and heart from the cold intellectualism of eighteenth-century reason, and in consequence a romantic outlook on life was sometimes combined with liberal views on politics. This was the case with Benjamin Constant in France, with Stein in Prussia, and at a later date with the brothers Gagern, who played so important a part in the German revolution of 1848. More often, however, romanticism in politics looked back upon the past, which it saw through rose-coloured spectacles as an age of faith and feeling and chivalry. Liberals in France quickly saw the dangers of these views, and most of them promptly attacked romanticism in all its forms. French liberal newspapers in the 'teens and 'twenties hotly defended classical literature against romantic literature; hostile criticisms of romantic poetry were given front-page importance, and an energetic liberal journalist, Armand Carrel, threatened to challenge Victor Hugo to a duel over the interpretation of a passage in Bossuet. The romantics, meanwhile, ranged themselves on the side of the restored monarchy, and encouraged Charles X to squeeze every ounce of power for himself out of the constitutional settlement of 1814. They encouraged him in romantic displays such as the return to the ancient form of coronation at Rheims, and touching for the king's evil, and many young romantics joined a secret society, the Knights of the Faith, whose double object was to restore Frenchmen to more faith and feeling and to restore absolute monarchy.

Elsewhere in Europe the antipathy between liberalism and romanticism was not so clearly demonstrated. Romanticism, for all its strange manifestations, sprang from generous sentiments, and the men who took to it were often ready to plunge into self-sacrifice on behalf of the oppressed. Hence romantics were to be found fighting on the side of the Greeks in the War of Independence and in similar exploits which caused them to be confused in the popular mind with the liberals. Metternich added to the confusion by persecuting both with equal vigour, since to him the fanatical young men who insisted on a return to chivalry seemed just as dangerous to the established order as the more ponderous gentlemen who asked for parliamentary institutions. But romanticism and liberalism were nevertheless distinct in essence, and more often than not mutually hostile, and in one sphere at any rate romanticism did great harm to the liberal cause. This was in Germany, where the movement for national unity had far more romanticism than liberalism in it from the beginning. The student societies which Metternich persecuted were inspired by romantic aims of uniting Germany so that she might return to her past greatness, rather than by liberal aims of uniting her so that the freedom of the individual might triumph. Whilst it is possible to find some liberalism in Germany in the early years of the century, liberalism did not really begin to get any sort of hold there until the 1840s, and even then many liberals mistakenly believed the romanticism of Frederick William IV of Prussia to be compatible with their own views. When the Frankfurt Assembly met in 1848 few people in Germany understood the liberal as distinct from the nationalist aspect of the Assembly's aims, and the Assembly was afterwards criticised for having spent too much time in pursuit of free institutions instead of trying to achieve German unity by hook or by crook.

The leading place amongst the opponents of liberalism must be given, however, to the Roman Catholic Church. The opposition of the Church appeared on two fronts, one practical and Italian, the other theoretical and European, and it lasted throughout the century.

In Italy, liberalism meant nationalism, for there seemed to be no hope of getting rid of the baleful influence of Austria, and the despotism of the petty princes of Italy, without some form of national unity. Nationalism in its most obvious form would mean the Church losing its lands in central Italy, and at the beginning of the nineteenth century the Pope still regarded the possession of these lands as necessary to the independence and hence to the spiritual authority of the Church. Nationalism was thus made to look like an attack not merely on the Church's temporal possessions, but on its spiritual power. In the 1840s a group of nationalist writers headed by Gioberti tried to solve the dilemma by suggesting that Italy need not become a unitary state; she could form a confederation, each state keeping its own ruler and each uniting with the others under some form of federal government. The proposal won a large number of adherents in Italy, but Mazzini and other radicals spurned it from the beginning as worse than useless to true nationalists, and it eventually collapsed in 1848 from its failure to cope with the Austrian problem. Theoretically speaking, Austria could have been allowed to keep Lombardy-Venetia and rule it as part of a new Italian confederation, but few Italian nationalists would consider any such proposal. The Austrians must be driven out of Italy, and when the Pope declined, as he needs must, to countenance any such movement, the initiative passed to Piedmont. Cavour began modernizing the Piedmontese state ready to play its part in the freeing of North Italy, and some of his earliest measures consisted of a serious reduction in the secular power of the Church, but he had no intention of attacking the spiritual power of the Church. Nor had he any intention of doing so in 1859 and 1860, when events drove him to annex the greater part of the Papal States. Cavour offered to Pius IX proposals for a settlement very similar to those accepted at a later date by Leo XIII, but Pius would have nothing to do with them. Italian unity had to be achieved in direct opposition to the wishes of the Church and by actually taking arms against her; and even when United Italy was an accomplished fact, Pius IX continued to demonstrate his hostility to the creation. This made many difficulties for the new Italian kingdom, which had a hard enough task anyway to win and hold the loyalty of the mass of the Italian people. It also made clear to liberals everywhere in Europe that Pius IX had dissociated the Church from what they regarded as liberalism's finest achievement.

Behind the Italian conflict lay a conflict of ideas which was of European significance. Liberalism undeniably contained many beliefs which were contrary to the teaching of the Church. The belief that man is born good, that his progress is inevitable, that he can by his own efforts reach perfection on earth—all these were contrary to the Church's teaching on Original Sin, on salvation through Christ, and on the sovereignty of God over earth and heaven. But there were other aspects of liberalism. A courageous French priest, Lamennais, tried to persuade his fellow churchmen that liberalism should be accepted and encouraged by the Church because it sprang from instincts which were truly Christian; for the desire to recognize the dignity of man born in the image of God, and from the desire to allow men the free use of the faculties given them by God. The French bishops were not convinced, and in November 1831 Lamennais journeyed to Rome, seeking a pronouncement from Pope Gregory XVI in favour of his views. Gregory at first temporized, and Lamennais returned to France in a hopeful frame of mind, but before he had actually reached France he received from the Pope an encyclical letter whose content amounted to a complete rejection of all that he had urged. In fairness to Gregory, one can show that he could hardly have done otherwise. It is not the duty of the Pope to keep abreast of prophets like Lamennais so much as to see that the flock stays within the fold, and liberalism at this time contained much that was likely to lead the ordinary man astray. One can show, too, that the responsibility for the encyclical rests as much, if not more, with Lamennais as with Gregory. For more than a year Gregory had turned a blind eye to the newspaper which Lamennais was publishing in France, and Lamennais should have been content to be tolerated. The encyclical *Mirari vos* made clear for the first time that liberalism, in spite of its many good qualities, could find no accommodation in the most spacious of all churches. Some fourteen years later liberals hoped for accommodation from a new Pope, Pius IX, who was said to have liberal sympathies, but their hopes were founded on an illusion. Pius IX carried out a few reforms in the Papal States, but this was because he was a kind-hearted man and a well-meaning ruler, not because he was a liberal. He allowed liberals in Italy to acclaim him as their leader, but this was because he was too inexperienced of the world to know what liberalism implied. When he discovered that liberalism contained elements of which he could not approve he turned against it in all its forms. In 1864 he denounced liberalism outright, along with pantheism, rationalism, indifferentism, socialism, communism, secret societies and Bible societies, as one of the errors of the age; ending his declaration with the pronouncement that it was a damnable error to suggest that the Pope could or should reconcile himself to liberty, progress, and recent civilization. Fortunately for liberalism, the Catholic mind rose to the occasion, and large numbers of Frenchmen and Italians, Belgians and Spaniards convinced themselves, by a triumph of adaptation, that they could obey the Pope whilst remaining liberal. Nevertheless, the opposition of the Catholic Church deprived liberalism of much moral force, and continued to harm the liberal cause in Europe to the last years of the century.

III

By 1870 the countries of western Europe had obtained something like the free institutions for which liberals had fought since the beginning of the century, and Europe entered upon what historians have called 'the liberal era'. Free institutions had never been regarded as an end in themselves, however; they were merely the essential beginning, and the time had now come to demonstrate to the world, and especially to those parts of Europe, notably Russia, which remained under despotic governments, that free institutions resulted in progress. Unfortunately the free institutions were by no means firmly founded, and the defence of them against enemies, old and new, might easily prove a task which allowed little room for progress.

Each country presented its own problems. In the Habsburg Empire, transformed by the 'compromise' of 1867 into the dual state of Austria-Hungary and ruled according to two separate constitutions, the maintenance of parliamentary government depended on the ability of the liberals to solve the age-old problem of conflicting national claims. In Austria the franchise was limited and organized in such a way as to debar the Czechs from any effective part in political life, and although the hostility which this provoked amongst the Czechs was a serious drag on the new constitutional régime, the liberals dare not try to allay it by extending the franchise. Any concession to the Czechs would have resulted in a policy to obtain similar rights for the Slavs in Hungary, and this would have reduced the power of the Magyars, who alone were strong enough to frighten Francis Joseph into keeping the constitutional settlement of 1867. The inability of the liberals to move towards any solution of the Czech problem, combined with the shock which the economic crisis of 1873 gave to their system of laissez-faire, gradually weakened their popularity even amongst the Austrian Germans, whose interests they were most likely to promote. Francis Joseph grew angry with them when they opposed his occupation of Bosnia-Herzegovina in 1878, and in the general election of the following year he used his influence to bring about the defeat of their candidates. The liberals never again, to the end of the century, achieved a majority in the parliament. For the next fourteen years they saw the conservative prime minister Taaffe making a mockery of parliamentary institutions, but their own policy of clinging to a narrow franchise and to an economic policy of laissez-faire which paid exclusive attention to upper middle-class interests failed to find wide enough support to enable them to put up any effective resistance. When the threat from the growing radical party caused Francis Joseph to dismiss Taaffe in 1893, the liberals could form a government only by allying with conservative groups, and the failure of their coalitions to pursue any effective policy either at home or abroad ended what little patience Francis Joseph had had with the constitutional system. By 1900 he had ceased to obey the most fundamental rules of the constitution, and the liberals were incapable of gathering sufficient strength to oppose his renewed absolutism.

In the new kingdom of Italy the liberal policy of Cavour devolved in 1860 upon the party of the Right, which controlled the destinies of the country for the next sixteen years. The members of the party were faced with the difficult task of assimilating into the parliamentary system the states of central and southern Italy which Cavour had not thought ripe for parliamentary government and which he annexed to his northern kingdom only because he was driven to do so by the activities of Garibaldi. The difficulty of the task was not lessened by the fact that the Right underestimated it. With the exception of Minghetti, the leading members of the Right had no direct knowledge of the central and southern provinces, and the traditions of the Risorgimento had not taught them to pay any attention to the social and agrarian problems of the peasantry. Obliged, in view of the high percentage of illiteracy amongst the Italian people, to keep to a narrow franchise which gave more votes to the northern provinces than to the rest of the country, the Right could hardly have escaped the accusation of dictatorship; but at least the dictatorship ought to have been used to raise the level of wealth and education amongst the mass of the people and thus to pave the way for the extension of political rights. Instead it was used primarily to enhance the greatness of the new kingdom in the eyes of the other powers of Europe. The discontent which prevailed in the south provided a fertile field for radical propaganda, and in 1876 the government of the Right fell before that of the Left. Extension of the franchise inevitably followed, and the results soon showed how little of liberal ideals the mass of the population had imbibed. The new voters were unable to understand their rights except as a means of obtaining corresponding benefits, and this tempted politicians into a system of patronage which quickly discredited parliamentary life. An outward respect for civil liberty and for constitutional forms preserved a façade of liberalism, and this concealed the decadence of the ruling class and the political ignorance of the masses to the end of the century, but it could hardly survive the disintegrating forces which came upon the country in later years.

In the new German Reich the constitution of 1871 established a parliament elected by universal suffrage and an Imperial Chancellor who must depend on parliament to pass the budget. The task of the liberals was to give these institutions more meaning than Bismarck intended them to have. A parliament elected by universal suffrage was more likely to prove a bulwark of authoritarianism than of liberalism, as had been proved in France during the Second Empire; and even if the electorate gave its loyalty to liberal ideals the parliament would have difficulty in making its influence felt upon ministers who were responsible only to the Emperor. In other words, the constitution was a doubtful concession to liberalism, and German liberals, far from being now in control of the political situation, were faced with a despotic power stronger than the despotisms of the early nineteenth century: stronger because it could claim brilliant achievements both at home and abroad, because it was administratively efficient, and because it appeared more forceful and progressive than a liberal creed connected in people's minds with the failures of 1848. Under these circumstances many liberals—indeed the majority of liberal politicians in Germany—saw no prospect of success in opposing Bismarck, and they joined those Prussian liberals who, in 1866, had rallied to Bismarck's support and called themselves the National Liberal Party.

The party contained some of the leading politicians in Germany —Lasker, Forckenbeck, Twesten, and Unruh, who had opposed Bismarck in the Prussian parliament in the early sixties; Bennigsen and Miquel who had led the liberal opposition in Hanover. Miquel announced, 'The time for ideals is past, and the duty of politicians is to ask not for what is desirable, but for what is attainable'. Yet the National Liberals were not wholly deserting their ideals when they joined Bismarck, nor even suspending them until happier times. Since the unfortunate experiences of 1848 many German liberals had come to distrust what they regarded as 'French' views on the proper position and function of parliament in the state. They turned back to the teaching of Hegel and Kant, and from this they imbibed a juridical concept of the state, defining liberty as consisting of legal rights granted by the state to the individual, and used by the individual in such a way as to prevent any encroachment from above or below. In England the common law had been given a place almost equal to that of parliament in the defence of individual freedom; and German liberals, obsessed by the insecurity which seemed to result from complete supremacy of the legislature, were ready to place more faith in the rule of law than in the rule of parliament. This kind of liberty, expounded in the second half of the nineteenth century by Gneist, Laband, Meyer, and Jellinek, might well be found in the political system established by Bismarck, which brought an element of self-government into the administration and allowed the parliament to exercise critical functions. The chief danger was that Bismarck might one day destroy the parliament which he had granted in 1871 as a grudging concession to liberal opinion, and thus place the rule of law in jeopardy. To guard against this danger the National Liberals opposed all Bismarck's attempts to make himself financially independent of parliament. Their success in this field proved to be their undoing, for Bismarck soon tired of allies so lacking in docility. In 1878-9, using to the full his remarkable gifts as a propagandist and political tactician, he destroyed their popularity with the electorate by making them appear disloyal to the Emperor, broke their political party by dividing them on the subject of protection, and discarded their alliance in favour of one with the Catholic Centre party. Bismarck's reliance on conservative groups during the 1880s accelerated the growth of social democracy, and it was with this force, which liberals had always distrusted, that the future of parliamentary institutions in Germany lay at the end of the century.

Even France, with its older tradition of parliamentary government, was no easy field for the liberals after 1870. The Third Republic began its career under the taint of national dishonour and social repression—the acceptance of the humiliating peace terms offered by Bismarck, and the suppression of the Commune. The fear of Jacobinism, which had broken out in Paris during the Franco-Prussian War, and the fear of communism, which most Frenchmen wrongly believed to have been responsible for the Commune, would have forced a conservative policy on future governments whether they had wanted it or not, and for twenty years vigorous advances either in foreign policy or in social legislation were out of the question. Left-wing groups, which combined democratic and socialistic views with intense patriotism, were likely to become increasingly hostile to a liberal Republic which seemed no different, in essentials, from the July Monarchy. In an attempt to give the Republic wider support the veteran liberal Thiers allied with the radical Gambetta in the elections of 1876, and the so-called 'opportunist' programme which resulted from this alliance was carried out energetically by the governments of the 1880s. Its main features were the extension of political rights and the establishment of free, secular, and compulsory education: there was a notable lack of any attention to reform of a purely social nature. In other words, liberalism compounded with democracy but refused to make any concession to the socialism with which democracy had been connected since the days of Louis Blanc. This refusal, along with an equally firm refusal to adopt a policy of revenge against Germany, provoked the dangerous outbreak of caesarism which took place in the name of Boulanger in the years 1886-9. Discredited further by the Panama scandal and the Dreyfus affair, the Opportunist groups were obliged to give way in the last years of the century to the radical ministry of Waldeck-Rousseau. From this time onwards the Republic underwent a much larger infusion of democracy and socialism than liberals would once have thought compatible with freedom of the individual.

Behind these failures, and similar failures elsewhere, lay an increasing doubt as to the efficacy of free institutions to achieve progress. In the early years of the century, when liberals had talked of the need to free the individual so that he could advance towards perfection, the meaning of progress had had a predominantly moral content; but by 1870 philosophy and its allied studies had surrendered pride of place to the exact sciences, and progress came to mean an increasing mastery over the physical universe and an increasing possession of the material benefits which this mastery afforded. These benefits could only be acquired by the individual if he had wealth. The middle classes settled down to the accumulation of wealth with all the hope and determination which they had once put into politics, and in the era of economic expansion which followed on the creation of the new nation-states they prospered. But economic prosperity now depended to a large extent on national security and power, and governments were often led into foreign policies little in keeping with the ideals of a liberal state.

At the same time, increasing industrialization brought the growth of urban proletariats anxious to obtain their share in the benefits which they saw around them. Their share did not come to them automatically, as Guizot had thought it would, by the mere force of circumstances; perhaps because the middle classes were more selfish than Guizot had believed, but more certainly because the new economic structure was more impersonal and more complicated than Guizot could ever have envisaged. Radical politicians urged that a reasonable standard of living for the workers could only be obtained by social legislation, but liberal politicians in the 1870s and 1880s held out against such demands, as Gladstone held out against Joseph Chamberlain in England. They gave as their reason their unwillingness to encroach on freedom of the individual, but opponents accused them of selfish class interest, and side by side the two ideas gained ground, that liberalism was a middle-class creed and that the interests of the middle class and the lower class were incompatible. Revolutionary socialism of one kind and another, inspired by Marx, Bakunin, and Blanqui, enjoyed a brief vogue amongst advanced politicians in most of the countries of western Europe in the 1870s. In time, however, the development of workingmen's associations and trades unions gave rise to a class of workmen skilled in leadership, trained in workers' politics, and accustomed to negotiating—a working-class intelligentsia, which took over the function performed earlier in the century by the middle-class intelligentsia and acted as a connecting link between the middle and the lower classes. Workmen were persuaded by these new leaders that nothing was to be gained by violence and that everything was to be gained by using the machinery of free speech and free association. By the 1890s there had appeared in most countries a parliamentary socialism of a type which had been developing slowly in England since the days of the Chartists. To this new socialism and its 'minimum programmes' liberal politicians felt obliged to make some concessions, telling themselves that they could do so without danger to parliamentary institutions. But concessions to socialism implied an amount of state activity which liberals of an earlier generation would not have countenanced, and the inescapable inference was that liberalism could only cater for the demands of the lower classes by sacrificing its own principles.

In one country of Europe the sacrifice called for seemed to be too great to be contemplated. This was in Russia, which proved to be the scene of liberalism's greatest failure. Very early in the nineteenth century Czar Alexander I had been attracted to liberal ideas, only to conclude that they were inapplicable in a country where large parts of the population remained under serfdom. Alexander II, more for reasons of state than for any liberal purpose, had emancipated the serfs in 1861, but had failed to assimilate them into the rest of society. The peasants remained a class apart, uneducated, inexperienced, incapable of concerted action to improve their own welfare, and with grievances which demanded attention on every ground of justice and humanity. Victorian doctrines of self-help were hardly applicable; the problem could only be answered by state intervention of a kind and on a scale which seemed to have little in keeping with liberal principles. The small liberal groups which appeared in the Duma of 1906, Russia's first national parliament, had no answer to suggest. They refused to support the proposal by the democratic 'Cadet' group, for the expropriation of land; and the field was thus left open for extremist elements of every kind.

By the end of the nineteenth century liberalism was a jaded force compared with what it had been in earlier years. Compromises with enemies old and new had shrouded its meaning, and other political parties, owing much in their origin to liberalism, but inimical to its existence as a political force, had obtained a wider electoral appeal. Optimism remained high, but it was insecurely founded and could not survive the disappointments following on 1918. The inevitability of progress, whether moral or material, appeared then to have been a delusion, and perfection had so far eluded men's grasp as to have passed beyond their hopes. Liberals still aimed at freeing the individual, but not in the certainty that he would achieve perfection so much as in the belief that freedom would enable him to do the best for himself and others in a difficult and unpredictable world. Liberalism had thus put aside many of the idealistic beliefs which had caused Karl Marx to ridicule it and the Catholic Church to denounce it, but in doing so it had lost much of its vigour. It was in a prevailing mood of doubt and despondency that liberalism faced, in the twentieth century, the two greatest threats it had yet seen—the rise of power politics in Germany and of communism in Russia.

BIBLIOGRAPHICAL NOTE

A useful introduction to this subject is to be found in H. J. Laski, *The Rise of European Liberalism* (2nd ed., London, 1947). Guido de Ruggiero, *The History of European Liberalism* (translated from the Italian by R. G. Collingwood, Oxford, 1927) is a difficult but rewarding book, dealing with the theoretical aspects of liberalism. It contains a detailed bibliography which is particularly good for contemporary sources. Benedetto Croce, *History of Europe in the Nineteenth Century* (translated from the Italian by H. Furst, London, 1934), presents the history of the century in the light of a struggle for freedom. It is valuable chiefly for the early chapters, in which the author assesses the forces on both sides of the struggle.

Among the many contemporary writings in which nineteenth-century liberals expounded their theories, two of the most important are Benjamin de Constant's *Esquisse de constitution* and *De la liberté des anciens comparée à celle des modernes* (published in a collection of Constant's works, under the title *Cours de politique constitutionnelle*, 2 vols., Paris, 1861). The *Esquisse*, first published just before the promulgation of the French Charter of 1814, indicates the kind of constitution regarded as desirable by one of the leading liberals of the time. Extracts from the works of some German writers of the early nineteenth century have recently been made available in English under the title *Political Thought of the German Romantics* (selected by H. S. Reiss, Blackwell's Political Texts, Oxford, 1955). These extracts from the works of Fichte, Novalis, Adam Müller, Schleiermacher, and Savigny, illustrate the dual relationship, part friendly, part hostile, between German liberalism and romanticism; also the stress, from the earliest days of German liberalism, on the authority of the state. F. Guizot, *De la démocratie en France* (Paris, 1849; also published in English, London, 1849), illustrates the hostile attitude which liberals in the first half of the nineteenth century usually took towards democracy, whilst John Stuart Mill, *Essay on Liberty* (first published in 1859; recently edited by R. B. McCallum, Oxford, 1946), denotes the anxiety of liberals in the second half of the century to adapt liberalism to the rising tide of democracy.

There are some interesting modern works dealing with particular aspects of liberalism. L. B. Namier, *1848: The Revolution of the Intellectuals* (London, 1944) criticizes the behaviour of liberals, especially in Germany, at a crucial point in the nineteenth century. A. R. Vidler, *Prophecy and Papacy* (London, 1954), deals with the attempt by Lamennais to reconcile liberalism and catholicism. V. Valentin, *1848: Chapters in German History* (London, 1940), gives a more sympathetic account of the German liberal revolution of 1848 than that propagated by pro-Bismarckian historians. D. Mack Smith, *Cavour and Garibaldi, 1860* (Cambridge, 1954), re-assesses the part played by the liberal Cavour in the making of United Italy. J. S. Schapiro, *Liberalism and the Challenge of Fascism* (New York, 1949), reconsiders liberalism in France and England in the first half of the nineteenth century. The social and economic back-

45

ground to liberalism in the early decades of the nineteenth century is analysed, from a neo-Marxist point of view, in E. J. Hobsbawm, *The Age of Revolution* (London, 1962).

Works in German have not so far been mentioned, as they are not likely to be readily available. But an exception should be made for Theodor Schieder's article, 'Das Verhältnis von politischer und gesellschaftlicher Verfassung und die Krise des bürgerlichen Liberalismus', *Historische Zeitschrift*, clxxvii (1954), pp. 49–74, of which a fuller version appeared under the title, 'Der Liberalismus und die Strukturwandlungen der modernen Gesellschaft vom 19. zum 20. Jahrhundert', in the 5th volume of the *Relazioni* of the Tenth International Congress of Historical Sciences (Florence, 1955).

ASA BRIGGS

1851

'We have got a Ministerial crisis', wrote Queen Victoria to the King of the Belgians in February 1851. 'This is very bad, because there is no chance of any other good Government, poor Peel being no longer alive. . . . Altogether it is very vexatious, and will give us trouble. It is the more provoking, as this country is so very prosperous.' This letter reveals the underlying contrasts and inherent frustrations of 1851. It was a year of national festival, the climax of early Victorian England, the turning point of the century. It was also a year of political uncertainty and ministerial instability. At the beginning of the year it was generally expected—and hoped—that Russell's Whig administration, known to be weak and tending to decline still further, would remain quietly in office throughout a season of Exhibition and carnival. The ministry did not even survive peacefully until the opening of the Exhibition on 1 May. It faced crisis in February, and although, after a great deal of political coming and going, it returned to office intact, its position was extremely precarious. It remained so throughout the year, and, after the dismissal of Palmerston in December, the way was prepared for its final break-up in 1852.

The Queen and the Prince Consort more than any other persons in the country felt both the full thrill of the Exhibition and the unsettling strain and inconvenience of ministerial instability. They saw quite clearly that 'the state of the country' and 'the state of the parties' were two distinct questions, and that economic prosperity and political fragmentation were unfortunately by no means incompatible. Yet throughout 1851 one of the causes of political instability was being steadily removed. Indirectly, increasing prosperity was influencing the Protectionists, who were unobtrusively dropping some of the slogans of 1846. Their gradual retreat took the sting out of politics. It also made life easier for the Queen, rather too late for her peace of mind in 1851. When Lord Derby told her in June 1852 that he considered Protection as 'quite gone', she wrote somewhat wearily that it was a pity he had not found this out a little sooner. 'It would have saved so much annoyance, so much difficulty.'

The annoyance and the difficulty were not entirely the fault of the Protectionists, even though they had been especially awkward not only about free trade, but also about the Exhibition. 1851 was a year of general pride and prejudice. The continued papal-aggression crisis roused public opinion to fever pitch and made ministerial politics extremely difficult. 'Parties were a good deal confused before thanks to Corn,' wrote Cobden, 'but the Catholic element has made confusion worse confounded.' In his view, the view of a small minority, it was unfortunate that England itself should be exhibited in the year of the Exhibition 'as the most intolerant people on earth', so that 'Europe cries shame on us, and America laughs at us'. The view of the majority was that in both the Exhibition and the religious crisis, national honour was deeply involved and had to be vindicated.

The Exhibition, the political crisis, the religious hysteria, all contributed to the temper of 1851. Behind the pride and prejudice there were doubts and dilemmas on all sides. How could you welcome crowds of foreigners, probably papists, to London to see the Exhibition while you thundered out against papal aggression? *Punch* depicted an old Tory, who knew one possible answer. He was shown hanging an Exhibition notice outside his house, 'ici on ne parle pas français'. Once the Exhibition was over, how could you reconcile its message of peace with the news of Napoleon's *coup d'état* in France and the knowledge of the alarming 'defenceless state of Great Britain', to which Sir Francis Head had drawn attention the year before? Palmerston's answer to that was to recognize the *coup d'état* as the least of many evils, but for welcoming Napoleon he lost his office. 'There *was* a Palmerston,' said Disraeli, while Prince Albert wrote that the year of contrasts closed with 'the, for us, happy circumstance, that the man who had embittered our whole life . . . cut his throat himself'. The verdict was premature. Within a short time, Palmerston was to turn out Russell, and his greatest political victories were still in the future. 'Lord Evergreen' was his nickname.

The doubts and dilemmas of 1851 were as important as its assurance and self-confidence. The Crystal Palace was no abiding city. 1851 was a good vantage point to take stock of half a century's progress, but the future was by no means clear, and all you knew was that the great world was spinning for ever 'down the ringing grooves of change'. Even when you paused to take stock, there were difficulties in your calculations. You might agree with *The Eclectic Review* that 'the year 1851, when compared with the year 1801, is as the palace of glass when compared with the houses built under the régime of the window duty', but you would realize that it all depended on your time scale. Tennyson's *In Memoriam*, a best seller for the crowds which attended the Exhibition, was as representative of the times as the glass house of the Great Exhibition itself, and it talked not of the visible triumphs of fifty years of industrialization, but of

> The sound of streams that swift or slow
> Draw down Aeonian hills, and sow
> The dust of continents to be.

II

From our present vantage point, in many respects a less satisfactory one than that of a hundred years ago, economics is a more familiar point of departure for exploring an age than religion. To contemporaries in 1851, however, the religious climate was more exciting and important than anything else. The amount of pamphlet and periodical literature devoted to religious questions was far greater than that devoted to economic or social problems, and the interest taken in the first religious census of 1851 was as great as that taken in the fifth general decennial census, which presented the statistics of material progress.

The statistics of material progress underlined the strength of Britain's industrial position. The Exhibition showed the nation's undisputed leadership in manufacturing. Its engines were the symbols of economic mastery:

> These England's arms of conquest are,
> The trophies of her bloodless war.

In commerce and finance, British supremacy was even more marked. Yet despite spectacular signs of progress in trade and industry, over a quarter of the male population of the country was engaged in agricultural pursuits, and one in nine of all females over ten was employed in domestic service. More men were employed as shoemakers than as coal-miners, and there were still only just over a quarter of a million professional workers of all types.

Amid the broad ranks of 'the middle classes', independent small men were the dominant group, not only in retailing, but in commerce and manufacturing. The virtues they prized were self-help, perseverance, thrift, and character. They conceived of self-dependence not only as a ladder to individual success, but as the mainspring of social improvement. All men could profit from it.

The middle classes were teaching these their own values to other groups in society, not without success. With the relaxation of the tension of the forties and the abandonment of some of the wild nightmares and utopias of a long period of conflict, some of the working classes, particularly 'the aristocracy of labour', were reaching up to seek middle-class virtues. 1851 was the year of the founding of the Amalgamated Society of Engineers, which claimed that its object was to do nothing 'illegally or indiscreetly, but on all occasions to perform the greatest amount of benefit for ourselves, without injury to others. . . . It is our duty to exercise the same control over that in which we have a vested interest, as the physician who holds his diploma or the author who is protected by his copyright.' As the working classes were looking up, the aristocracy was looking down. Middle-class ideals set the standard for the nation, and while the upper ranks of society 'were beginning to live in fear of the butcher and the grocer', the Queen and the Prince Consort were providing a model of happy family life.

Along with the spread of middle-class values went a rise in middle-class comfort. John Store Smith's *Social Aspects*, a new book in 1851, noted how 'the middle-class family now possesses carpets and hangings, which would have excited great wonderment even at so recent a period as the American War, and not a few of our London middle-class tradesmen possess a better stock of family plate and linen than many a country squire, even of the last generation'. Porter's 1851 edition of *Progress of a Nation* painted the same picture of the prosperous middle-class household, the walls covered with paintings and engravings, and the whole setting 'full of evidences that some among the inmates cultivate one or more of those elegant accomplishments which tend so delightfully to enlighten the minds of individuals and sweeten the intercourse of families'.

While the industrial and commercial middle classes were enjoying prosperity in the spring of 1851, the landlords and farmers were still disgruntled. Agriculture was in the doldrums, and although it provided employment for a very large proportion of the nation, it was no longer conceived of, except by 'the landed interest' itself, as the backbone of national prosperity. Early in 1851 the division of interest between landlords and manufacturers—Disraeli's 'unhappy quarrel between town and country' and Roebuck's 'master-key' to British history since 1832—was the most important source of conflict within the political arena. Disraeli's motion on agricultural distress was only defeated by 14 votes in February 1851, when disgruntled farmers in East Anglia were saying that they would rather march on Manchester than on Paris. In May the Protectionists held a giant rally in Drury Lane, where they copied 'the arts and violence of the agitators' that they had so much deplored.

Their power was extremely limited. The balance of forces was such that there could be no easy return to any form of agricultural protection, even if it were disguised in the new language of relief and amelioration. In 1851 over nine million quarters of grain were imported into the British Isles: in other words, one quarter of the people's bread was foreign. These immense imports of foreign grain and flour were consumed, as Graham did not fail to point out, 'by millions of mouths that otherwise would not have been fed'. 'Though Peel is dead, he still speaks, and from the tomb I hear the echo of his voice.' Wise Tories could not ignore these figures, and clever politicians could not afford to ignore one of the most important elements in all political calculations, that if the Protectionists came back into office the threat of a new agitation outside Parliament, on the lines of the Anti-Corn Law League, would make a reversal of 1846 hazardous and probably impracticable. The north of England was still on the alert. As *The Manchester Guardian* put it, 'The moral effect of free trade supplies a theme, which years of agitation have not staled, nor the eloquence of Mr. COBDEN exhausted'.

By the end of 1851, after a good harvest, there were unmistakable signs of agricultural revival, and Protectionism looked to be less and less necessary. Granby, a prominent Tory leader, visited Hughenden in November 1851, staying long enough, Disraeli wrote, to have time to ask the village butcher whether any land had gone out of cultivation in the neighbourhood. 'The astonishment of Redrup, who had just sold his barley for 30s. per quarter, might be conceived.' It was not only Disraeli and his friends who thought that Protection was dead. A little later, even *The Quarterly Review* was writing that 'the prospects of British agriculturists are not of a nature to lead to despondency', and explaining with largeness of gesture that Protectionism did not mean protection of landlords, but protection of the interests of the poor, of the labour of young people, and of the Christian character of the state.

1851 was the critical year in the reshaping of British agricultural prospects. It ushered in a period of agricultural prosperity, largely dependent upon the opening up of the railway system and the increase in incomes generated by industry. Whatever part gold had in the unfolding of the boom, contemporaries in 1851 saw the new supplies from California and Australia as the basic force, giving, in the words of *The Times*, 'an electric impulse to our entire business world'. While the crowds at the Exhibition admired a piece of gold from California, at the other end of the Empire, in Australia, the gold rush was 'drawing even clergymen to the exciting scene, and not in every case did they confine themselves to their calling'. In excited anticipation of a new period in history, Ashley wrote in his Diary that California had led the way and Australia followed. '*Auri sacra fames*. What no motive, human or divine, could effect, springs into life at the display of a few pellets of gold in the hands of a wanderer. This may be God's chosen way to fulfil his commandment and "replenish the earth".'

In the period after 1851 many men and women thought that they caught a glimpse of the Promised Land. Certainly something of the tension disappeared from the relations both between landlords and captains of industry, and between masters and men. The way was prepared for what Professor Burn has called 'The Age of Equipoise'. The fiction of the day reflected the change. There was a shift in writing from 'novels in which the basic structure of society was discussed in terms of bitter satire and deep passion to those in which personal problems were discussed against the background of a society whose structure was assumed to be sufficiently stable'.

In politics, frequently abortive skirmishes between interests absorbed more energy than struggles concerning large measures of constitutional or social change. The tone was set in 1851 by the opposition to Wood's budget, far more hotly discussed than Ashley's 'Inspection and Registration of Lodging-Houses Bill', which Charles Dickens described as 'the best law that was ever passed by an English Parliament'.

Wood was handicapped by the very prosperity of the country. The budget surplus amounted to £2,521,000. Disgruntled agriculturalists wanted a share of it: impatient manufacturers wanted to see 'the final abolition of the inevitable and inquisitorial income tax', still standing at 7d. in the £. Wood, who was no Gladstone, satisfied neither interest, although he did suggest the abolition of the Window Tax, with a House Tax to take its place. Opposition to his budget proposals played an important part in the background of the ministerial crisis of February, and, after the crisis was over, the government was again defeated on a Radical motion, limiting the imposition of the tax to one year, and setting up a Select Committee to inquire into the mode of assessing and collecting it. The men who defeated the government were neither fiery extremists nor Manchester men. They were, as *The Daily News* remarked, 'the quiet, steady representatives of mercantile communities, who are, in general, chary of extremes'. They were the men who were to count most in the period after 1851, men frightened of taxation and suspicious of government. As trade remained prosperous and agriculture improved, they felt that they could rely upon themselves better than upon politicians.

There was thus an underlying distrust of government, which continued to mould the shape of politics until the passing of the Second Reform Bill. Self-help came first: government, except as an agency for dealing with foreign relations and for facilitating self-help, came very low on the list of daily preoccupations.

III

It certainly came below religion. Religious questions shared the headlines with news of the Exhibition throughout the first half of 1851. There was a sustained religious crisis—so it was called by contemporaries—which began with Wiseman's announcement 'given out of the Flaminian Gate of Rome' of the papal decision to restore a regular Roman Catholic hierarchy in England. Russell, 'the historic champion of religious liberty', made himself the mouth-piece of indignant Protestant exasperation. The noise and excitement of the public reaction to the Pope's action surprised even Ashley, who had long foreseen a religious crisis of this type. 'What a surprising ferment!', he wrote, 'it abates not a jot; meeting after meeting in every town and parish of the country. . . . It resembles a storm over the whole ocean; it is a national sentiment, a rising of the land! All opinions seem for a while submerged in this one feeling.' Other less partisan observers remarked that there had been no similar popular outcry since the brief period when the Reform Bill was considered to be in danger, and that in 1851, as then, the middle classes, 'those who were usually the calmest and most reflecting section of the community', were at the heart of the movement.

The flames were fanned by those who pointed not to the external but to the internal danger—the threat from within the Church of England of Puseyite traitors, attempting to lead 'their flocks step by step to the verge of the precipice', and of ritualists like Bennett, forced from St. Paul's, Knightsbridge, in 1851 to a quiet living in Somerset. *The Times* warned against the 'terrible danger of the renegades of our national Church' restoring 'a foreign usurpation over the consciences of men to sow dissension within our political society'. The danger was an ever-present one. Even while Parliament was debating legislation against papal aggression, Archdeacon Manning was moving over from the Church of England to the Church of Rome. 'Lord, purge the Church of those men,' wrote Ashley in his

53

Diary, 'who while their hearts are in the Vatican, still eat the bread of the Establishment and undermine her.'

Russell realized the strength of the Protestant cry, and in February 1851 introduced his Ecclesiastical Titles Bill in an effort to curb papal claims by legislation. His bill was too mild to satisfy militant Protestant feeling inside as well as outside the House of Commons. At the same time, the very idea of legislation on this topic alienated the Catholic Irish group in Parliament on whose votes the fate of the Whig Ministry depended. Irish members were lobbied by their constituents against the measure just as strongly and strenuously as were English members in its favour. The member for Cork, for instance, described how his constituents, 'who were as calm as a summer sea when compared with the excited inhabitants of other parts', had passed a resolution calling upon him to vote against the Whig government on every occasion, no matter what the principle in-involved. Such congenial advice was willingly accepted by most of the 'Pope's Irish Brass Band', who found a leader for the occasion in 'the pocket O'Connell', John Sadleir. It was the consequent loss of Irish support which was the most important factor weakening the Whig government in 1851. Russell found himself in an impossible parliamentary situation. So indeed would any other leader have done, for as Cobden wrote, 'any government that perseveres in the anti-Papal policy will be opposed by the Irish members on every subject, and if an Administration were to come in to do nothing against the Pope, they would, I suppose, be turned out by the English. So that we are in a rather considerable fix.'

The Ecclesiastical Titles Bill was not only indirectly responsible—through the defection of the Irish—for the defeat of the Government and the ministerial crisis. It also prevented the Whigs, during and after the crisis, from coming to terms with the Peelites to set up a coalition government. The Peelites and some of the Radicals, particularly Bright and Roebuck, were resolutely opposed to legislation concerning ecclesiastical titles. If the Peelite *Morning Chronicle* had been the property of Cardinal Wiseman himself, wrote one Protestant, it could not have advocated his cause more thoroughly or with more apparent zeal. The Peelites gave as their main reason for not joining a coalition their opposition to new legislation on the Catholic question. 'Who could now assert that the Pope has no power in England?' asked Ashley. 'He has put out one Administration and now prevents the formation of another.'

When the Whig ministry returned unchanged after its political crisis, Russell shortened and modified the Ecclesiastical Titles Bill, leaving it, as Sir Robert Inglis said, rather like the play of Hamlet with the part of Hamlet left out. The second reading of the measure in its mutilated form, was carried by the enormous majority of 438–95, but in Committee it underwent many vicissitudes. With the Irish contingent 'significantly and ostentatiously abstaining' from speaking and voting, the Protestants succeeded in carrying extreme amendments against the Government. Thesiger, the Protestant leader, whose arguments were described by his opponent Gladstone as 'formidable indeed', proved himself a more effective tactician than Russell. The Bill was finally carried, plus its Protestant amendments, by 263 votes to 46.

There were spirited protests from the Peelites and a handful of Radicals. Gladstone made the most telling speech against it. He said that he had disliked 'the vaunting and boastful character' of the papal pronouncements, but he disliked the bill even more. It was hostile to the institutions of the country on four counts. It would teach the established religion to rely on other support than that of its own spiritual strength and vitality which alone could give it vigour. It would undermine and weaken the authority of the law in Ireland. It would disparage 'the great principle of religious freedom upon which this wise and understanding people had permanently built its legislation'. Finally, 'it would destroy the bonds of concord and good will which ought to unite all classes and persuasions of Her Majesty's subjects'. Grattan went further and suggested that the title of the measure should be amended to read, 'A Bill to Prevent the Free Exercise of the Roman Catholic Religion in the United Kingdom'.

The opposition opinions were far from representative of popular opinion. There were more people both in the country and in Parliament who felt that the bill did not go far enough, and merely attempted to vindicate 'the wounded honour of our illustrious Queen' in pounds, shillings, and pence. Although the Queen herself regretted 'the unchristian and intolerant spirit' abroad in the land and 'the violent abuse of the Catholic religion', there was little she could have done to damp it down. Even a large number of nonconformists, who disliked the Establishment as much as they disliked the Papacy, and stressed the 'Dissidence of Dissent' alongside 'the Protestantism of the Protestant Churches', proclaimed themselves Englishmen first, and attacked the idea of a foreign potentate—'be he Pope or King—assuming to divide our kingdom according to his pleasure'. Charlotte Brontë complained that with the arrival of Cardinal Wiseman in England, 'London will not be where it was, nor will this day or generation be either *what* or *where* they were. A new Joshua will command the sun not merely to stand still, but to go back six centuries.' The panic persisted. In less oracular vein, Scholefield, one of the members of Parliament for Birmingham, claimed that cells were being built in Newman's Oratory 'for the forcible detention of some of Her Majesty's subjects'. He was not convinced when Newman replied that the 'cells' consisted merely of a larder and a kitchen.

The manifestations of alarm and hysteria were probably shared by many who had few profound religious convictions at all. Indeed *The Ecclesiastic*, a Puseyite magazine, warned the Evangelicals that their alliance with the 'godless crowds' of the large towns could at best offer only a temporary source of strength, and that before very long anti-Catholicism might turn into anti-Christianity. Certainly, even in 1851, despite the excesses of religious enthusiasm, there was a submerged mass of religious apathy and indifference. The religious census of 1851, which presented statistics of numbers of people attending churches and chapels on a random Sunday, 30 March, showed that more than half the population had not been to a church or chapel at all, and that only 20 per cent had attended an Anglican service. Furthermore, what was perhaps even more serious, even had they wished to go, there was only available sitting space in the churches and chapels for 58 per cent of the population—in Birmingham, for only 28·7 per cent of the population, and in London, 29·7 per cent. However easy it might be in a wave of national emotion to justify England to the Pope, it was more difficult, in Charles Kingsley's phrase, 'to justify God to the people'.

The blackest areas were the working-class districts of the large cities, where although Roman Catholic and Nonconformist church building was proceeding at a more rapid rate than Anglican building, there were large groups of people scarcely touched by Christian influences at all. These were the people outside the pale of both Church and Constitution, with few opportunities to become either members of the 'pays légal' or sons of the Church. They had been offered cheap food and little else, and as *The Eclectic Review*, a nonconformist journal, thought it necessary to point out, there was no necessary connexion between the repeal of the corn laws and a religious revival. Indeed, in a rapidly changing world, politics and religion might pull in opposite directions. Kingsley's *Alton Locke*, a new book in 1851, was raising these and similar questions. 'It is the book of an age,' wrote one reviewer, 'it is a kind of concrete thrown up from the vast cauldron of civilization, in which luxury and filth, brutality and art, virtue and intellect, tyranny and wretchedness seethe tumultuously together.'

IV

It was against such a background of light and shade that the ministerial crisis of February and the Great Exhibition stand out, the first an affair of private meetings and secret conferences, the second a festival of crowds, bustle, and publicity.

But the ministerial crisis does not make sense if it is left entirely unrelated to the national background. It was the budget, with its inadequate sops to the increasingly vocal interests clamouring outside Parliament, which made the government tremble. It was the Ecclesiastical Titles Bill, growing out of the national religious panic, which robbed Russell of essential Irish support. It was parliamentary reform, the threat to the balance of the whole political structure, which, in Lansdowne's phrase, provided 'the last drop which made the cup flow over'.

On 20 February the government was defeated on Locke King's radical motion, proposing that the conditions of franchise in the counties should be the same as in the boroughs. Locke King proposed his 'simple, moderate, and practical plan' as the prelude to a great and comprehensive measure by Russell. He claimed that it would crown the victory of 1846 by finally destroying the political bastions of Protectionist privilege. And was not Protectionism still a threat to society, 'akin to communism in its worst shape, for protection might be regarded as the few taking from the many, and communism as the taking from all'? Locke King was supported by Joseph Hume, who argued in similar terms, that the measure was necessary 'to neutralize the opposition of the landed interest'.

Russell attacked Locke King's motion. Simple it might appear to be, but in reality it was opposed to the spirit of the 1832 Reform Bill, on which all reform of the franchise should be based. 'We should not attempt to construct a new and fanciful edifice, but endeavour to add to the symmetry and convenience of the old.' He pledged himself, however, to bring in a reform bill during the next session, if he were still in office. Locke King accepted this promise and did not wish to divide the House, but Hume and Bright insisted, urging that, 'if you don't divide and beat him, he will throw over his promise and do nothing'. The Radicals shared Bright's fears and voted solidly against the ministry. Most of the Irish and Protectionists stayed away, and the government was defeated by 100 votes to 54. According to Stanley, the minority consisted of 17 Protectionists, 27 'official men', tied to the government in various ways, and only 10 'independent' Whig members.

There was general surprise in the House of Commons when Russell chose to resign on this defeat. 'Not a creature in or out of the House,' wrote Greville, 'expected he would regard such a defeat as this as a matter of any importance.' The ministers themselves were divided about the propriety of going out of office. The Queen understood the cause and sympathized. 'Though it was not a question *vital* to the Government, Lord John feels the support he has received so meagre, and the opposition of so many parties so great, that he must *resign*! This is very bad, because there is no chance of any other good Government, poor Peel being no longer alive . . . but Lord John is *right* not to go on when he is so ill-supported, and it will raise him as a political man, and will strengthen his position for the future.'

The position of a Whig Prime Minister was, had been, and was yet to be, an extremely difficult one, and this particular crisis, behind its special features, was symptomatic of a chronic weakness in the existing structure of politics. The Tory *Quarterly Review* offered a shrewd, if one-sided, analysis of the problem. In the first place, a Whig Prime Minister faced the dilemma of being at once the leader of a 'movement and agitation party' and the head of a government, 'the essence of all government being restraint and resistance'. Quite apart from the extreme Radical tail of the movement party, there were many 'independent members', who were unwilling to support the government merely because it was a Whig government. They might be won over by patronage, but patronage could not meet all the demands on it. From 1846 onwards Russell had governed precariously 'from hand to mouth—that is, by what the Treasury *hand* puts into the *mouth* of the hungry member'. Where patronage could not be offered or would not work, expedients were constantly necessary. From the time of the Lichfield House Compact of 1835, Irish support had been essential for Whig power. As a result of constant recourse to such expedients, 'what was called *governing* the country came to be nothing else than the art of keeping this heterogeneous and discordant body together and in any kind of discipline—which could only be accomplished by a constant subterranean traffic of patronage with private jobbers, and by frequent sacrifices of Church and Constitution to Dissenters and Radicals. This was the real difficulty of the case and the cause of every Ministerial crisis.' The condition was a chronic one, and could not be attributed to any individual or sequence of events. Indeed the day before Locke King brought forward his motion, Disraeli wrote that notwithstanding the efforts of all persons and parties to keep them in, he doubted whether the government could stand.

Russell's resignation led to several days of hectic excitement. 'Such was the confusion of the ministerial movements and political promenades,' wrote *Punch*, 'that everybody went to call upon everybody. The hall porters were never known to have had such a time of it, but though knocking at doors continued throughout the whole day, nothing seemed to answer.'

The Tories were unable to form a ministry. However right *The Quarterly Review* might in its thesis on Whig weakness, there was no doubt at all about the even weaker position of the Tories. The Whigs could claim on their side two great advantages—experience of office, the knowledge that they could form and wanted to form a government of seasoned ministers; and the slogans of free trade and progress, which kept them aligned with 'the spirit of the age'. When free trade was threatened, they knew that they could not only close their own ranks, but widen the basis of their support. 'Upon the first proposition of a Stanley Government,' Aberdeen and Graham told the Queen, 'the junction of the Parties would be contemplated, and there would be only *one* strong opposition.' The cry of 'Free Trade in Peril' would rouse the country and make the work of a Protectionist government impossible. 'I am *l'homme impossible*,' Stanley told Russell when the crisis was over.

If the continued identification of the Tories with Protection handicapped them in the eyes of the outside world, their differences of opinion about its practical application led to division and paralysis in their inner councils. With the notable exception of Disraeli they were neither prepared for nor willing to accept the responsibilities of office. 'It was by no act of mine or one of my friends that the late Government fell,' Stanley told the House of Lords, 'I felt no exultation at the event, and I felt no undue anxiety to seize the offices they had held.' He begged the Queen 'that he might not be called upon to take office except as a *dernier ressort*'.

The Tories could not form a ministry: the Peelites by themselves were impotent, nor at this stage did they feel disposed to join in a coalition with the Whigs. They raised so many issues besides the Ecclesiastical Titles Bill that it seemed as if some of them, particularly Graham, 'did not wish to complete any combination'. They were unwilling to reach any understanding with Stanley and the Tories, for apart from the shadow of Peel and the barrier of free trade, they felt that the Crown and the country were only safe 'in these days, by having the Liberals in office, else they would be driven to join the Radical agitation against the institutions of the country'. Throughout the crisis they talked of the possibility of joining the Whigs at some unknown date in the future. They were in fact waiting for another and bigger crisis, for as *The Quarterly Review* remarked, 'coalitions of this (Whig-Peelite) nature are reluctantly taken in cold blood'. They developed out of a *mêlée* rather than a *pas seul* or *pas de deux*.

The Queen tried all existing possible combinations. She was not in favour of a dissolution as a means of breaking the deadlock and refused to give Stanley a positive assurance that she would dissolve, saying that 'she would discuss the question when the emergency arose'. She was anxious, as were many other people, to avoid a dissolution in the year of the Exhibition, but quite apart from this special consideration feared stirring up commotion in the country before it was strictly necessary. The Queen's attitude was widely shared and there was little interest in an 'appeal to the country'. After the crisis was over, Greville claimed that the only thing which would obtain anything like forbearance for the government was 'the general dread of a dissolution and the anxiety of members to stave it off'.

The only possible answer to the deadlock was to follow the advice of the Duke of Wellington and restore the Russell ministry to office. They came back on 4 March not triumphantly but as a *pis aller*. They were 'damaged, weak and unpopular'. 'No bonfires were lighted, no bells were rung, no living man, save those personally interested, rejoiced in the fact. The Administration had worn out the endurance of the nation; not a particle of enthusiasm remained. Amongst its followers a dull dead feeling of indifference prevailed. . . . The country was incredulous. They could not believe that the Ministry, *as a whole*, were reinstated.'

The return of Russell marked no final solution of the parliamentary deadlock. 'It is the unique distinction of the present dilemma,' wrote *The Times*, 'that it was always foreseen, and that in similar circumstances, it must inevitably recur. There exists no political party competent, at the usual challenge, to receive from others the reins of power. We possess no Opposition convertible into a Government, and we feel the effects of the privation in the negligence and imperfections of a Ministry so long as it acts, and in the absolute paralysis of the State when it can act no longer.'

If you were a reader of *The Quarterly Review*, you would see the dilemma as part of the price of 1832, a permanent feature of the new constitutional framework. 'How can the Royal Government be carried on?' Wellington had asked. The answer was that it could not. If you were a Peelite or the Queen, you would see the deadlock as largely personal, in terms of the premature death of 'poor Peel'. If you were a Radical, you would see it as a chapter in an unfinished political revolution. 'The family coteries of Whiggery require to be broken up,' wrote *The Eclectic Review*, 'and what has occurred will hasten this. . . . What we have witnessed is only one of the many scenes which will be enacted before the common right of Englishmen in the business of legislation is admitted. . . . The times for oligarchial rule are passed. We have as yet seen only the initial struggle. The real contest is to come. . . . We must secure talent and public virtues by whomsoever exhibited, and in whatever class seen, without regard to the interested cliques which claim a monopoly of political wisdom.' According to this view, so long as cliques controlled politics at Westminster, they would while away their time in merely factious struggles, irrelevant to the progress of the nation. This was the view of bodies like the Parliamentary and Financial Reform Society, trying to stir up radical opinion in the provinces.

Caught among all these interpretations of the crisis, Lord John was in his usual uncomfortable position. 'His mishaps have almost exhausted metaphor. One day he *overturns the coach*, another day he *swamps the boat*, then he *breaks down*, then he *blows up*, in council he is *squirrel-minded*, and finally, it is *impossible to sleep soundly while he has command of the watch*. Admiral Byron did not better deserve the sobriquet of *Foul-weather Jack*.' And his troubles were by no means over. Although he was to ride safely into a new year, at the heavy price of losing Palmerston, he met his *tit for tat* in 1852. The Palmerston crisis was politically more significant than the February crisis, for it was Palmerston and not Russell who was to show in face of the recurring parliamentary deadlock how the impress of a powerful personality might impose some sort of order and continuity on half-reformed English politics. And it was by means of foreign policy and not by offers of parliamentary reform that Palmerston was to cast his spell.

V

Between February crisis and the fall of Palmerston came the Great Exhibition. To Disraeli, with both eyes fixed on parliamentary problems and prospects, it was 'a godsend to the Government . . . diverting public attention from their blunders'. To those less interested in the promptings of political ambition, it was a national triumph. The *frondeurs*, who had ridiculed both the idea and the site of the Exhibition in 1850—'an industrial exhibition in the heart of fashionable Belgravia to enable foreigners to rob us of our honour' —prophesied public indifference and financial failure. As events proved, there were over six million visitors between the opening and closing days. Cheap excursions ensured the success of the enterprise. Visitors poured in from all parts of the country and overseas. Never had such quiet—and orderly—crowds been seen in London before. They made the most of the occasion. 'I never remember anything before that everyone was so pleased with, as is the case with this Exhibition,' wrote the Queen.

Part of the delight lay in the inspiration of Joseph Paxton's glass mansion itself. The enormous conservatory of glass and iron— 1,848 feet long, 408 feet broad, and 66 feet high—with transepts so constructed as to contain indoors some of the finest elms growing in Hyde Park, was designed to capture the public imagination:

61

As though 'twere by a wizard's rod,
A blazing arch of lucid glass
Leaps like a fountain from the grass
To meet the sun.

Paxton had won the prize for the design of the Exhibition building
in face of 245 designs and specifications sent in by professional
architects from all parts of the world. His adaptation of the late
Georgian iron conservatory, with which he had already experi-
mented as the Duke of Devonshire's gardener at Chatsworth, was
elaborated by architects and ornamentalists. Barry, for instance,
whose new unfinished Houses of Parliament were being admired by
the crowds, was responsible for introducing the barrel-roofed
transept. But it was Paxton who took credit for the conception. As
John Summerson has said, 'he was a type of creator as new and as
characteristic of the Age as the building he had designed. Paxton, the
expert gardener, the observer of nature, the man of affairs, the
engineer, the railway director, the prompter of newspapers and
magazines, seemed as much the "complete man" of Victorian
England as Alberti had been of Renaissance Florence'. He was the
epitome of self-help, showing, as the Queen remarked, how the
lowest were able to rise by their own merits to the highest grade of
society.

The building itself was thought to offer a solution to the difficult
problem of finding a distinctive nineteenth-century style in architecture. 'We have been saved from a hideous and costly mass of bricks
and mortar,' wrote one commentator, 'and have a graceful and
beautiful creation in its stead, and a new and suggestive *fact*, a step
taken along a fresh track. . . . Architecture has had to wait for help
from a botanist. Quite in keeping is the building with the age. It is
the æsthetic blossom of its practical character, and of the practical
tendency of the English nation.' *Practical* and *magical* were not considered as incompatible. Disraeli knew the right sort of language to
please when he called the building 'that enchanted pile which the
sagacious taste and the prescient philanthropy of an accomplished
and enlightened Prince have raised for the glory of England and the
delight and instruction of two hemispheres'. Douglas Jerrold's
brilliant name *Crystal Palace* was the perfect designation: it seemed
to catch not the workaday realities but the hidden dreams of England
in 1851.

The Crystal Palace was a symbol of the age. It represented the
triumph of human thought and of human work. Paxton had prepared the scheme from the first flash of the idea to the drawing up of
the blue-prints during just over a month, from 11 June to 15 July

1850. The achievement of the contractors was equally remarkable. The ground was handed over to them on 30 July; the first column was raised on 26 September. Within seventeen weeks of the start, nearly a million feet of glass had been fastened on to the web-like structure of 3,300 columns and 2,300 girders. The exhibits started pouring in from the beginning of 1851, and on 1 May, the official day of opening, the only exhibits which had not arrived were those from Russia.

There were over 13,000 exhibitors, one half of the total Exhibition area being occupied by Great Britain and the Colonies, and the other half by foreign states, of which France and Germany were the most important. There were four distinct classes of exhibits—raw materials, machinery, manufactures, and fine arts. Looked at as a whole, the Exhibition represented the meeting of old and new. Machinery was in the ascendant, but handicrafts were not yet in general eclipse. Alongside a sewing machine from the United States and cotton machines from Oldham, there was fine black lace from Barcelona and pottery from Sèvres.

The machines fascinated the visitors. While a crowd of men in smocks admired the agricultural implements, the Queen was particularly impressed by a medal-making machine which produced fifty million medals a week where it had only been possible to produce a million fifteen years before. She marvelled too at the electric telegraph, and sent messages to loyal subjects in Edinburgh and Manchester. Other visitors, interested in mechanical progress, contrasted the functional beauty of the English locomotives with the ornate 'make-believe of your rococo side-board with its false outlines and incongruous ornament', and compared the creative energy of the machines with 'the dead mechanicalness of barefaced copies of Gothic screens'.

1851 had two faces. It was producing not only locomotives, but Gothic replicas, and set aside from the rest of the Exhibition, 'looking dark and solemn', was Pugin's mediæval court, 'for the display of the taste and art of dead men'. You could look either forwards or backwards. While Dr. Whewell, Master of Trinity, looked to machines and interchangeable spare parts to create an age of mass-production, Pugin lingered longingly in the fourteenth century. Both attitudes were fashionable. When the Queen visited the Guild Hall in July to celebrate with the City the success of the Exhibition, supper was served in the crypt, which was fitted up as an old baronial hall, figures in mediæval armour being scattered about, carrying lights which illuminated the chamber. Candles and gas-light and dreams of electricity: mediæval armour and Birmingham hardware: buildings of glass and Gothic shrines—all these were part of 1851; and many recent writers have considered that the mediæval preoccupations of the men of 1851 were at least as fruitful as their confident expectations of continued material progress. It is difficult to judge. Of two young men called William, who visited the Exhibition, one, William Whiteley, aged 20, was so inspired by the glass building that he began to dream of large shops, 'universal provider's' shops with plate glass fronts. The other, William Morris, three years younger, was moved enough by the Exhibition to call the whole display 'wonderfully ugly'.

Both old and new, revival and anticipation, had to be represented if the Exhibition were to fulfil the objective laid down by the Prince Consort of presenting 'a true test and living picture of the point of development at which the whole of mankind has arrived . . . and a new starting point, from which all nations will be able to direct their further exertions'. The Exhibition was conceived of as providing a running commentary on the age. But its purposes went further than that. It was a running commentary interrupted by constant object lessons. Two themes were repeated more than the rest—the gospel of work and the gospel of peace.

The Exhibition was designed to honour 'the working bees of the world's hive' and to cast tacit reflexion on the drones. This was the great popular lesson—'the workers, of all types, stand forth as the really great men'. The Exhibition medals bore the words, *pulcher et ille labor palma decorare laborem*. In such a festival, not only the entrepreneurs but also the manual labourers had to be remembered. Indirectly the Exhibition focussed attention on the same set of problems as had been raised in *Alton Locke*. 'Shall we ostentatiously show off all manner of articles of luxury and comfort and be ashamed to disclose the condition of those we have to thank for them?' This was a question which could no more be shelved than the other great question of the day—the divergence and reconciliation of material and moral progress. 'For what shall it profit a man if he shall gain the whole world and lose his soul?'

The gospel of peace was stressed with as much fervour as the gospel of work. There had been many industrial exhibitions before 1851. The Society of Arts itself had exhibited its prize awards for agricultural and industrial machinery since it first instituted them in 1761. In 1849 there had been a big industrial exhibition in Birmingham. The special feature of the 1851 Exhibition was that it was universal. 'Paxton, go forth,' *Punch* depicted Prince Albert as saying, 'take glass and iron, and, beauty wedding strength, produce the Industrial Hall of Nations.' Out of the honest rivalry of industry and skill, countries would find a new brotherhood. The Crystal Palace was thought of as a Temple of Peace, where all nations would meet by appointment under the same roof, and shake each other by the hand. *Paxton vobiscum.* 'The tree of trees to be planted is a gigantic olive that is expected to take root in the Paxton Palace of Hyde Park; an olive strengthened, sheltered, and protected by the glass walls and roof, that admit the commercial trophies of all the world—a veritable Peace Congress, manufactured by the many-coloured hands of the human family. We do not see why there should not be an Order of the Olive. Will Prince Albert think of it?'

The emphasis on peace had an avowedly Christian colouring. The Archbishop's opening prayers reminded the first distinguished visitors not only that all wealth had come from God, but also that England could be specially thankful for 'the peace that is within our walls and plenteousness within our gates'. They should pray that God might help them in their noble purpose of 'knitting together in the bonds of peace and concord the different nations on the earth'. The earth was the Lord's and all that dwelt therein. Queen Victoria was pleased with a 'nice sermon' which she heard three days after the opening of the Exhibition, when the preacher alluded to the ceremony, and took as his text, 'And he hath made of one blood all nations of men to dwell on the face of the earth'.

The hopes of peace were soon dashed. They had seemed too grandiloquently phrased for many of the writers of the time. Some of them could not forget that the 'order' of 1851 rested on the repression of the revolutions of 1848. Others were sceptical about the future. *The Eclectic Review* referred to 'stern facts weltering beneath the rose pink surface', and pointed out how the 'Federation of the Universe' propaganda of the French Revolution had served as a prelude to a generation of war. 'The "tears of joy" were turned to tears of blood, and with their plenteousness watered the earth. A great farce proved the opening scene of a great tragedy.' These words were not intended to suggest that similar terrors were imminent, but by the end of the year, scarcely before the contractors had begun to dismantle the fabric of the Crystal Palace, events in France rudely shattered the confidence in a new world. At the same time also, they shattered the summer-time equilibrium of Russell's government.

VI

The Great Exhibition had been designed in part to reveal to foreigners the attractions of the British Constitution. 'We all agreed,' the Duchess of Gloucester wrote to the Queen the day after the opening of the Exhibition, 'in rejoicing that *Foreigners should* have witnessed the affection of the *People* to *you* and *your Family*, and how the *English people* do *love* and respect the *Crown*.' Foreigners did not appear to learn the lesson. On 30 September the Queen wrote to the King of the Belgians that 'the position of Princes', which was difficult in those times, would be much less difficult, 'if they would behave honourably and straightforwardly, giving the people gradually those privileges which would satisfy all the reasonable and well-intentioned, and would weaken the power of the Red Republicans. Instead of that, *reaction* and a return to all the tyranny and oppression is the cry and the principle—and all papers and books are being seized and prohibited, as in the days of Metternich.'

The Queen and the Prince Consort had strong views concerning not only the duty of Princes but the methods and responsibilities of Foreign Secretaries. They had clashed frequently with Palmerston in 1850, the Queen persistently urging Russell to transfer him to a different office or to remove him from the Cabinet. The February crisis seemed to offer an easy opportunity, but Russell refused to consider any immediate change. 'Our party is hardly reunited, and any break into sections, following one man or the other, would be fatal to us.' He knew and confessed that he, Russell, was the element of weakness in the government, and Palmerston the element of strength, on account of his great popularity with the Radicals; and that to remove the Foreign Secretary would break up the administration. He promised that he would try to get rid of Palmerston during the Easter recess, but, when Easter came, declared that this was again impossible. Palmerston's departure was indefinitely postponed, and the Exhibition overshadowed all other problems.

It had scarcely come to a close, when the visit of Kossuth to England led to renewed antagonism between the Queen and the Foreign Secretary and to open conflict between the Foreign Secretary and the Prime Minister. The visit of Kossuth was one of the big events of the year. He met with enormous cheering crowds wherever he went, in the provinces as well as in London, and fulsome tributes were paid to his defence of liberty and to his eloquent presentation in fluent English of the salient features of the international situation. The Queen feared a meeting between Palmerston and Kossuth, and Prince Albert feared that if that did not happen 'something worse' would. Russell 'positively requested' Palmerston not to receive Kossuth, and the Foreign Secretary replied tartly that he did not choose to be dictated to as to whom he might or might not receive in his own house. 'I shall use my discretion. . . . You will, of course, use yours as to the composition of your Government.' The Cabinet backed Russell, and Palmerston did not see Kossuth, but he did receive radical deputations from Finsbury and Islington, who used colourful language in his presence to describe the actions of the Emperors of Austria and Russia.

The Kossuth affair was still being discussed when news of Napoleon's *coup d'état* reached London. The *politique de bascule* was over in Paris: midnight military violence had taken its place. Behind a carpet which had been shown at the Exhibition, twelve persons were killed. England could not escape the shock of the French *coup d'état*, the last big event in the sequence of revolution and counter-revolution which followed from the events of 1848. 'We are destined to feel the electric shock of every explosion or convulsion that France undergoes,' wrote *The Quarterly Review*.

News of the French *coup d'état* reached England by the newly laid electric telegraph. There were immediate rumours in *The Daily News* that Palmerston had quarrelled with his colleagues: 'along with the alarming despatch from Paris has come a report that Lord Palmerston is no longer in the Cabinet'. The rumours were soon forgotten, and on 16 December the newspapers reported that ministers were quietly leaving London for their Christmas holidays, 'congratulating themselves, no doubt, on the very comfortable state of things in England compared with France'.

Beneath the surface things were very far from comfortable in the cabinet. Two days after the *coup*, Queen Victoria wrote to Russell explaining that it was of very great importance to instruct Normanby, the British ambassador in Paris, to remain entirely passive, and to take no part and make no comments on what was happening. The Queen's advice came too late. Palmerston had already expressed 'private' approval of the *coup d'état* to Walewski, the French representative in London, and was writing to Normanby rebuking him for his hostility to Napoleon, and telling him to report more sympathetically on the course of events in Paris.

Normanby's brother-in-law, Colonel Phipps, was Prince Albert's secretary, and Lady Normanby plied him with information concerning Palmerston's peculiar and 'most flippant' conduct. He had been wilder than ever before. 'He ridicules the idea of the Constitution; turns to scorn the idea of anything being done to the Members of the Assembly; laughs and jokes at the (English) Club being fired into, though the English people in it were within an ace of being murdered by the soldiers; says that Normanby is pathetic over a broken looking-glass, forgetting that the same bullet grazed the hand of an Englishman, "a Roman citizen". . . .'

On 13 December the Queen wrote to Russell, enclosing a Normanby despatch about Walewski's conversation with Palmerston, and asked, 'Does Lord John know anything about the alleged approval, which if true, would *again* expose the honesty and dignity of the Queen's Government in the eyes of the world?'

Russell received an extremely unsatisfactory explanation from

Palmerston, offered him the Lord Lieutenancy of Ireland in place of the Foreign Office, and finally, after Palmerston had refused this greatly inferior position, replaced him by Granville 'the Polite', a friend of the Prince Consort, with whom he had worked as a member of the Royal Commission for the Exhibition of 1851. A Cabinet meeting on 22 December backed up Russell, and two days later the news of Palmerston's fall was announced in *The Times*. It came as a shock to the public despite the previous rumours of resignation. 'The change had been made, and all but formally ratified, with the secrecy and celerity of the Parisian *coup d'état*.' Many people did not believe the report in *The Times* and waited for the evening's *Globe* to see if a mistake had been made.

The cause of the dismissal of Palmerston was not immediately clear to the public. *The Morning Chronicle* spread the report that it was because he had quarrelled with the Austrian and Russian ambassadors about England becoming 'a place of asylum' for foreign refugees. It was not until a little later that the news came through, first, that the French question had led to a 'divergency of action, amounting to the opening of two distinct and discordant channels of communication with the French Government', and, second, 'that of late Lord Palmerston assumed an independence and singleness of action altogether inconsistent with the fact that the whole Cabinet shared the responsibility of his acts'.

While the readers of the press were bewildered and perturbed by the fall of so highly-valued a Foreign Secretary, the Queen was delighted with this ending or apparent ending to a long chapter of recklessness and disaster. 'I have the greatest pleasure,' she wrote to the King of the Belgians on 23 December, 'in announcing to you a piece of news which I know will give you as much satisfaction and relief as it does to us. *Lord Palmerston is no longer Foreign Secretary*.' Seven days later, she philosophized about the news. 'It is too grievous to think how much misery and mischief might have been avoided. However, now he has done with the Foreign Office for ever, and "the veteran" statesman, as the newspapers, to our great amusement and I am sure, to *his infinite* annoyance, call him, must rest upon his laurels.' This was one occasion on which Queen Victoria was amused, although the amusement did not last long.

The Queen and the Prince Consort felt themselves strengthened by Palmerston's fall: Lord John Russell's administration was undoubtedly weakened 'unto death'. Russell chose the occasion of Palmerston's fall with as much care as he could, and he acted swiftly. As Disraeli wrote to Lady Londonderry, 'the success of Napoleon seems to have given Johnny a taste for *coup d'états*'. Russell hoped that not all Radicals would adopt the same friendly approach to the new French government which Palmerston had done, and that their opposition to blood-stained dictatorship would more than counterbalance their faith in Palmerston as a Radical bulwark in European politics. He hoped further—and in this he was right in the very short run—that Palmerston's waywardness towards his colleagues, and, though it could not be said too openly, towards the Queen, would meet with general disapproval. But all these hopes could not disguise the loss of the one powerful personality, who could win the loyalty of the Radical and 'independent members'. 'Palmerston's good nature, courtesy, and hospitality,' wrote Clarendon, 'made him many friends, and he was able to turn away the wrath of opponents as no other member of the Government can do.'

In the last few months of 1851 all the paradoxes in the Radical support of Palmerston had been most striking. While he was listening to addresses referring to the Emperors of Russia and Austria as 'odious and detestable assassins' and 'merciless tyrants and despots', he was opposing Russell's plans for a new Reform Bill, that same Reform Bill which Russell had promised Locke King in February. The fate of the Reform Bill became very problematical after the fall of Palmerston, and so did the fate of the government. There was yet another Morton's fork confronting the Prime Minister. If he proposed a comprehensive reform bill in such quiet times, it would be talked out or thrown out; if he proposed anything temperate, 'the movement party would spring at him like hounds'. Disraeli knew the answer to that dilemma. 'He ought to resign.'

The only possible way of averting defeat and resignation was to explore yet again the rejected alternatives of February 1851. The one thing which stood out after December was the prospect of a Whig-Peelite coalition, but it did not prove possible to secure it at once. It was not Graham or Herbert or even the Duke of Newcastle who filled the vacant place in the Cabinet, but Vernon Smith, who had voted for Locke King's motion in February. The government was not strengthened, February again proved a cruel month, and Russell was forced to resign in February 1852, when Palmerston threw his weight against him, this time to make way for a short-lived Protectionist ministry. Derby's hopes of drawing in Palmerston again failed, although they seemed a good deal more realistic than they had done a year earlier. Indeed the expectations of the Protectionists, although still very hazardous, were becoming rather more realistic in general. The dissolution of 1852 freed them from thraldom to a dogma, and allowed them to take the first step in the long and difficult process of becoming a popular party. That first step was a necessary condition for a return to a two-party system. The absence of this system in 1851 had made English politics strangely similar to more recent politics in France, and the Queen's great fear in contemplating a further dose of parliamentary reform was whether 'the strengthening of the Democratic principle will upset the balance of Constitution, and further weaken the Executive, which is by no means too strong at present'.

VII

The weakness of the Executive might alarm the Queen, but it cheered large sections of the community. While the Queen rejoiced at Christmas 1851 in the fall of Palmerston, the community as a whole rejoiced in a year of prosperity and progress. *The Manchester Guardian* interpreted the events and the spirit of the year for the benefit of its Christmas readers. 'The best contribution that anyone can make to the happiness of a Christmas circle is to show its members that they have good grounds for satisfaction, for hope, and for self-approval. We are glad, therefore, to be able to say that English society had never a better right, than at the present moment, to sit quietly under a sermon, with that pleasing moral. In all our relations, we have at least as much, if not more, substantial reason for contentment and thankfulness than at the close of any past year in our history.'

It went on to give the reasons for this happy state of affairs. First, there was cheap food in plenty, and with it 'clothing, fuel, shelter, and transition from place to place—within the reach of all, except those whom demerit, or extraordinary misfortune has reduced to complete destitution'. Second, 'we have complete domestic tranquillity, and as much amity abroad, as is compatible in these days with the maintenance of self-respect'. Third, the tone of the country was right, and it was still set on a road of progress. 'The last twenty years have witnessed an unprecedented growth of interest and good feeling among our widely separated classes, a great improvement in national manners and public morality, the introduction of a more humane and popular spirit of legislation, and, in general terms, a patient, but earnest desire of progressive improvement in all ranks of the people.' Finally, 'it would be unseasonably invidious to institute a minute comparison between our own and our neighbour's pudding; but we cannot refrain from saying that there are few Christmas parties in Europe to which we can turn a momentary glance, without greatly heightening the satisfaction with which we turn again towards home'.

The qualifications introduced into the catalogue of national blessings are important in catching the spirit of 1851. The phrase 'except those whom demerit, or extraordinary misfortune had reduced to complete destitution' recalls once again the submerged ranks of the nation, dismissed in terms of social theory or inevitable accident, but no longer frightening enough to be regarded as a second nation in themselves. The phrase 'as much amity abroad as is compatible with the maintenance of self-respect' recalls the limit placed even in this year of peace on national appeasement. There was a recognition in the words of Prince Albert that 'we are entering upon most dangerous times in which Military Despotism and Red Republicanism will for some time be the only Powers on the Continent, to both of which the Constitutional Monarchy of England will be equally hateful. That the calm influence of our institutions, however, should succeed in assuaging the contest abroad must be the anxious wish of every Englishman.'

The recognition of dangerous times ahead on the continent did not go far enough, however, to disturb the mood of self-satisfaction. As Sir Llewellyn Woodward has said, 'the Victorians were living dangerously, far more dangerously than they knew. The world was much stronger than their machinery, and the nature of man more fragile and at the same time more unfathomable.' The elements of doubt had not yet been fashioned into a pattern of self-criticism. That was to be the work of the future. The criticism has been pushed so far since 1851 that men are beginning to react against it, and to feel increasingly nostalgic about the loss of the world which reached its triumphant peak in the year of the Great Exhibition.

D. C. SOMERVELL

The Victorian Age

ANYONE who writes under such a title as this must encounter a preliminary scepticism. Are any features, any details, characteristic of the Victorian Age as a whole? In other words, is the Victorian Age a fact, or a figment which the otherwise non-significant facts of a Queen's accession and demise have imposed upon our imaginations? No doubt all the 'Ages' and 'Periods' with which historians have articulated the chaos of their raw material belong to the realm of fiction rather than of fact. They have been invented for the convenience of the student. 'The Middle Ages' or 'The Renaissance' are both of them easily analysed out of existence, and every 'Age' has in turn pleaded guilty to being an 'Age of Transition'. Nothing stands still, least of all since Watt invented (or improved) the steam engine. Acceleration is one of the keynotes of all that Modern Age of which the Victorian is the central section. It would be possible to take each Victorian decade in turn and to devote this essay to showing how strikingly it differed, not only in incident but in atmosphere, from its predecessor. Any picture of the Victorian Age must be a picture in the Hollywood rather than the National Gallery sense of the term. On that point there would be general agreement. The question at issue is rather this: would a series of such pictures, beginning somewhere in the thirties and ending with the end of the century, have sufficient unity within itself and sufficient distinctness from what comes before and after to deserve serious historical treatment as a 'period'? Let us, by an examination of the beginning and the end of the alleged Victorian Age, see what evidence can be collected in favour of its existence.

I

It is customary to date the opening of the Victorian Age from the passage of the Reform Bill of 1832. That measure has offered an easy target to the iconoclasts. They have shown that, numerically, it added less than a quarter of a million to the electorate, and that it made the franchise in certain boroughs not more but less democratic than before; that it did not perceptibly alter the social type dominant in the House of Commons, and so on. All these things are true, but they miss the main points. The Act proved that the franchise was alterable, that public opinion, armed with arguments and if necessary with brickbats, could coerce the government into coercing the House of Lords; that in fact the English Revolution, so often discussed since Waterloo, would not be required and would therefore not take place. Instead, the House of Commons, if socially still the same, would reveal its political difference. The age of inquiries, commissions, and blue books was about to open. Epochs always overlap and the Chartists of 1839 revived for a few months the Peterloo atmosphere, but they were quickly beaten off the field by the Anti-Corn Law Leaguers. The Age of Cobbett gave place to the Age of Cobden, and the latter name is as certainly Victorian as the former is certainly not.

Still more obviously does the accession of Victoria coincide with the appearance of one of the salient features of modern life and landscape, the railway. Stockton-Darlington and Liverpool-Manchester were earlier, but these were almost isolated forerunners separated by nearly a decade from the main movement. Then in 1836 the accumulated savings of five good harvests poured forth into the first railway boom, and in 1836–7 thirty-nine acts legalizing railway projects, among them five rival projects for a Brighton line, passed through Parliament. In 1838 lines from London reached Birmingham and Maidenhead, in 1840 Southampton, in 1844 Dover. Indeed, by the end of the forties, the outlines of the modern system were completed by the efforts of local companies, soon to coalesce into the larger concerns whose names were familiar down to the end of the 1914–18 War. An inscription on a railway bridge outside Kendal— 'Lancaster and Carlisle railway 1847'—supplies both a fact and its date. That the railways revolutionized passenger transport goes without saying. They also revolutionized the transport of goods and were probably a more important factor than the repeal of the Corn Laws in establishing the famous 'Victorian prosperity', which opened in the last years of the forties. They also offered the public a new and hitherto unequalled opening for speculative investment, and provided, roughly speaking, the model on which the productive industries were going to organize themselves after the passage of the limited liability acts of the sixties.

Nor were railways the only mechanical improvements to coincide with the opening of the Victorian Age. Innovations trivial in themselves may, if they come home sufficiently closely to men's business and bosoms, claim some social significance. Of this order are the substitution of steel for quill pens, of blotting-paper for sand, of 'little paper bags called envelopes' for seals, of matches for tinderboxes. All these can with very little pressure be synchronized with the Queen's accession. Also the penny post, and postage-stamps— and the habit of eating chocolate, hitherto regarded only as the ingredient of a beverage. Cadbury advertised 'French Eating Chocolate' in 1842. I remember reading somewhere that 1580, known to Macaulay's schoolboy as the date of the arrival of the first Jesuits in this island, was also approximately the date of the arrival of the cockroach (or was it the bed-bug?). It is characteristic of school history to record the lesser and overlook the greater misfortune, just because the latter had nothing to do with politics. Let it then be recorded of 1842 that, while a Conservative government gave us the income tax, a family long to be associated with the Liberal party gave us something better.

If one regards the appearance of new men as an essential feature of the establishment of a new age, the course of British politics offers no encouragement to our quest. Peel, Palmerston, Russell, and Aberdeen, all of them pre-Victorians, are in no haste to make way for their successors. But if one turns from politics to literature one finds the Victorian Age marked off from its predecessor with a very peculiar distinctness. What one may call the Waterloo generation dies off with surprising suddenness and unanimity. Keats, Shelley, Byron, Wordsworth, Coleridge, Scott, Bentham: all but one of these was dead several years before the Queen's accession, and Wordsworth, though he had not ceased to produce poetry, had ceased to be a great poet. Then ensued a kind of pause, a silence before the early Victorian lions began to roar and the early Victorian nightingales to sing. Of the greater Victorian writers only one, Macaulay, was conspicuous before the passage of the Reform Bill; his first essay appeared in the year of Byron's death and he 'awoke to find himself famous'. With the thirties, the new figures step forward and enter upon careers of persistent productivity, extending in some cases well onwards towards the end of the century. These may almost lay claim to be whole-time Victorians. Such was Tennyson, the most intimately Victorian of all, whose first volume appeared in 1830 and his last in 1892. Carlyle's *Sartor Resartus* appeared in 1833 and his *French Revolution* in 1837. *Pickwick* and *Paracelsus* in 1836; *Oliver*

Twist and *Strafford* in 1837. Darwin's *Voyage of the 'Beagle'* in 1839. If lighter fare be called for, there is *The Ingoldsby Legends* in 1840, and the founding of *Punch*, that quintessentially Victorian periodical, which has raised a million laughs and never brought a blush to a maiden's cheek, in 1841. A few years more bring the first novels of Thackeray and Charlotte Brontë and the first volume of *Modern Painters*.

Such are some of the marks of the opening of the Victorian Age. When we look for the signs of its close they are as easily found. Thirteen months before the end of the reign occurred that unforgettable Black Week—Stormberg, Magersfontein, Colenso; tragedies in minature by later standards, they none the less effectively pricked and deflated that late Victorian imperial complacency against which the major prophet of imperialism had, only two years before, warned his vast public in his Jubilee Recessional. And no reinflation followed, for it seems in retrospect that after Black Week nothing could go right for long. The South African War itself, instead of ending with a bang as wars should end, prolonged itself in a wearisome geurilla in which all the honours and all the fun were with the defeated. Then the leading statesman of one party focused attention on our dying industries, and a few years later the leading statesman of the other set himself to fan the flames of class warfare. The Lords challenged the Commons, the Kaiser challenged the British Navy, the Suffragettes challenged the male sex, Dublin and Belfast threatened each other and both threatened Westminster, and the leading trade unions in Triple Alliance threatened a General Strike. Whatever one may think of these things one can hardly think them Victorian.

Black Week befell at the end of 1899. A much less noticed event earlier in the same year might be taken as the conception, though not yet the birth, of post-Victorian party politics. In that year the Trades Union Congress joined with certain socialist societies to establish a Labour Representation Committee, with Mr. Ramsay MacDonald as secretary. Powerfully assisted by the agitation following the Taff Vale judgment in 1902, the Committee succeeded in getting 29 candidates into the parliament of 1906. As these were immediately joined by 22 'Lib-Labs' (Labour candidates elected with Liberal support), the new party commanded fifty seats. The old aristocratic parliamentary cricket match, Whigs and Tories, Liberals and Conservatives, alternately batting and fielding, enjoying and never overstepping the rigours of the game, was nearing its end. One sometimes fails to realize how exclusively Victorian that system was. Before the first Reform Bill the Tories had held office for nearly fifty years. Under the first two Georges the Whigs had held office for an equal period. Only in the Victorian Age, the Melbourne-Peel-Russell-

Derby-Palmerston-Disraeli-Gladstone-Salisbury age, did the system of regular alternations between two groups, socially equal and politically similar, prevail. It is one of the distinguishing features of the period.

The age began with the coming of the railway; it ended with the coming of the motor, and it is unfortunately typical of the developments that lie within the Age itself that, whereas the railway was an all-British invention, which subsequently conquered the world with British engines and British iron rails, the internal combustion engine was patented by a German and the first practicable cars were built in France. The once notorious Red Flag Act which made motoring impossible on English roads was repealed in 1896 and the event was celebrated by a processional expedition from London to Brighton. The crowd jeered the new toy good-humouredly, for some of the cars failed to start; but others performed the journey without mishap. Most of us who are old enough to have such memories would find, if we researched, that our first contact with the new transport coincided fairly closely with the end of the reign, though in 1900 the personal possession of a car was still almost as exceptional as the personal possession of an aeroplane today. In the history of transport the Victorian Age might be defined as the age of the eclipse of the road, and therewith the roadside inn. What the coaches had lost the cars and later the motor-buses and motor-lorries brought back. This was to mean many non-Victorian things, among them the resumption of arterial road planning at the point where Telford and his colleagues had left it: it also meant, for thousands of investors, a slump in railway stocks and dividends.

The same year (1896) that legalized the motor-car saw the establishment of Harmsworth's *Daily Mail*, followed in 1900 by Pearson's *Daily Express*, and in 1904 by Harmsworth's *Daily Mirror*, a picture paper suitable for such as found reading difficult, and intended, as its name suggests, mainly for women. The 'new journalism' had for some years previously been experimenting with weeklies of the *Tit-Bits* type, but its advance into the realm of the dailies was a portent. Cynics have remarked, with justification, that it was a direct result of the Education Acts which provided compulsory schooling and ensured universal literacy while unable, in the nature of the case, to ensure universal education. Finer food for cynicism might be found in the fact that the new type of paper was found to satisfy the demands of so large a percentage of the class whose education had cost so much more and pretended to go so much further. Only a few of the older papers were strong enough to refrain from copying what was bad as well as what was good in the new model. That there was good in it need not be denied. If a modern reader of *The Times* were to be presented once again with his favourite oracle in its Victorian guise, he would find it impossibly stodgy.

This is a depressing subject. So turn once again to that most fertile 1896, and we find that for the first time the state museums and galleries were thrown open to the public on Sundays. This fact might open up a series of reflexions on either religion or art, but we will hold the former in reserve for the present. In art and music the Victorian reputation does not stand high. Perhaps it has been made too much of an Aunt Sally, but one cannot deny that the most conspicuous features are Revival Gothic (which, as has been said, bears the same relation to real Gothic as Madame Tussaud's waxworks bear to human beings), allegorical pictures by Watts and Hunt, and monster performances of the *Messiah* and *Elijah*. Carlyle says somewhere that the English were a dumb nation, 'their only Mozart Sir Henry Bishop'—and the said Sir Henry was the composer of 'Home, Sweet Home'. In these departments, as in so many others, the Victorians of the later generation worked hard at cures which their successors deem themselves to have completed. The æsthetic movement, a wholly Victorian affair, was at its best an assertion that art was not primarily concerned with preaching other people's sermons. By the end of the Victorian Age we were beginning to realize the significance of modern French art, but this came slowly. The *Encyclopædia Britannica* of 1911 has no article on, and only one casual mention of, Cézanne, though the famous Post-Impressionist Exhibition had been held some years before. The musical revival was well under way. Perhaps the only two works of modern English music which have established themselves as first-class classics fall on the dividing line between Victorian and modern times, Elgar's *Enigma Variations* in 1899 and his *Dream of Gerontius* in 1900. It is significant that the latter received its first adequate performance in Germany. What was more significant for the future was the establishment in 1895, in the newly opened Queen's Hall, of the Promenade Concerts, under the direction from the first of that apparently perennial benefactor of humanity, Henry J. Wood. Real music was to be rescued here from the leading strings of piety, society, and 'variety'.

Having marked the beginnings and the endings of our period it might be well to consider its internal divisions. There alternative traditions are available for our choice. The terms Early, Mid, and Late Victorian are in common use. If we adopt these terms we must find an essentially Victorian core or centre, and a prologue and epilogue on either side of it. Mid or essential Victorianism would be found to begin with the outbreak of the Great Victorian prosperity in the later forties, the final enactments of free trade, the completion of the main railway system, the final failure of revolutionary Chartism in 1848, and the establishment of the Queen's personal prestige, secured, one may say, by Prince Albert's labours in connexion with the Great Exhibition of 1851. The Great Victorian prosperity was rudely interrupted in the middle seventies and not resumed until the year of the first jubilee. Within that decade events could be found which could be taken as lines of division between the Middle and the Late periods. The death of Disraeli and the crushing defeat of Gladstone; the emergence of new political techniques with Joseph Chamberlain and Randolph Churchill and Parnell; the first stirrings of the socialist societies and (just beyond the dates indicated) the rapid spread of the New Unionism among unskilled workers, grouped according to the industries they served rather than the crafts they practised; in general the growing audibility of protest against Victorian standards of respectability and a consciousness of declining hold within the Churches. The ridiculous epithet of 'naughty', adhesively because alliteratively attached to the nineties, proclaims that Victorianism was dying before Victoria was dead. On the whole, however, the practice of recent historians is in favour of a twofold division, 'Early' and 'Later', dividing the reign between them. Having watched the dawn and the sunset, let us look for the signs of the passing of the zenith.

The middle year of the reign can be proved by arithmetic to be 1869, the first full year of Gladstone's first premiership—Gladstone with the first definitely Liberal (rather than Whig) majority, the product of the new semi-working class franchise, and girding himself up for his first struggles with the Irish problem, the House of Lords, and the Queen; the year also of the publication of *Culture and Anarchy*, a book in which Early Victorian habits of mind were attacked along lines which in retrospect we recognize as distinctively modern. Without straying very far on either side of that date, we shall find it very easy to collect sufficient facts to indicate the nature of the watershed between the Early and Later Victorian Ages. We shall look backward down a slope stretching beyond Victorian limits towards a horizon where Waterloo can be descried, and onwards down another slope reaching again beyond Victorian limits to 1914, and, in fact, towards the mingled anxieties and enlightenments of our own day.

Conspicuous beyond all other events is, of course, the Franco-Prussian War, when Europe, as the saying was, exchanged a mistress for a master. The ultimate corollaries of this event are too obvious to call for comment. Retrospectively, it brought to an end the Early Victorian or Palmerstonian phase of British foreign policy, because it abolished the conditions in which that policy could effectively operate. Those conditions were, in one word, inefficiency. Governments were casual, administration chaotic, movement dilatory, armies unreliable. Not one word in ten was intended to be followed by a blow. In such circumstances a great deal could be done by bluff backed by prestige. The Napoleonic wars had given England prestige, and Palmerston was the greatest of all masters of bluffing. Hence the effectiveness of his operations in Belgium, Italy, and elsewhere. His age predeceased him by a very few years, and the fiasco of his methods as applied to Schleswig-Holstein after Bismarck's accession to power showed what was coming. Gladstone has borne the blame, not altogether deservedly, for the decline of British influence upon European events which followed. The new epoch was driven back on 'splendid isolation' and a concentration upon exploiting the resources of the empire, brought nearer by the growth of steamship transport which is another feature of the 'watershed'. British steam tonnage, less than a million in 1870, was nearly two million in 1875, three million in 1881, and four million in 1885. Within the same period tonnage under sail had shrunk from four and a half to three and a half million.

The significance of the victory of Sedan was plain for all to see. Other facts, equally important for us, were only revealed by subsequent statisticians. Somewhere very near 1870 the British lead over all competitors in world trade attained its maximum, and a very extraordinary lead it was. In 1870, British imports and exports exceeded in value those of France, Germany, and Italy combined. For decades the hackneyed phrase, 'the workshop of the world', expressed not an aspiration but an established fact. Thenceforward, though our figures continued to increase, those of others increased faster, and our share of the whole diminished. The turnover from iron to steel, a feature of the seventies, gave an advantage on technical grounds to Germany and America. In the decade 1871–81, Britain for the first time produced less than half the world's supply. The slump which set in with the middle seventies was a world-wide phenomenon, but the profound agricultural depression caused by the opening up of the American prairie wheat-fields was all our own, partly because our own agriculture, though the most advanced in technique to be found anywhere, was more vulnerable, partly because, unlike nearly all our Continental neighbours, we took no measures to protect it. The Later Victorian Age was increasingly aware, as the Earlier Victorian Age was not, that the same course of events that had established our industrial pre-eminence would, in the course of nature, take it away. Protection began to be talked about long before Joseph Chamberlain's post-Victorian campaign. But the early protectionists were as insignificant for all purposes of practical politics as the early socialists. Free Trade had become a dogma of the Englishman's religion, for was not 'freedom' an essentially

British virtue? In any case, the foreigner had still a long way to go.

Another set of figures is, it must be granted, an affair of the eighties and not the seventies, but it is too significant to be omitted here. The annual birth-rate, which had stood at about 35 per thousand of population ever since registration of births was established in the first year of the reign, fell to 33 for the years 1881–5, and thenceforth continued to fall slowly and steadily. The practice of birth-control had begun, and spread downwards through the social scale. This did not mean an immediate decline in the rate of net increase, for the decline in the death rate, due to the progress of public health, fully kept pace for a time with the decline in the birth-rate. It meant something more important than any merely quantitative measurement can be. The most fundamental of all Victorian institutions, the large Victorian family, had seen its best days. The first edition of Malthus's *Essay on Population* had correctly described the factors—plague, pestilence, and famine—which had limited, not the fertility, but the posterity of parenthood in earlier ages. Now the remedy of his second edition was to be applied—prudential restraint.

So vital a cause was bound to produce effects in many directions. One that concerns us here is the emancipation of women, the earlier stages of which fill the whole of the Later Victorian Age. The connexion between the two things is unmistakable, even though it be not consciously a connexion of cause and effect, even though steps were taken towards woman's emancipation before birth-control had begun to operate. Through countless ages of human history the prime of the average woman's life had been entirely occupied with the bearing and rearing of children. The so-called bread-winning male had been much less exhaustively occupied, and, in fact, he had invented the luxury we call civilization in his spare time. Whether woman was to be admitted to membership was long a moot point. George Meredith said that woman was, or would be, the last thing to be civilized by man. As soon as woman began to be relieved of half her duties in the matter of bearing and rearing children, her claim to 'sex-equality' became irresistible. All ignorant of this argument of the future, the pioneers were preparing to equip woman to claim her place. In 1869, which we marked down as the middle year of the Victorian Age, Girton College was founded (at Hitchin), and the Endowed Schools Commission published its report on the education of girls. In 1870, Miss Buss founded the first public day school for girls. Miss Beale was already enthroned at Cheltenham, where she reigned, as awful a figure in her own sphere as Victoria herself, till beyond the limits of the Victorian Age.

That the Victorian Age was one of increasing urbanization goes without saying, and the steady growth of London and the industrial towns hardly calls for comment. The appearance of other types of new town, characteristic of the Later, but not of the Early Victorian Age, deserves notice. Bournemouth 'practically dates from 1870, when the railway first reached it'. At the other end of England, Blackpool began to be talked about at nearly the same time.[1] These names, and others could be adduced, stand for changing habits in the spheres respectively of capital and of labour. The typical Early Victorian capitalist was, in the terminology of the old economic text-books, an entrepreneur, a hard-faced, hard-fisted man who relied upon his own money as well as upon his own brains and, if he ground the faces of the poor, ground them in the sweat of his own brow. Railways, limited liability and, later, municipal enterprise, multiplied the numbers of a very different kind of capitalist, an idle rich class living on investments, and doing neither good nor harm to anyone. For such the Bournemouths provided happy homes, though it has been unkindly said that the contribution of these towns 'to the nation's general culture has been less perhaps than might have been expected'. They have, at least, provided safe seats for Diehard Conservatives. As for the Blackpools, they are evidence of the growing prosperity of the working classes and the enterprise of the railway companies which, having attained their Victorian maximum, or nearly so, in the matter of speed, set themselves to gratify their customers in other ways. Is it altogether unworthy of notice that our central year, 1869, saw the introduction of the first dining-car, on the Great Northern?

Urbanization and railway travel between them are the background of the immense development of organized games, which is one of the most important social features of the Later Victorian Age. The sports of an earlier and predominantly agricultural age were shooting and fishing, hunting and racing; as for fresh air and exercise, these were quite literally all in the day's work. Urban life demands, and does not of itself supply, fresh air and exercise; indeed it supplies only confined spaces where these may be obtained. Hence games, which the Arnoldian public schools, themselves a product of the railway age, brought to perfection and presented not only to their own Old Boys but to the larger and less privileged public. Railways facilitated inter-club matches and necessitated the standardization of rules. The innumerable local diversities of football crystallized into Association (1863) and Rugby Union (1871) and 'international' matches under both sets of rules began almost at once. Anyone who examines the issues of an old school magazine for the early seventies will find, as likely as not, a triangular controversy between the advo-

[1] They are the only two English towns that have been added to the list of hosts of the British Association in the present century.

cates of Soccer and Rugger, and those who wanted to go on under their own local rules in spite of the growing protests of visiting teams. 1869 (the central year again) witnessed the coming of age of W. G. Grace. In 1874 Major Wingfield invented lawn tennis, and three years later his rules were revised by the Wimbledon All England Croquet and Lawn Tennis Club. Golf reached Hoylake from Scotland in 1869, and thence spread over the southern kingdom.

Dickens, who knew not Soccer and Rugger and golf, and whose cricket is far removed from W. G., died in 1870. He had created more characters whose names are household words than all the other English novelists from Samuel Richardson to Aldous Huxley taken together. His works are a mine of information about the Earlier Victorian period, and the stately tomes of *The Early Victorian Age* make ninety quotations from them, apart from thirty-six other allusions to their author. His death would not matter to us here, if it were not for the fact that his England was itself at the same date obsolescent. It was the England which Matthew Arnold had summarized in the previous year under the terms, 'Barbarians, Philistines, and Populace': upper, middle, and lower classes distinct and separate. 'The Barbarians' were beyond the range of the Cockney Shakespeare; the Philistines and the Populace, in their London manifestations, he knew inside out. What has become of them since 1870? They have been transformed by many agencies, but most of all by education, the Philistines by the Arnoldian public schools and the Populace by the elementary schools of Arnold's son-in-law's Education Act. The public schools have been a potent engine for the transformation of the Philistines into a very colourable imitation of the Barbarians, and the elementary schools have transformed the old Populace into a lounge-suited, Homburg-hatted, and (to vary the sex) silk-stockinged imitation of the Philistines. We are, to adapt Sir William Harcourt, all bourgeois nowadays, except perhaps in some remote mining districts. A large section of the old Middle Class has gone 'Upper-Middle'—pleasing compound of pride and modesty—and though we do not talk of a 'Middle Lower' class we well might. In his last novels Dickens scents the change. He has an elementary schoolmaster, who commits murder, or tries to, and his favourite pupil, who has been described as the most unpleasant character in the whole range of Dickens's works. There is also, in Miss Bella Wilfer, a forerunner of the new feminism who does not want to live in a 'doll's house'—a phrase which afterwards provided the title of Ibsen's propagandist play, though I do not know whether Ibsen took the title from Dickens; and Mr. Crisparkle, a Church of England clergyman, who is a pleasantly drawn example of the new public school type.

Something has already been said about art in connexion with the final Victorian date, but it is tempting to look for a date on the dividing line. It must surely be 1878, the year in which Whistler, that master of the modern school and of the modern art of self-advertisement, brought his famous libel action, and made Ruskin, the pundit of Art and Morals, look supremely foolish. Why Ruskin should have swallowed the Turnerian camel and strained at the Whistlerian gnat can be explained on no general principles; it is due to the fact that Turner was of the generation before Ruskin and Whistler of the generation after him.

Enough, perhaps more than enough, has been said to separate the Later from the Earlier Victorian Ages to mark a line of division fairly near the central date, and to show the Later as altogether very much more akin to ourselves. It is indeed the England of the Prince of Wales as distinguished from the England of the Prince Consort.

II

Under the guise of a search for dates we have introduced a good many features of the Victorian scene. It is time to come to grips with essentials. Where are they to be found? What are the substantives to which the adjective Victorian is most commonly attached? One might have 'Victorian piety', and therewith 'Victorian prudery' and 'Victorian hypocrisy'; the æsthetically sensitive will add 'Victorian ugliness'; *laudatores temporis acti* will retort with 'Victorian energy', 'Victorian optimism', and 'Victorian achievement'.

The characteristic Victorian piety was, of course, Evangelicalism. It has been analysed so often, with authority and eloquence, that it seems better to quote than to pretend originality. Mr. Ensor writes: 'No one will ever understand Victorian England who does not appreciate that among highly civilized, in contradistinction to more primitive, countries it was one of the most religious that the world has known. Moreover, its particular type of Christianity laid a peculiarly direct emphasis upon conduct. . . . The essentials of evangelicalism were three. First, its literal stress on the Bible. . . . Secondly, its certainty about an after-life of rewards and punishments. If one asks how nineteenth-century English merchants earned the reputation of being the most honest in the world (a very real factor in the nineteenth-century primacy of English trade), the answer is: because hell and heaven seemed as certain to them as tomorrow's sunrise, and the Last Judgment as real as the week's balance-sheet. . . . Thirdly, its corollary that the present life is only important as a preparation for eternity. . . . It made other-worldliness an everyday conviction and, as we say, a business proposition; and thus induced a highly civilized people to put pleasure in the background, and what it conceived to be duty in the foreground, to a quite exceptional degree.'[1]

Or take M. Halévy: 'Men of letters disliked the Evangelicals for their narrow Puritanism, men of science for their intellectual feebleness. Nevertheless, during the nineteenth century Evangelical religion was the moral cement of English society. It invested the British aristocracy with an almost stoic dignity, restrained the plutocrats newly risen from the masses from vulgar ostentation and debauchery, and placed over the proletariat a select body of workmen enamoured of virtue and capable of self-restraint.'[2]

Or Mr. G. M. Young, in the opening paragraphs of his brilliant *Portrait of an Age*: 'Evangelical theology rests on a profound apprehension of the contrary states: of Nature and of Grace; one meriting eternal wrath, the other intended for eternal happiness. . . . This is Vital Religion. But the power of Evangelicalism as a directing force lay less in the hopes and terrors it inspired than in its rigorous logic, "the eternal microscope", with which it pursued its argument into the recesses of the heart and the details of daily life, giving to every action its individual value in this life and its infinite consequence in the next. Nor could it escape the notice of a converted man that the virtues of a Christian after the Evangelical model were easily exchangeable with the virtues of a successful merchant or a rising manufacturer, that more than a casual analogy could be established between Grace and Corruption and the Respectable and the Low. To be serious, to redeem the time, to abstain from gambling, to remember the Sabbath Day to keep it holy, to limit the gratification of the senses to the pleasures of a table lawfully earned and the embraces of a wife lawfully wedded, are virtues for which the reward is not laid up in Heaven only.'[3] In fact, a sky-scraping theology issuing in a table of commandments as humdrum as they were rigorous, and the Way of Salvation proving to be at the same time the Way of Respectability.

The Victorians did not discover Evangelicalism; they inherited it in the days of its zenith and assisted in the first stages of its decline. Perhaps its zenith, the period in which it was still gaining more at the lower end than it was losing at the upper end of the social and intellectual scale, may be placed in the forties and fifties, though it was as late as the seventies and eighties that three successive Lord Chancellors were regular teachers in Sunday schools. If we are to look for

[1] R. C. K. Ensor, *England, 1870–1914*, pp. 137–8.
[2] E. Halévy, *History of the English People in the Nineteenth Century*, iii, 165.
[3] *Early Victorian England*, ed. G. M. Young, ii, 414; also G. M. Young, *Portrait of an Age*, pp. 1, 2.

its beginnings we must go back a hundred years to the Wesleys and Whitefield and their like resolutely bestirring the dry bones of Walpolian England. What most people think of as Victorianism is, in fact, Wesleyanism or Methodism come to its full fruition, one of the very few great movements of the modern mind that has confined itself almost entirely within Anglo-Saxon limits. This Evangelicalism overleapt all sectarian divisions of church and chapel. My own grandparents were devout Evangelicals, and wherever they went they set themselves to find the place of worship which gave them most nearly what they needed; in some places it was a parish church, in others a Nonconformist chapel. My father writes: 'It seems to me as I look back to those early days that the preaching of the "plan of salvation" formed the whole of the sermons we heard. I daresay this was not actually so, but I think we heard very few sermons from which it was left out. Certainly it was so much insisted on that every detail of it was familiar to me by the time I was six years old.'[1]

This Evangelical outlook is out of fashion today. Indeed, it is so far out of fashion that we are hardly in a position to judge it dispassionately. The Evangelicalism of Victorian parents has been visited upon post-Victorian children whom it did not suit, and many of them have recorded their sufferings before a sympathetic audience. Hence the widespread application of the epithet Victorian to such terms as hypocrisy, prudery, ugliness—the connexion of the last with piety is not obvious, but it has been assumed to exist. The charge of hypocrisy may be briefly dismissed. Hypocrisy is the shadow cast by idealism, and the higher the idealism the longer the shadow. Very likely no age was so fertile in the production of hypocrites as the thirteenth century—that 'Age of Faith', so much admired by many who have little but contempt for Victorianism; such at least is the conclusion suggested by the works of Dr. Coulton. In a society where all eat and drink because tomorrow they will die there will be no hypocrites, because there is nothing to be hypocritical about.

The prudery is a much more distinctively Victorian feature, for it was a fashion of the age as a whole, not merely a vice of its weaker brethren. The Victorian Age is, in literary history, the Age of Expurgation, even though the most famous of the expurgators, Thomas Bowdler, had died as early as 1825. Bowdler produced an edition of Shakespeare in which 'those words and expressions are omitted which cannot with propriety be read aloud in a family'. Thereby he did more than any previous editor to popularize the poet for family reading, and, if we clear our minds of anti-Victorian cant, we shall

[1] *Robert Somervell: Chapters of Autobiography*, edited by his sons, p. 17.

find that he did the text very little damage. But expurgation covers much more than the application of censorship to the classics; we include under it the fact that nearly every successful writer of the Early Victorian Age excluded from any but conventional treatment the whole subject of sex. How the Victorian novelists got on under such an embargo their successors may well wonder. There is some evidence that Thackeray found the restriction galling.

The last of the Great Unexpurgated was Byron, who died in 1824. Expurgation reaches its climax with the Evangelicalism of which it was a by-product. Where are the first signs of its decline? On the watershed between the Early and Later Victorian Ages we find Swinburne's *Poems and Ballads* (1866), and the Rossetti volume of 1872, which was the special bugbear of a pamphlet by Robert Buchanan, entitled *The Fleshly School of Poetry*. And what was it that Buchanan found so fleshly? Do we dare to quote? I think we might venture, for this was one of the couplets specially stigmatized:

And as I stooped, her own lips rising there
Bubbled with brimming kisses at my mouth.

A wet kiss apparently, but nothing to worry about otherwise, one would think. Swinburne was described by John Morley in a review as 'an unclean fiery imp from the pit', and as exhibiting 'the feverish carnality of the schoolboy', for Morley was one of those who, like Huxley, retained all the Evangelical's morality while rejecting all the Evangelical's religion.

And ugliness. That the Victorians have imposed upon us a great many very ugly buildings is plain for all to see. It is rash to dogmatize on matters of taste, but in our view, at any rate, most of their furniture and their pictures were as bad as their building. Are we to attribute this ugliness to their piety? I really do not know why we should, except that the Evangelicals would never have supposed or admitted that beauty of design was a matter of much importance. They would certainly not have set Beauty beside Truth and Virtue as one of the three co-equal ends of life. But is it certain that the builders of the Gothic cathedrals set any more store by Art and Beauty as things in themselves? Victorian ugliness, in architecture at least, can be traced in the main to two sources, and neither of them has anything to do with Evangelicalism. One was the Gothic Revival, which began long before as a fad of aristocrats and antiquarians and, in so far as it made contact with religion at all, found its home in the Anglo-Catholic movement. The other cause of ugliness was the industrial revolution and modern transport.

Before the railways came the builder, aiming, as all builders must, at cheapness, had relied on local materials, the use of which had long been moulded by tradition into harmony with one another and with their environment. The railways altered all this. It was henceforth cheapest in almost all parts of the country to build walls with brick and roofs with slate, an ugly combination at the best. The cheapening of glass encouraged better ventilation and lighting, in themselves excellent things, but pointing towards the gable and the bow-window which have proved the most fruitful sources of ugliness. At the same time machinery encouraged the mechanical repetition of meaningless ornament, affecting both building and furniture. The age of steel made cheap springs possible and introduced into every sitting-room that æsthetic abomination, the really comfortable 'lounge' arm-chair. There is here a real dilemma between elegance and comfort, and a resolute return to elegance often favours the eye at the expense of other parts of the person. The modern fashion for strictly rectangular all-wood garden seats is a case in point. They are undoubtedly less comfortable than the ugly Victorian type, where wooden planks were affixed to curved metal supports, for the seated human form does not achieve a right-angle.[1]

We seem to have strayed rather far from Evangelicalism. Its heyday filled the Early Victorian period. It inspired the dreams and sanctified the business of nearly all those tight lipped, bushy whiskered individuals who stare at us wanly from the faded photographs of old family albums—for it was among other things the Early Photographic Age, though the invention in this case was not English but French. Even Carlyle, the most drastic critic of its dreams and its business alike, its money-making, its philanthropies, its ideas of freedom and progress, was himself more than half an Evangelical, a Puritan uncertain of his creed, and though he satirized 'Hebrew Old Clothes' and made fun of the Thirty-nine Articles, his rhapsodical invocation of Eternities and Immensities, Everlasting Nays and Yeas and what-not—so wearisome to us who value him, if at all, as a sardonic humourist—made him welcome to his generation. He was himself swathed to the neck in Hebrew Old Clothes, as comfortably incomprehensible as Isaiah. The dissolvents of Evangelicalism must be sought elsewhere.

There was, in the first place, the rise within the Church itself of an alternative form of religion, starting from the Oxford Movement (1833–45) and issuing in Anglo-Catholicism. The Oxford Tracts were addressed to the clergy, and the Movement always appealed more to clergy and to women than to men, though great Anglo-Catholic lay-men can, of course, be cited: for example, Gladstone and Salisbury; but Gladstone was notoriously an amalgam of incompatibles, and he

[1] Most of this paragraph, but not the final illustration, I owe to Ensor, *England, 1870–1914*, pp. 152–3.

retained to the last an Evangelical accent and therewith the support of the Nonconformist conscience. A census of religious observance taken towards the end of the reign reveals the fact that the percentage of males in the congregations of Anglo-Catholic churches was much below the average elsewhere. Moreover, Anglo-Catholicism tended towards Rome, and anti-Popery has been for centuries a popular English tradition. Anglo-Catholicism did not only recruit itself at the expense of Evangelicalism; it introduced an atmosphere of insecurity and recrimination within the common fold to which both varieties of religious experience belonged. It distracted the defence which might have been unanimously concentrated on the foes without.

The most easily discernible of the foes without passes under the name of Science. First came the new geology which, through fossils, led to the new biology—Darwin versus Moses—and then the new history which insisted upon treating the sacred documents, the inspired Word of God, as it treated all other historical documents, asking when they were written and by whom, with what purpose, with what bias, and under what human disabilities. The Bible was put in the witness-box, and under cross-examination contradicted itself again and again. The Pentateuch was dissolved in J, E, and P; Isaiah into a goodly fellowship of prophets; a new evangelist was disinterred and dubiously labelled Q, and the Gospel of St. John was disrespectfully referred to as 'the Fourth Gospel'.[1]

Of the many storms raised by these issues, none is more instructive than the case of Robertson Smith, son of a Scots minister and a brilliant scholar in many fields, who, when Professor of Oriental Languages and Old Testament Exegesis at Aberdeen, was invited to contribute articles on biblical subjects to the 1875 edition of the *Encyclopædia Britannica*. These articles (I quote the article on Robertson Smith in the 1927 edition of the same work) 'distressed and alarmed the authorities of the Free Church. In 1876 a Committee of the General Assembly of that Church reported on them so adversely that Smith demanded a formal trial, in the course of which he defended himself with consummate ability and eloquence. The indictment was dropped, but a vote of want of confidence was passed and Smith was removed from his chair. At the end of the trial he was probably the most popular man in Scotland.' Many, in fact, considered that the leaders of the Free Church had acted with disingenuousness and timidity; that they had condemned opinions with which they were secretly in agreement, from fear of what would now be called the Fundamentalists among the rank and file of their con-

---

[1] Dr. Welldon, Evangelical Headmaster of Tonbridge (1843–75), regarded reference to 'the Fourth Gospel' as next door to atheism; he also called brewers' vans 'the devil's coaches'. He was a very good headmaster.

gregations. Smith's career was by no means blasted by this reverse. He became a professor at Cambridge, and his popular lectures on biblical criticism were received with applause. In fact, there was already a wide public with what was loosely called a Broad Church view, which recognized that the so-called warfare of science and religion was a conflict of false issues; that history and biology could correct and clarify opinion on historical and scientific subjects without touching the vital core of religious belief; that popular Christianity was encrusted with what Matthew Arnold called *Aberglaube* (over-belief; Arnold, like Carlyle, was fond of dropping into German), and the sooner it was stripped off the better for all concerned, including religion. But perhaps this notion was too simple.

> First cut the Liquefaction, what comes last
> But Fichte's clever cut at God Himself?

says Browning's sceptical Roman Catholic bishop. Where was the line between essentials and *Aberglaube* to be drawn? Certainly Arnold's own attempt to draw it was acceptable to few.

Thus religion because uncertain of itself, and the greater its intelligence the greater its uncertainty. Tennyson found 'more faith in honest doubt, believe me, than in half the creeds', and could do no more than 'faintly trust the larger hope'. Science suffered from no such tremors; it was as arrogantly sure of itself as Calvin or Tertullian, and Samuel Butler, who disliked biologists more than he disliked bishops, foresaw that a time would come when it would be said that Science sent down His only begotten son, Darwin or Huxley, that all who believed in Him, etc.

The most subtle of the scientific dissolvents of religious dogmatism, the new psychology, scarcely touched the Victorian Age, though that far-sighted man of genius, Walter Bagehot (died 1877), foresaw its coming; also Samuel Butler in a famous chapter of *Erewhon* (1871).

But the most formidable enemy of the Evangelical ethos was, after all, something quite other than science. Science was for the few; those who did not like it were wonderfully successful in pretending that it was not there, and those whose religion was alive and robust could accept the findings of the biologists and the biblical critics, and reconcile the new learning and the old faith in a higher synthesis. The most formidable enemy was what Mr. Ensor calls 'the new hedonism', and its standard-bearer, if it had one, was the Prince of Wales, who 'sponsored and perhaps invented the week-end'. The transition from the Early to the Later periods is the passage from Albert to Albert Edward. Victoria survived, no doubt, through both epochs, and after the temporary eclipse of her prolonged withdrawal she grew in stature throughout the Jubilee period. That is but a reminder that though Evangelicalism was losing force in the Later period, it lost ground but slowly, and the last of the great Victorian prophets, Rudyard Kipling, is more than half an Evangelical himself. His belief in the British race as a Chosen People, his most widely used slogan, 'the White Man's burden', his 'Recessional' which went straight into the hymn-books—all this was simply Evangelical idealism applied to the new pride in 'dominion over palm and pine'. None the less, Evangelicalism was in retreat. It had denied the claims of pleasure, and pleasure began to refuse to be denied. The change is something like that which occurred in the Renascence. For fundamentally the Renascence was a reassertion of worldliness, of the feeling that this world is the only world we know anything about, and that we may as well enjoy it while we can.

The cult of pleasure: the pre-Victorian Benthamites had constructed a whole philosophy on the basis of pleasure, which they treated as a synonym for happiness. John Stuart Mill, the last and finest Victorian flower of their garden, had been driven to conclude that happiness and pleasure were not at all the same, and that happiness was to be found only by turning one's back on pleasure and pursuing a scheme of life which was Evangelical in everything but creed, and his view found curious confirmation in Fitzgerald's *Rubáiyát of Omar Khayyám*. Omar counselled pleasure, while admitting that it was a counsel of despair. This most musical and melancholy of Victorian poems issued from the press almost unnoticed in 1859. Its immense popularity at the end of the century—or perhaps it would be more exact to say in the first decade of the present century —is a measure of the advance of 'the new hedonism'.

The Renascence was followed by the Reformation—but history does not always repeat itself.

III

Victorian party politics continues to be, for many of us, a source of almost inexhaustible entertainment. That long succession of storms in the parliamentary tea-cup, what a feast of good reading they have provided, and continue to provide. Take a single decade, the eighties: Midlothian, the G.O.M. back again after all; Hartington and Chamberlain; Bradlaugh and the Fourth Party; Parnell, Kilmainham, Phœnix Park; Alexandria, Tel-el-Kebir, Khartoum; the Caretakers' Government, Parnell, Carnarvon, Randolph; Unauthorized Programme, Hawarden Kite, Home Rule Bill; Bloody Balfour, Parnell Commission, Pigott, O'Shea, Committee Room Fifteen: where else in history, ancient or modern, will you find as good a story? Nowhere, some will think; but the best stories are not always the most important ones. The attractions of Victorian party politics and its gladiators have overshadowed the fame of the men who were doing the real work, while those others talked—Chadwick, Southwood Smith, Simon, Kay-Shuttleworth, and all the mute inglorious Chadwicks and village Simons, the men who each in his own locality played his part in the long battle with muddle and waste and ignorance and filth; the men who halved the death rate,[1] and laid the foundations of the modern social service state.

Dicey, in his well-known *Lectures on the Relations between Law and Public Opinion in England in the Nineteenth Century*, divides his subject chronologically into three parts of fairly equal length; the age of Tory stagnation and legislative quiescence, which is wholly pre-Victorian; the age of Benthamite Reform, lasting, roughly speaking, to the date we are already familiar with as the dividing line between Earlier and Later Victorianism; and the age of Collectivism, which is very much what Socialists called Fabianism, piecemeal legislation in a socialistic direction, extension of state control, organization, and expenditure, redistribution of the national income by means of increased taxation for the financing of social services, the kind of legislation which Joseph Chamberlain advocated and Gladstone resisted, and which led Harcourt in the nineties to exclaim somewhat ruefully, 'We are all socialists now'.

Dicey makes allowance for a considerable overlap in the movements that give his periods their names, but even so it is doubtful whether the distinction between Benthamism and Collectivism was as sharp in principle as the main scheme of his book suggests.[2] What was this Benthamism or Utilitarianism which, as all the books assure us, dominated Early Victorian political thought almost as completely as Evangelicalism dominated its religion and morals? Primarily it was a revolt against traditionalism, a determination to judge every social problem and legislative proposal on lines of common sense and expediency alone, and ruthlessly to clear away every existing institution and enactment which would not stand such tests.

---

[1] There is a touch of poetic licence here. The death rate has, in fact, been halved in the hundred years since 1837—reduced from 24 to 12 per 1,000. About half of that reduction falls within the Victorian Age. Every provincial town had its 'village Chadwicks'. For example, we in Tonbridge should, but mostly do not, remember with honour Dr. John Gorham and his brother William Gorham, solicitor. See our excellent local history, *The Tonbridge of Yesterday*, by A. H. Neve.

[2] Dicey corrects this suggestion in the short, but very important, chapter entitled 'The Debt of Collectivism in Benthamism', from which quotation is made below. I have often wondered whether this chapter was an afterthought in Dicey's scheme.

This may seem platitudinous today, but it was clean contrary to the 'thin end of the wedge' argument with which reforms had been effectively countered in the thirty years after the French Revolution, clean contrary to the final philosophy of Burke, who came near upholding the divine right of what existed to continue, on the ground that what was old thereby proved that it worked and created a presumption that something different would not work as well.

Benthamism manifested itself in two slogans, 'the greatest happiness of the greatest number' and *laissez-faire*. The French formula was not, as it has sometimes become since, a translation of Melbourne's, 'Can't you leave it alone?' It was the very opposite of that. It was an ambitious programme of liberation, a crusade for the abolition of every measure which shackled individual freedom, every measure which restricted the individual from pursuing his 'greatest happiness' (of which he was himself the best judge) in his own way. Under this heading come all the measures for extending freedom of trade, freedom of opinion, religious equality, reform of judicial procedure, and much more besides. The various measures establishing sex equality from the Married Women's Property Act onwards, though they belong to the Later period, constitute perhaps the last big instalment of *laissez-faire*.

But there was another side to Benthamism, for one does not need to be a socialist to discover that, over a large range of activities, the 'greatest happiness' cannot be secured merely by abolishing impediments to individual activity. The principle of utility is the principle of efficiency. The Benthamite abhorred muddle and waste, slums, dirt, disease, and these things could only be tackled by a policy curtailing individual liberty. No sooner had the Benthamites given a man freedom to choose his own church and his own market than they took away his freedom to dispose of his own sewage. There was, indeed, as Dicey remarks, 'a despotic or authoritative element latent in utilitarianism', and this despotic element, the zeal of the new bureaucracy, becomes the Later Victorian collectivism without any perceptible transition, long before the Fabians arose to point out that it was socialism by instalments. John Stuart Mill was universally recognized as the oracle of Victorian Benthamites, and none of them attached greater spiritual value to individual spontaneity. His essay on 'Liberty' is the best of his books (except his Autobiography), and it is not too much to say that it is the nearest thing to Milton's 'Areopagitica' to be found in Victorian literature. None the less in each successive edition of his *Political Economy*, published in 1847, and several times reissued before Mill's death in 1873, the chapter on 'The Limitations of the Principle of Laissez Faire' grew longer.

And, indeed, the state of public health and housing in Early Victorian England was beyond the limits of modern imagination. We will not recapitulate horrible statistics of the lives and deaths of the poor in the thirties, forties, and fifties, when even so small and apparently inoffensive a town as Tonbridge witnessed five outbreaks of cholera. It is enough to remind ourselves that in the houses of the rich, smelling the drains was regarded as a sign of oncoming rain; that the windows of the Houses of Parliament had to be shut at certain states of the tide on account of the smell of the Thames; that the houses on the north of Hyde Park emptied their drains into the Serpentine, where 'as late as 1850 an evening stroll by the waters sometimes ended in sudden fever, collapse, and death'. It is worth also remembering that the most scarifying account of the horrors of the Early Victorian slums, especially those of the new industrial towns, was written by Engels, subsequently the colleague of Karl Marx; and what were Engels's principal sources of information? They were the reports of the Royal Commissions which the reformers had recently secured. Engels's deduction was that such evils could only be cured by revolution. He might, with more discernment, as the future showed, have deduced that a system of government capable of producing such unexpurgated reports would also prove capable of abolishing the evils which the reports laid bare.

The reformers were driven to undertake their herculean[1] and often heartbreaking labours by two kinds of motive which operated with different degrees of force on different individuals; pure philanthropy, generally inspired by Evangelical religion, and Benthamite zeal for the elimination of muddle and waste. The typical illustration of the first motive is Lord Shaftsbury, of the second Edwin Chadwick. Shaftsbury figures, very rightly, in every school text-book; Chadwick is almost forgotten, and a brief commemoration of him may not be out of place in an historical essay, the more so as his limitations were as characteristic as his virtues. Shaftsbury himself, with his passion for Sunday observance by legal compulsion and otherwise, and his horror of rationalism and of Rome, is scarcely more remote from our own day. At any rate, Chadwick was the typical Victorian Benthamite in action as J. S. Mill was the typical Victorian Benthamite of letters. Bentham himself, who died in 1832, had employed Chadwick as secretary, left him a handsome legacy, and expressly regarded him as a destined executor of his ideas. As for Chadwick's ideas, they were expressed in a remark to Louis Napoleon which is quoted by Mr. G. M. Young. The Emperor asked Chadwick what he thought of his improvements in Paris, and Chadwick replied: 'Sire, it was said of Augustus that he found Rome brick and left it marble.

[1] The epithet is appropriate, for one of the labours of Hercules, the cleansing of the Augean stables, may be accounted a sanitary reform.

May it be said of you that you found Paris stinking and left it sweet.'

In 1833 he became a member of the Royal Commission appointed to examine into the operation of the poor laws, at that date encumbered with the notorious 'Speenhamland system'. As principal author of the Report, he was also the architect of the Poor Law Amendment Act of 1834, and became secretary to the Poor Law Commissioners. He was thus prominently associated with the most important, the most unpopular, and the least obviously philanthropic of the social reforms of the thirties. Its purpose was frankly economy, and it was the cause of economy which directed Chadwick's energies to public health. In 1838 the Poor Law Commissioners presented a Report on the great burden thrown upon the rates by sickness and epidemics due to insanitary conditions, and they urged that it would cost less in the long run to reform these conditions than to continue relieving the poverty they caused. Thereupon the Commissioners were instructed to report on the sanitary condition of the country. This gave Chadwick his opening, and the Report he drafted has been described by Mr. and Mrs. Hammond as 'one of the most powerful documents ever issued from a Government department'. By this time (1842) others were drawn into the crusade, medical experts such as Southwood Smith and Kay-Shuttleworth, philanthropic members of parliament such as Lord Ashley. The usual complications and delays ensued. Another Royal Commission, on the health of towns, was appointed with Chadwick again in control. Fifty large towns were examined; in forty-two the drainage and in thirty-one the water supply was 'decidedly bad' and in most of the others it was no more than moderate. The Report insisted that local authorities must be armed with wider powers, and that the Crown must have powers to supervise their sanitary measures.

We have reached the middle forties. In 1846 Cobden's crusade issued, owing to circumstances over which he had no control, in the repeal of the Corn Laws; in 1847 Ashley's crusade resulted in the Ten Hours Act for factories; in 1848 Chadwick's turn came, and the first Public Health Act, creating a General Board of Health, reached the Statute book. It was a badly conceived measure, and its defects were characteristic of its principal author. Chadwick had as little faith in democracy as Ashley. He was of the straitest sect of the bureaucrats. He could not bear to leave popularly elected bodies to make their own mistakes, and the powers of interference entrusted to his General Board of Health were such as to ensure the maximum of friction. The Board was abolished in 1854, with the enthusiastic approval of *The Times*, whose leader writer declared that 'we prefer to take our chance of cholera and the rest than to be bullied into

health' (there speaks the other sort of Benthamite). 'It was a perpetual Saturday night, and Master John Bull was scrubbed and
rubbed and small-tooth-combed till the tears ran into his eyes, and
his teeth chattered, and his fists clenched themselves with worry and
pain.' It was the end of Chadwick's official career, though he was
only fifty-four and lived to be ninety. Three years before his death
someone wrote a book about his work; the authorities were reminded of his existence, and at the age of eighty-nine he received a
K.C.B.

There is about this award an almost comic inadequacy, for the
great crusade for the organization of public health, in which Chadwick had been the prime mover, scarcely checked by the reverse of
1854, had gone on from strength to strength. Disraeli had coined the
slogan, 'Sanitas sanitatum, omnia sanitas', in the sixties, and those
who made fun of his 'policy of sewage' were already old-fashioned.
The youthful Chamberlain had shown the possibilities of enlightened
local government in Birmingham, and even the aged Bright, once
champion of the strictest school of non-interference, had declared
that local government ought to be 'more expensive', because it could
not do its work unless it had more money.

The Victorian achievement in the sphere of administration, as one
looks back on it from the end of the Victorian Age, might be summarized as follows: Not only had a variety of social evils been
tackled with results which, however inadequate we may regard them,
were beyond the most optimistic imaginings of the Age of Grey and
Peel; two instruments of administration, both almost non-existent
at the time of the Queen's accession, had been created as efficient
instruments of the indefinite extension of social reform—the modern
civil service and modern elective local government.

This, it will be said, is altogether too sweeping and too favourable
a verdict. It is certainly not the verdict in fashion; for the Victorians
were, we think, overpleased with their own performance, and we are
not going to make the mistake about them which they made about
themselves. Also, we are today living in a world all awry, and the
Victorians, as our immediate predecessors, may fairly be blamed for
that. Perhaps a great deal of the blame may, on analysis, be debited
to two men, the German Bismarck and the Jew Marx, and both were
Victorian in date though not among Her Majesty's subjects.

For the case against the Victorians, as stated by one who knows
them well enough to appreciate their merits, we may turn to Mr.
Wingfield-Stratford's *Victorian Tragedy*. In chapter after chapter,
always brilliant and often profound, he gives his Victorians all the
good marks they deserve, yet in the last one, like an inverted
Balaam, he unfolds the sinister significance of his title—Why a

Tragedy? 'If we are to judge,' he writes, 'solely by what was done at the time, without any relation to what might or ought to have been done, a fair case could be made out for describing the four mid decades of the nineteenth century as more fruitful than any other period of our history.' Very handsome, but there is clearly more to follow; let us see.

'The conditions confronting the Victorians were just those which biology has shown to be the most dangerous with which living organisms can be faced. The environment of *homo sapiens* was being not only changed but revolutionized. . . . Without being conscious of what he was about, Man, by means of his newly invented machines, was changing the conditions of his life with a rapidity which would have constituted an inevitable death sentence on any other animal. It remained to be seen whether discourse of reason, or whatever might be comprehended in the word "soul", would enable him to play the part of Œdipus in answering this last and most terrible riddle that he himself had propounded. . . . That was the central theme of the Victorian Tragedy. Could the people of this island and, particularly, its dominant middle class, with its moral earnestness and seemingly limitless resources, bring about the miracle of adjusting human life and western civilization to the new conditions?'[1]

Mr. Wingfield-Stratford answers his question in the negative, and, of course, one could compile a formidable catalogue of things which we, looking backward with the wisdom that comes after the event, could wish the Victorians had had the foresight to anticipate and provide for. On these grounds every age could indict its predecessor, and be indicted in its turn. But if we are to meet our author's challenge we would say, first of all, that the Victorians were not dealing with a changed but with a changing environment, and that, rapid as the process of change was, the process of political and social adaptation more than kept pace with it. The leeway of adaptation was not greater in 1900 than in 1830, but much less. When we follow Mr. Wingfield-Stratford into his second volume, *The Victorian Sunset*, we find that he hardly does justice to this theme. Catholic as are his tastes and omnivorous his curiosity he is perhaps less interested in the machinery of administration than in—shall we say female adornment? For example, Workmen's Compensation Acts are not to be found in his very efficient index, nor the London County Council.

And in the second place we would say, Do not talk of Tragedy till the play is over. Even 1914–18 is not the last act of the play.

But one is tempted to probe a little deeper. What is it that Mr. Wingfield-Stratford demands and the Victorians fail to supply? He

---

[1] E. Wingfield-Stratford, *The Victorian Tragedy*, pp. 279–80.

demands, I think, that Victorian society should have envisaged itself as an organic whole, with an indefinite future ahead of it, that it should have framed a policy *sub specie æternitatis*, and fixed its attention not upon the immediate but the distant future, not on itself but on *us*. This is a thing which few societies have ever tried to do, and if any has tried it has failed. Least of all can it be done under a system of Liberal democracy, and Liberal democracy was, for good or ill, the cornerstone of Victorian theory and practice. A totalitarian state may take Cromwell's maxim, 'Not what the people want but what's good for them,' and not for them only but their issue in perpetuity. Tentative hankerings after totalitarianism of various shades may be detected in certain Victorian schools: the Anti-Liberalism of the Early Oxford Movement as expressed in Keble's Assize sermon and the youthful Gladstone's 'Church and State', which, as he confesses, he soon found that nobody wanted; Carlyle's 'Hero-worship' and glorification of Prussia; Matthew Arnold's 'Culture' as an antidote to Liberal Anarchy; Cecil Rhodes's crude fancies, expressed in his earlier testamentary dispositions, for buying up the whole world and painting it red. But whatever Victorianism may positively have been it was negatively the opposite of this; it was a muddling along, and, as I have tried to maintain, on the whole a muddling through.

And now, as I draw this paper to a close, a goodly company of shades is gathering around me, shades of estimable topics undiscussed and even unmentioned, peevishly inquiring why I have not found room for them. Nothing has been said, for example, of Victorian Scotland or Wales, of which we hear too little; nothing of Victorian Ireland, of which we have heard too much; nothing of Victorian Empire expansion and evolution. Victoria's accession coincided with the Canadian rebellions, which were followed by the Durham Report; her death coincided with the Federation of the Australian Commonwealth. What a theme to have neglected! But I am very sorry, my dear shades, I can do nothing for you; other and better men are engaged at this season on the same subject as I. Go and pester them, and good luck to you.

But there is one point that can hardly be overlooked. Whatever we may think of the Victorians, they represented our country at a time when its influence upon the fortunes of the world was greater than it had ever been before, greater perhaps than it will ever be again. Try to visualize an historian of the thirtieth century, located in whatever may then be the centre of civilization, and engaged upon an Outline of World History. What will he find to be the salient features of a period as far away in time from him as the Age of Hildebrand is from us? He will note that it was the age of steam power and industrialization, the age of an unprecedented expansion of population, the age which extended the rudiments of European civilization into the furthest corners of the earth, the age of a great and widespread experiment in Liberal parliamentarism; perhaps he may even condescend to notice that it was the age which popularized organized games; he will certainly notice that its later decades witnessed the development of scientifically organized militarism. And he will record that in every one of these developments, except the last named, England was the pioneer. We are not ashamed of the exception.

H. MOYSE-BARTLETT

From Sail to Steam

From the time when primitive man first went adrift on a bundle of reeds or learnt to balance himself on a floating log, to the days when his descendants, no more than a few generations ago, raced scrambling aloft to trim the towering sails of a full-rigged ship, the skill of the sailor remained the same: the application of the forces of nature in wind, tide, current, and human muscles to the propulsion of his craft. Throughout this long period, although the principle involved remained unaltered, the ingenuity of man brought about a number of developments of even wider scope and more far-reaching importance than in the case of travel on land. Prior to the seventeenth century the record of such changes, especially as regards the ships of merchant traders, is imperfect and incomplete. The evidence available, however, is sufficient for a broad outline of the principal stages in the evolution of the sailing ship, an understanding of which is a necessary preliminary to any account of its last and most famous days.

Ancient Britain abounded in well-timbered river banks, so her earliest craft were dug-out canoes. By a crude process of pegging extra pieces of wood along their edges to secure greater freeboard, these evolved into plank-built boats, of which the original canoe became merely the heavy keel. Before the coming of the Romans the Britons probably used plank-built vessels similar to those of the Veneti, as described by Caesar. Boats of skin stretched over wooden frameworks were also in use in southern England.

The early vessels of Northern Europe owed nothing to Mediterranean influence. Such evidence as we have shows that the ships of the Scandinavian seafarers differed in several important particulars from the contemporary Mediterranean galley. Bow and stern were similar in the Viking ships; steering was effected by a single paddle on the starboard quarter instead of by double paddles; clinker building, i.e. with overlapping planks, was the method of construction as opposed to the Mediterranean carvel building with flush planking. An interesting feature of the later type of Viking ship lies in the thorough understanding shown of underwater hull design to reduce resistance in the water. No such practice is apparent in the design of medieval sailing ships, and it was not until comparatively recent times that the principle was again scientifically applied in ship construction.

The earlier Norman ships appear to have differed little from the Scandinavian. The Bayeux Tapestry (c. 1120), however, affords evidence of a development which, though simple in itself, was of considerable significance. The Tapestry shows vessels of a clinker-built type, propelled by oars and by a square sail set on a single mast, and in a few instances what are apparently shrouds. These do not appear previously on any known representations of ships. So long as a vessel was expected only to run before the wind, shrouds would not be necessary, and their appearance, therefore, is indicative of a real advance in the practice of navigation, enabling advantage to be taken of a beam wind.

With greater dependence on wind and less upon oars, the fine lines of earlier craft disappeared, and for some three hundred years the average length of ships remained at about three times their beam. There was not as yet any difference between ships designed for war and those intended primarily for trade, though fighting-castles fore, aft, and on the mast, which eventually became permanent features of construction, were originally erections for the accommodation of soldiers. During the thirteenth century the bowsprit (the original purpose of which was to enable the bowline to be carried further forward) and the stern-rudder, made their appearance in Northern Europe. These two innovations carried the evolution of the sailing ship a stage further. As a result of the former, the windward leech of the sail was held taut so that the vessel could sail closer to the wind. The latter made the ship more easily controllable when sailing with a strong wind on the starboard quarter, which had hitherto been difficult or even impossible, as the heeling of the ship tended to lift the old starboard side-rudder right out of the water. With these improvements the vessels of Northern Europe can fairly be described as ships, for such craft required considerable skill in handling.

From the fifteenth century onward, progress in the art of ship construction was rapid. By far the most important development was the adoption of more than one mast. The two-master, essentially a Mediterranean type, never became popular in Northern Europe, perhaps because the balance of the ship was upset, as the mainmast was still stepped in the same central position as before.

The earliest representation of a three-masted ship appears on a seal of Louis de Bourbon, dated 1466; the first three-masters cannot have appeared much earlier. They carried a large square sail on the mainmast, a small square sail on the foremast, and a 'lateen', a triangular sail that had become very popular in the Mediterranean during the ninth century, on the mizzen. To this rig there was added later in the century a small spritsail, the function of which was to keep the ship's head off the wind. The three-masted ship, with its greater powers of manœuvre and its ability to sail with the wind on the beam as well as to take full advantage of a favourable breeze, thus became sufficiently handy to navigate all the waters of the globe. A variety of reasons contributed to bring about the great era of maritime exploration that began in the fifteenth century, but one of the main reasons why this development began when it did lay simply in the adoption of two extra masts in the medieval ship. Vessels of this type made possible the voyages of Vasco da Gama, Columbus, and Magellan.

The maritime activity of the Tudor period resulted in a steady increase in the size of ships, and the adoption of a greater keel-length and finer lines. At this time the size of ships was calculated solely as a measurement of carrying capacity, either as 'tons burden' (capacity when carrying wine in barrels) or as 'tuns and tunnage' (capacity in bulk cargo, a somewhat higher figure). On this basis, the merchant ship of the period probably did not as a rule exceed 400 tons, though the royal ships were often considerably larger. The increase in the proportion of length to beam was seen in the 'galleon', distinguished also by its projecting beakhead in place of the old, lofty forecastle. Under Henry VIII the warship became a separate type, owing to the king's insistence on the mounting of heavy guns capable of smashing the hull of an opponent, which led to the supersession of clinker by carvel building, and necessitated other modifications in design to ensure added strength. The heavy arming of merchant ships, making them sometimes practically indistinguishable from men-of-war, did not come until later, during the period when English merchants were engaging in unofficial wars in distant waters against their continental rivals. Meanwhile a more elaborate sail-plan was introduced including topsails and even topgallant-sails on the larger ships.

Tudor ships were usually decorated with painted designs on their upper works and with carved figureheads, but the era of elaborate decoration really began with the big three-deckers of the Stuarts, which were famous for their carved and gilded stern galleries. So lavish was the decoration of the *Sovereign of the Seas*, built out of the proceeds of ship-money in 1637, that it actually amounted to a fifth of the total value of the ship. An order of 1703 attempted to check such extravagance, at any rate so far as the royal ships were concerned, but the movement was a reflection of the nation's intense pride in its maritime strength.

Throughout the seventeenth century there was a steady movement towards finer lines, and a continuous elaboration of sail-plan and rig. Owing principally to the interest and industry of Samuel Pepys our knowledge of such developments is placed on a much sounder basis with respect to the post-Restoration period. But it must be remembered that the improvements thus recorded in the large warships of that time were only very slowly followed by the smaller merchant ships.

Early in the eighteenth century the steering-wheel replaced the whipstaff, or pivoted vertical lever that for nearly two hundred years had been used to move the tiller. During this century the dimensions of the different classes of men-of-war were standardized, and showed a steady increase in size. But the most important development was the great elaboration of the sail-plan. The forward part of the lateen yard and the lateen sail that projected beyond the mizzen were cut away, so that the yard became a gaff and the sail a 'spanker', or 'driver'; jibs and staysails became common, and topgallant-sails on all three masts. By the end of the century the full-rigged ship carried nearly forty sails. The larger merchant ships were by then very similar to men-of-war, though built on more generous line to secure greater cargo capacity and without the characteristic 'tumble-home' that narrowed the top deck of the warship to preserve stability in view of its heavier armament.

The long series of naval wars that began in the middle of the eighteenth century and ended in 1815 was responsible for a notable advance in the speed, size, and manœuvrability of the sailing-ship. During the nineteenth century she was destined to come to her finest, fastest, and most beautiful form in the clipper. By that time, however, the new principle of mechanical propulsion was already well established. Throughout the nineteenth century there can be traced three parallel movements: the final, splendid evolution of the sailing ship, brought about by an unprecedented demand for fast passages that had its origin in the abolition of old trade monopolies and the growth of new colonies; the replacement of wooden by metal hulls; and the development of the steam engine, first as auxiliary, then as dominant partner, and finally as superseder of sail.

At the close of the Napoleonic War there were three main types of English merchant vessel. Those of the East India Company, which were generally built to a stereotyped naval pattern, though somewhat roomier and designed rather for comfort and for carrying capacity than for speed (a matter of secondary importance to a company in possession of exclusive trading rights), had then attained an average size exceeding 1,300 tons. At this time the company was running a fleet numbering more than a hundred vessels, chartered as a rule from private owners, who were often themselves members of the company. The West Indiamen, engaged principally in the important sugar trade with the West Indies, were much smaller, usually between 300 and 500 tons. The only other ships built in any numbers with a view to a particular class of trade were those engaged in the east coast coal traffic, which embraced also the major Baltic ports. These vessels were smaller still.

The loss of the East India Company's monopoly, which freed the trade with India in 1813 and with China in 1834, was followed by a period of intense commercial activity which in its turn brought about a major development in the construction of merchant ships. The new competition in eastern commodities led to a demand for fast passages; speed suddenly became no less important than capacity. The best-known ships of the new type evolved to meet this demand were those constructed at the Blackwall shipbuilding yard, which had been in existence since the early years of the seventeenth century. Since the time when the first ships had been built there by Henry Johnson, a cousin of Sir Phineas Pett, this yard had been responsible for the construction of many famous East Indiamen, and now, with the growth of a demand for a faster type of ship, it began producing hulls of much finer lines than ever previously attempted in the construction of large merchant vessels. The 'Blackwall Frigates', as they were usually called, attained a proportionate length of 4·7 in relation to beam, and as successors to the Old East Indiamen proper, continued to hold the regular passenger and cargo trade with eastern waters until the century was well advanced. They retained their characteristic stern windows and quarter galleries long after these features had disappeared from other types.

In the early years of the century the eastern trade was of far greater importance than that of the Western Ocean, which had not yet recovered from the effects of the American War of Independence. When it did revive, it remained for some time almost entirely in the hands of American sailing companies. The Black Ball Line began the first regular service between New York and Liverpool in 1816. The Red Star, Swallow Tail, and Dramatic Lines on the same route, and the Black Cross Line on the route between New York and London, followed soon after. The keen element of competition introduced by the operation of so many rival companies was enhanced by the desire to secure the mail contracts. It was the captain, and not the company, who profited by the allowance of two pence (or two cents) a letter; and it was the captain, rather than the ship, who was selected by the intending emigrant, anxious, since he had to provide his own food, to cross the Atlantic in the shortest possible time. So hard were these ships driven that only the most seasoned of Liverpool 'packet rats' would willingly stand up to such conditions. The east-bound passage, usually accomplished in about half the time necessary for the west-bound, was reduced in a very short time from an average of three weeks to less than a fortnight. Thus on the western as well as the eastern runs the early years of the century witnessed the rise of a competitive demand for fast passages on a scale previously unknown in the history of sail. At the height of the emigration boom following the middle of the century a passage to America could be bought for as little as three pounds ten shillings.

The result was the production for the first time of a class of merchant vessel designed primarily for speed. The Americans led the way with the *Ann McKim*, built in Baltimore in 1832. This ship was copied and improved upon until by the eighteen forties the real clipper (of which the first is usually held to be the *Rainbow*, built at New York in 1845), with her distinctive bow, modified stern (which slipped through the dead water instead of holding it), high proportion of length to beam—rising eventually to as high a figure as 6·7—and her imposing array of between thirty and forty sails, including such extra devices as skysails and studdingsails, brought the full-rigged ship to the peak of perfection. After the repeal of the Navigation Laws such vessels began to appear in English waters in increasing numbers in search of trade.

The cession of Hong Kong as a free port after the Anglo-Chinese War of 1839–42 and the opening of Shanghai to foreign trade in 1843 encouraged still further the growth of the eastern trade. The quality of tea was considered to deteriorate while in the hold of a ship, and amid the growing demand for still faster passages the American clippers found their opportunity. The first to break into this trade was the *Oriental*, launched in 1849 at New York, a clipper that set up a record on its first voyage from the Far East by accomplishing the passage to London from Hong Kong in ninety-seven days. The Blackwall Frigates stood no chance against such opposition, and British shipowners began ordering clippers from American yards. But the British yards were not slow in producing clippers of their own. In 1850 Green of Blackwall built the *Challenger* and Hall of Aberdeen the *Stornoway*, which in the following year made two fast passages, of 102 and 103 days, to Hong Kong. Similar ships followed, still faster and finer in their lines. During the next twenty years many records were made and broken in the famous tea-race from China. Comparisons of alleged records must always be examined with care, and the resulting conclusions sometimes accepted with reservations, for at this period there were no 'recognized courses' such as that now admitted for the Atlantic Blue Riband. The many claims put forward by owners on behalf of their ships are not always the best means of assessing their qualities under sail. But the spectacular tea-race gave rise to a good deal of interest. One of the most exciting of these races took place in 1866 between the *Ariel*, *Taeping*, and *Serica*, all built by Steele of Greenock. They left Foochow-foo together, and docked in London on the same tide ninety-nine days after. Still faster passages were recorded before the opening of the Suez Canal finally drove the clippers from the China trade altogether.

The Australian gold rush of 1851 offered another opportunity of which the American clippers attempted to take advantage. Within six years of the discovery of gold, nearly a quarter of a million people emigrated to Australia, creating a demand for shipping that could only be met by resort to extraordinary measures. Tonnage was diverted from the eastern trade, bought on the American market, and ordered urgently both from American and British yards. A problem no less serious was the provision of crews, who developed a tendency towards wholesale desertion in Australian ports. Special precautions were necessary to keep them aboard, particularly at Melbourne, and it was not unknown for ships to make the homeward passage with crews brought up to strength with convicts drafted from Australian prisons.

Much of this emigrant trade lay in the hands of the Liverpool shipowners, among whom James Baines, owner of the Black Ball Line, was particularly active. Before the rush the passage to Australia had usually taken about four months, but with three American-built ships, the *Marco Polo*, *Lightning*, and *James Baines*, he successfully lowered the record to sixty-three days. The last-named ship is reputed on one occasion actually to have exceeded for a short while a speed of twenty knots.

As the gold rush died down the importance of the Australian trade was maintained by the development of exports of timber, gum, hides, tallow and, above all, wool. Here also there was a particular motive in desiring fast passages, for wool sales were held in England on fixed dates, and the wool clippers often left Australia with the express intention of catching them. As the tea trade passed into the hands of the new steamship companies, many of the China clippers were diverted to the Australian run. Famous passages were made by the *Thermopylæ*, *Sir Lancelot*, and *Cutty Sark*, the last-named averaging over eight knots on her best voyage, for the tea clippers were as a class generally faster than the wool clippers, though their smaller capacity was a drawback in handling so bulky a cargo.

The introduction of metal hulls was a factor of considerable importance in enabling Britain to maintain her maritime position in the face of serious challenge from abroad. From the days of the earliest sea-going craft of the Egyptians, with their hogging-truss of twisted rope passing under bow and stern and over Y-shaped posts on the centre line, the provision of longitudinal strength had constituted one of the main problems in the construction of wooden ships of any size. If a certain length were exceeded, the vessel was very liable to break her back, especially in rough weather or on going aground. Sir Robert Seppings made an effort to solve this problem by introducing a system of diagonal framing into the construction of wooden warships. But added strength was only gained by this method at the cost of a certain clumsiness that materially reduced sailing speed, and it was evident that the solution to the problem, and with it the possibility of a substantial increase in the size of ships, must lie elsewhere.

Although it was early recognized that an iron pot would float just as easily as one made of wood, it was for long contended that an iron ship could not prove satisfactory on the grounds that it would be far too heavy and cumbersome for easy handling. Actually, iron construction resulted in a saving of more than a third in weight, while enabling more sail to be carried in a head sea without fear of straining the ship. Iron was tried for shipbuilding soon after the Napoleonic War. In 1829 the famous shipbuilder John Laird of Birkenhead launched his first iron ship, and during the next decade his lead was followed in other yards, for any development conducive to hard driving was sure of serious trial. These were sailing ships; it was not until 1837 that the first iron sea-going steamer appeared, the *Rainbow*, of 600 tons. It soon became apparent that a stranded vessel could be refloated without serious damage in circumstances that would have resulted in the total loss of a vessel made of wood. One of the principal advantages enjoyed by American yards in their keen competition with British shipbuilders during the middle of the century was a handy supply of plentiful timber. It was in an endeavour to counteract this advantage that many of the new British clippers, laid down especially to compete with their American rivals, were constructed of iron. These clippers owed their speed not only to their longer lines, which exceeded those of the American soft-wood ships, but also to their proved ability to stand the strain of hard driving in heavy seas.

The introduction of iron hulls was a movement affecting the development of sailing ships and steamers alike. On certain routes in tropical waters, however, there was an intermediate stage before iron vessels generally replaced those of wood. One of the earliest problems confronting traders to countries such as China and Australia was the fouling of the hull. The only effective (though very expensive) remedy lay in sheathing the vessel below the water-line with copper or yellow metal. The use of iron nails to secure the copper had been found impracticable on account of the corrosion caused by electrolytic action between the two metals when immersed in salt water. In consequence it was at first held that iron vessels would be useless in the China trade, since their hulls could not be sheathed. To overcome this disadvantage a type of building known as 'composite' was evolved, the iron framing of the ship being covered with planks, and these again with a copper sheath secured by copper nails. Eventually the introduction of anti-fouling preparations made such devices unnecessary; copper sheathing fell into disuse, and composite building went with it.

The success of iron hulls was productive of advantages to British shipping more far-reaching than mere technical improvements in design and speed. In the middle of the century, just at the time when British shipowners were feeling the increasing effects of American competition, the Irish famine brought about the repeal of the Corn Laws, and also the suspension of the Navigation Laws in order to accelerate the rapid importation of grain. In February 1847, a committee was appointed to examine the system. There followed an immediate outcry from shipowners all over England, led by the Shipowners' Society of London. It was argued that British shipping owed its success mainly to the operation of these laws; that the bulk of the British carrying trade would inevitably fall into foreign hands; that a decrease in shipping would undermine our naval supremacy by weakening trained reserves. In spite of these arguments, the bill passed its readings in the Commons, though with a dwindling majority, and the Navigation Laws were repealed in June 1849. The immediate result was undoubtedly a setback to British shipping, which suffered a temporary decline. The situation was restored, however, by the unusual demand for shipping created by the Australian gold rush and the Crimean War, followed later by the withdrawal of American competition as a result of the Civil War. But recovery was also assisted by another factor, the influence of which has not been so generally recognized: the replacement of wooden by iron ships in a country which, although poor in timber, possessed what was at that time the most highly-developed iron and steel industry in the world. Thus the lean years were tided over. The general adoption of iron hulls was followed by the introduction of iron masts and spars, and of still greater importance, steel rigging. During the eighties steel hulls also came into general use, lighter by some fifteen per cent than those made of iron. Owing to the early development of steel processing in Britain, this still further increased the advantage enjoyed by British shipyards. The first ocean-going vessel built of steel was the *Rotomahana*, launched in 1879.

The demand for fast sea passages created by the rapid expansion of trade and emigration in the nineteenth century was at first met chiefly by developments in the design of sailing ships. It was many years before the marine steam-engine offered a serious challenge to the clipper, and it is a source of some gratification to ship-lovers that the full-rigged ship was able to reach such heights of beauty and speed before being driven from the seas by the rise of mechanical power. At first regarded as of no more value than to propel a tug, the steam-engine gradually won recognition as a convenient asset for manœuvring in narrow waters. Then came a stage when sail was auxiliary to steam as a useful means of saving coal when winds were particularly favourable. By the end of the century the steamship had triumphed by practically ousting the full-rigged sailing ship from every important trade route on the seas.

The first British steamer went noisily afloat in 1788, when William Symington fitted a two-cylinder engine to a twenty-five-foot boat and attained a speed of five knots on a Scottish loch. In 1802 he produced his second effort, the *Charlotte Dundas*, which was driven by a large paddle-wheel aft and met with some success towing boats on the Forth and Clyde Canal. Similar experiments were in progress in America at about the same time. The first steamboat to carry passengers in this country was the *Comet*, of twenty-four tons, which appeared in 1812. She was described in her owner's advertisement as 'a handsome vessel to ply upon the River Clyde from Glasgow, to sail by the power of air, wind and steam', a feat accomplished by the use of a three horse-power one-cylinder engine and of a large square sail, set on the funnel. Her career ended eight years later, when she went ashore at Craignish Point. In 1815 the *Marjory*, a paddle-steamer of seventy tons, began a similar service between London and Gravesend, to be quickly followed by several others. So far the new invention had been confined to inland waters, as the uncertain machinery and flimsy paddle-wheels were not considered capable of withstanding the rough usage of the open sea.

But the experiment was soon made, and made successfully. In 1816 the first sea-going steamboat, the lugger-rigged *Hibernia*, began a service between Holyhead and Ireland. Within the next five years there was a rapid increase in steam tonnage. Properly speaking, however, these early cross-Channel boats were not steamers at all, as they were built on the same lines as sailing ships, and, of course, carried one or more sails, either on masts or on the funnel. The real distinction began when David Napier, after a series of experiments with models, introduced the wedge-shaped bow. The effectiveness of steamers having been proved on short voyages in home waters, it was not long before some of the more enterprising shipowners began experimenting with steam on the Atlantic passage. It is hardly possible to give an exact date for the first crossing of the Atlantic under steam, but auxiliary engines were used as early as 1819, when the *Savannah* made a passage from New York to Liverpool. Most of the voyage was made under sail, but her engines were in use until the fuel ran out, as testified by her captain's entry in the log of 'no cole to git up steam' as the vessel approached the British Isles. During the course of the next twenty years many similar passages were made by other sailing ships fitted with auxiliary engines, which were used for varying periods in accordance with the type of weather encountered. The most popular sail-plan for these early steamers was the barque rig. Their engines were of the beam type, with low-pressure boilers; paddle-wheels were in any case unsuited to the application of high pressures. For many years the difficulty of stowing an adequate supply of coal strictly limited the use of engines.

It was obvious that much work must be done on the development of the marine engine before steamers could hope to break the monopoly of the fast sailing packets operating along the Atlantic routes. But the crossing is, after all, comparatively short. Sailing ships, however hard driven, could only advertise their date of departure; the date of arrival could never be forecast with any certainty. So far as passenger traffic was concerned, reliability, if it could be ensured, might prove an even greater attraction than speed.

The first serious attempt to attain this object on any scale did not come until 1838, when the *Great Western* of 1,320 tons made her maiden voyage. She was constructed especially for the North Atlantic passenger service, and fitted out on a lavish scale. There were actually bells in the staterooms to summon the stewards. Such efforts to improve conditions of travel were long overdue, though some time was still to elapse before the matter was brought under proper control. Passengers were still too often regarded as necessary evils rather than the basis of the owner's profits. Those wealthy enough to pay for staterooms were sometimes forced to provide bedding and even furniture. Steerage passengers were usually supplied only with water and fuel, and received no other service whatever. During the great emigration rush of the fifties, which brought into the passenger trade many ships totally unsuited for the purpose, serious overcrowding aggravated these evil conditions until it was not unknown for steerage passengers to die of hunger, when a particularly bad passage made them too ill to cook or swallow their dwindling supplies of food. Improvement began in earnest with a series of laws to regulate the emigrant trade, one of the most important of which was the Passenger Act of 1855, which gave wide powers to emigration officers to check overcrowding and secure arrangements for proper feeding. The enforcement of these regulations afterwards became the duty of the Board of Trade.

Perhaps the chief impetus towards the early establishment of regular steamer routes lay in the competition to secure the mail contracts, on account both of the financial rewards and the constant effort and efficiency needed to ensure fulfilment of the contract terms. The success of the *Great Western* and of two similar ships, the *British Queen* and *President*, in making more regular passages than the sailing-packets led the British government to issue an invitation for tenders. The contract went to a new undertaking, specially formed to secure it by Samuel Cunard of Halifax, Nova Scotia. The original fleet of what came eventually to be known as the Cunard Line numbered four wooden steamers of over 1,000 tons, the *Britannia*, *Acadia*, *Caledonia*, and *Columbia*. Within eleven years nine more ships, successively larger and more powerful, were added to the fleet, and provided a service of weekly sailings. This service was not established without provoking strenuous competition from America. The subsidized American Collins Line, which came into existence in 1850, began running an excellent fleet of five steamers. But two of these were lost at sea, and with the withdrawal of the subsidy in 1858 the Collins Line ceased operations.

Early competition with sailing ships on the longer eastern routes offered a more difficult problem. On the Cape route the cost of providing coal at intermediate stations was at first prohibitive; even on the shorter Mediterranean route, which was broken by portage across the Suez Isthmus, it was an expensive undertaking. None the less, the East India Company very soon showed its interest in the new development, for the matter was under consideration as early as 1822. Here again mail contracts played an important part, and led to the offer of a grant by the company for the establishment of a steamer service by either route, held to be successfully accomplished after two round voyages, with a maximum of seventy days allowed for the passage.

In 1825 two vessels, the *Enterprise* and the *Falcon*, both fitted with engines, left for Calcutta. The latter used her engines so little that her passage could hardly be considered a genuine attempt. The former, a paddle-steamer of 479 tons register, spent 103 days at sea. She was purchased by the company and employed with success on the Calcutta-Rangoon service. This experiment was followed by the use of river steamers on the Hughli and Irrawaddy, and further trials with steam on the run between India and China. Some of the later Blackwall Frigates, such as the *Vernon* and *Earl of Hardwicke*, were equipped with engines and paddle-wheels, but they depended chiefly on the fact that they were full-rigged ships, and generally used their engines for brief periods only.

In spite of early disappointments, the East India Company continued to persevere. During the thirties a steamer service was started between Bombay and Suez. It was expensive and irregular, though less affected by the monsoon than the former service run by sailing ships, and provided timing arrivals and departures was reasonably accurate, made the Mediterranean-Red Sea route unquestionably the quickest way to India. In 1837 a mail contract was secured by the Peninsular Steam Navigation Company, which for three years had been operating between London, Spain, and Portugal. In 1840 the company added two new steamers to its fleet, changed its name to Peninsular and Oriental Steam Navigation Company, and extended its service to Malta and Alexandria. In 1842, in spite of opposition from the East India Company, which maintained its Suez-Bombay service until 1854, the P. and O. inaugurated a new service between Suez, Madras, and Calcutta with a large new paddle-steamer, the *Hindostan*. The result was a considerable improvement in the passage between this country and India, and an increase in the number of passengers electing to travel by the Mediterranean route. This was reflected in the added provision made for their comfort on the overland portion of the journey, for which they had originally been required to make their own arrangements. Anything up to 3,000 camels might still be needed for transporting the cargo of a single vessel, but for passengers camels and donkeys were replaced by horses and two-wheeled carriages; river transport was arranged where practicable; and after 1843 a chain of hotels and rest-houses was organized at staging posts. Similar improvements continued up to the time when it became evident that the long-discussed canal was about to become a fact. But there were always some passengers who preferred the more leisurely journey round the Cape.

Within a few years further mail contracts had enabled the P. and O. to extend its services to the Far East, running at first to Penang, Singapore, and Hong Kong, and later to Shanghai, Swatow, and Amoy. Other steamer lines followed, such as the Calcutta and Burma Steam Navigation Company, which began carrying mails for the East India Company in 1857, and later, under its present name of British India Steam Navigation Company, absorbed most of the coastal trade of India, the Persian Gulf, and the east coast of Africa. Meanwhile an attempt by the P. and O. to establish a service with Australia was temporarily suspended owing to the Crimean War, but was resumed later in competition with the Royal Mail Steam Packet Company, both concerns running services that eventually included Sydney, King George's Sound, and Melbourne. Several attempts were also made during the early fifties to run steamers to Australia via the Cape, but it was as yet too early for the steamer to challenge successfully this final stronghold of the clipper. Difficulties enough were still experienced over coal supplies on the other route, where the P. and O. employed over two hundred sailing colliers annually to supply its needs. It was not until the opening of the Suez Canal on 17 November 1869, that the success of the steamer on the Far Eastern and Antipodean runs was fully assured, at the expense of the regular lines of sailing ships to China and Australia. Fewer than five hundred ships passed through the Canal during the year following its completion, but this number was nearly trebled in the next five years, and went on increasing steadily as steam tonnage multiplied. One by one the sailing-ship companies running to Australia and New Zealand turned over to steam, or retired from the contest. The Orient Line became the Orient Steam Navigation Company in 1878, and began a fortnightly service to Australia in conjunction with the Pacific Steam Navigation Company. The latter was succeeded for a time in the service by the Royal Mail, until the Orient Line bought out other interests and assumed responsibility for the Australian mails on its own. The Aberdeen Line began replacing its clippers with steamers in 1881. A similar policy was followed a few years later by a new company formed from the amalgamation of the old Shaw, Savill, and Albion Lines.

In a region so vast and remote from organized fuel supplies and repair workshops as the Pacific, it might be expected that the sailing ship would have remained unchallenged by steam until the century was well advanced. In 1840, however, owing to the efforts of an American named William Wheelwright, who had failed to obtain the necessary support for the project in his own country, a royal charter was granted to the Pacific Steam Navigation Company for the operation of a service 'along the shores of North and South America in the Pacific Ocean'. The company started with two small paddle-steamers of about 700 tons, the *Chili* and *Peru*. Here again mail contracts helped the company through its early struggles. For a time the service was confined to the Pacific coast. In 1865 it was extended to the River Plate, via the Falkland Islands, and three years later a direct service, that before long consisted in regular fortnightly sailings, was inaugurated between the Pacific coasts and England.

But it was the Western Ocean runs that were responsible for the real development of the steamer. A year or so after the foundation of the Cunard Line, the Royal Mail Steam Packet Company, which had come into existence in 1839, obtained a contract for carrying mails to the West Indies, Mexico, and the former Spanish Main. Fourteen steamers were soon in use on this service, which was of so onerous a nature that the company was for many years in financial difficulties. However, the contract was renewed in 1850, and the company extended its service to Rio and the River Plate. During the next twenty years many more steamship lines appeared on the Atlantic routes: the Inman Line to the United States, which was soon engaged in a healthy rivalry with the Cunard Company; the Allan Line to Canada; Alfred Holt to the Caribbean; the African Steamship Company to the West African coast; and the Union Line, which secured the Cape mail contract in 1857, four years after its foundation.

During the latter half of the century competition between steamship companies, especially on the Atlantic routes, grew very keen. In 1867 a new White Star Line succeeded to the house-flag of a line of sailing ships that had borne the same name. This company entered the Liverpool-New York service in 1871 with a new steamer, the *Oceanic* of 3,707 tons. Within five years four more ships, the *Adriatic*, *Celtic*, *Britannic*, and *Germanic* had been added to the fleet, and a new service was being developed in the North Pacific between San Francisco, Japan, and China. By concentrating on the provision of better accommodation, especially for steerage passengers, the company soon became well established, and was the first to install gas-plants for lighting, though the experiment did not prove a success.

The rapid multiplication of new steamship lines during the two decades that followed the middle of the century was the outcome of a great stride in marine engineering. The advantages of the streamlined hull were not confined to clippers, and in steamship design followed the introduction of the wedge-shaped bow. Constant improvements in the manufacture of iron and steel made possible the construction of tubular boilers, capable of withstanding high pressures, and the development of the expansion engine, in which steam was expanded successfully in more than one cylinder. The use of this type of engine, which was tried out as early as 1854 in the steamer *Brandon*, resulted in greater economy in fuel, reduced the stress on bearings, and gave greater regularity to the turning movement. Experiments were somewhat protracted, but triple-expansion engines came rapidly into use after 1880.

The most important improvement, however, was the invention of the screw propellor. The advantages of the screw over the more vulnerable and clumsy paddle-wheels had long been realized, but there were certain practical difficulties to be overcome in the design of stern and rudder to permit of proper steering without undue interference from the screw, and in the casting of bearings sufficiently hard to withstand the constant wear of the shaft. In 1837 experiments by Francis Smith with a thirty-foot boat on the Paddington Canal gave promise of commercial success, and two years later the first screw-propelled sea-going ship, the *Archimedes*, of 232 tons, was launched by a syndicate formed for the purpose. As a result of her success the Great Western Steamship Company in 1843 fitted their new steamer, the *Great Britain*, of 3,500 tons, with a screw instead of paddle-wheels. On her maiden voyage across the Atlantic she averaged nine and a half knots.

At this time steamers on the Western Ocean routes did not exceed four thousand tons, and were usually smaller. In 1858 an experiment was made that gave rise to such interest that its importance has since been greatly exaggerated. This was an attempt, with the launching of the *Great Eastern*, of 18,914 tons, to discover whether a vessel so very much larger than anything previously built would prove more economical than several smaller ones. She was built on the longitudinal system, with transverse bulkheads separating her into compartments each sixty feet in length. In addition to carrying sails she was propelled both by screw and paddles, under the power of which she could steam at fifteen knots. Valuable lessons in marine engineering were learnt during her construction, but commercially she was a failure. As her name indicates, she was originally intended for the eastern trade, but it was difficult to find a service on which she could profitably engage. After several transatlantic voyages she was employed in cable-laying in the Atlantic and Indian Oceans and ended her career as a show ship before being broken up in 1890.

The screw propellor was the decisive factor in converting the Navy from sail to steam. At an early stage in the history of steam the Admiralty had acquired a number of small steam vessels for general purposes, but owing to the vulnerability of paddles, reliance continued to be placed on the old wooden sailing ship as a fighting unit. In 1843 the sloop *Rattler* was launched, a screw steamer of 1,078 tons. A tug-of-war was arranged between her and the *Alecto*, a paddle-steamer of approximately the same tonnage and power, in which the *Rattler* towed her opponent backwards at over two knots. The first warship designed as a steamer was the *Agamemnon*, launched in 1852. The Crimean War proved beyond doubt the obsolescence of the old line-of-battle ship. Wooden hulls gave place to iron at about the same time; the last wooden warship, the *Victoria*, an auxiliary steamer of 121 guns, was launched in 1859. During the succeeding decade the first ironclads, large vessels carrying no sails at all, made their appearance, though many years were still to elapse before cruising under sail disappeared from the Navy altogether.

The nineteenth century witnessed the rise and growth of a code of marine legislation that materially improved the conditions of merchant seamen. The disappearance of the East India Company's Maritime Service had struck a blow to the prestige of the mercantile marine. The tradition of this great seafaring service, with well over three hundred years' experience to its credit, was scattered after 1834, and only gradually rebuilt. 'No respectable people send their children to sea now,' remarked an old shipowner during the discussions preceding reform of the Navigation Laws, recalling sadly the days when the Maritime Service had been considered a fit occupation for the best families in the land. There was no lack of individual commanders who insisted on some measure of smartness and efficiency, but the realization that apprentices could be used as a means of securing cheap labour contributed to a general lowering of the status of officers, and in most ships it was customary for the second mate to take his turn with the men in all but the most menial tasks. In the early years of the century the conditions under which the crews lived were often as bad as, or even worse than, in the days of Elizabeth.

In 1850 the first major act was passed for improving conditions and maintaining a proper discipline among merchant seamen. Nine superficial feet of space was to be allotted to the accommodation of each member of the crew; a supply of medicine was to be provided; an examination was made compulsory for the master and mates of all foreign-going ships; proper articles of engagement were to be drawn up, and regulations enforced to ensure a regular method of engagement and discharge. Another act passed four years later gave the Board of Trade chief control over maritime affairs with power to hold courts of inquiry into the circumstances of wrecks and vessels lost, and laid down a number of provisions dealing with the safety of life at sea. In 1870 Samuel Plimsoll, Liberal M.P. for Derby, took up the cause of merchant seamen in the House of Commons. The violence of his views undoubtedly led to a certain disregard for fact in his book, *Our Seamen*, published in 1873. But this did little to diminish its widespread influence, and Plimsoll secured a strong backing in the country, resulting in the incorporation of provisions for a compulsory loadline in the Merchant Shipping Act of 1876. After 1890 the position in which this 'Plimsoll mark' was painted was no longer left to the owner's discretion. It must be remembered, however, that long before this time the Board of Trade had been empowered to prevent a ship from sailing if it was considered unfit to proceed to sea.

On the long ocean routes to Australia, New Zealand, and the Pacific, for which the early paddle-steamers were unsuited and where coaling was expensive, the sailing ship continued in some measure to hold her own until the last decade of the century. For such trades the clippers had usually been built on somewhat roomier lines, and often exceeded 3,000 tons. By the late eighties they could no longer compete with steamships as a means of fast transport, and as they went out of commission were not replaced. For a time, however, the building of sailing ships continued for the Chile guano trade and for general cargo, and even experienced a revival in the four-masted barque, square-rigged on the fore, main, and mizzen, and fore-and-aft rigged on the jigger. Speed being no longer the first consideration, all such extra aids towards the spread of canvas as skysails, studding-sails, and jib-booms disappeared. With them went the finer clipper lines, and the roomy barques of this period sometimes attained a size of well over 5,000 tons. Much romantic interest has centred on such of these ships as were still in commission during the present century, but to the sailor who remembered the heyday of the clipper they were no more than clumsy steel boxes. The last of these deep-sea sailing ships to fly the British flag was the *Garthpool*, launched as the *Juteopolis* in 1891. She remained in commission till 1929, when she was lost on the Ponta Reef, off the Cape Verde Islands.

A comparison of tonnage may serve as a broad illustration of the rate at which the supersession of sail by steam was accomplished. In 1829 nearly three hundred ships, totalling some 30,000 tons register, had been fitted with steam-engines. At mid-century, sailing ships totalled about 3¼ million tons, and steamers about 165,000. During the next twenty-five years sailing tonnage increased to well over 4 million. Steam tonnage was then less than half that figure, and did not equal sailing tonnage until about 1880. Sailing tonnage was by then declining at an ever-increasing rate until by the end of the century it accounted for no more than a quarter of the total British tonnage.

There is one aspect of the maritime progress of the nineteenth century that should not be overlooked. Owing to the rapid expansion of overseas trade and of colonization, British oceanic policy became worldwide in intention and in fact. Our shipping was enabled to fulfil the requirements that this entailed by successive improvements in design, by a technical skill that developed the new inventions in propulsion, by an enterprising spirit that accepted financial risks and successfully overcame initial difficulties, and by the advantage enjoyed by Britain as a producer of coal, iron, and steel. A further factor was the preoccupation of her only serious rival with domestic issues during the critical mid-century years. But behind all this lay a deeper, more far-reaching significance. From the time when its authority ceased any longer to meet with serious challenge during the

Napoleonic War, British naval power assumed a position in world affairs far transcending the mere implications of what is known as 'foreign policy'. In the suppression of slavery, the policing of the seas to stamp out piracy, and the surveying and charting of distant waters, the Navy assumed an international rôle that came to be accepted by Englishmen as a part of its natural function. This could not have been accomplished had Britain failed to meet the growing demands made on her mercantile shipping after 1815. For naval power cannot be created by the mere voting of taxes; nor can it flourish except on the basis of a sound seafaring tradition. This the Merchant Navy provided during the nineteenth century on an expanding scale commensurate with the needs of a growing Empire. Historians have stressed at length the exploits of Tudor and Stuart seamen in the history of British expansion, but similar influence on the growth of the Empire in more recent times is often too little regarded. To suppose that the maritime growth of the nineteenth century was no more than the necessary fulfilment of the law of supply and demand is not in accordance with the lessons of history: we need only to study the fate of Spain as a world power for ample proof that the needs of empire will not of themselves create that maritime strength on which the cohesion of the whole so largely depends.

SHORT BIBLIOGRAPHY

There are no books dealing both completely and satisfactorily with the period under review, though there have been many more exponents of the later history of the sailing ship than of the early development of the steamer. The following, however, will prove useful for those aspects indicated by their titles.

G. S. Laird Clowes:

   Sailing Ships: Their History and Development as illustrated by the Collection of Ship-models in the Science Museum.

      Part I., Historical Notes (1931)

      Part II., Catalogue of Exhibits, with Descriptive Notes (1932)

      (An authoritative and fairly technical account of the history of ship construction.)

   The Story of Sail (1936)

      (A brief and simple introduction to the subject, outlining the principal stages in the evolution of the sailing ship, with a series of excellent drawings by G. C. Trew, showing many types of past and present craft.)

Romola and R. C. Anderson:

   The Sailing Ship: Six Thousand Years of History (1926)

      (A concise, well-illustrated account from the earliest times.)

B. Lubbock:
The Blackwall Frigates (1922)
The China Clippers (1919)
The Colonial Clippers (1921)
The Western Ocean Packets (1925)
The Last of the Windjammers (1929)
(A well-known series, dealing in some detail with the different types of the later period, and the trades in which they were engaged.)
E. K. Chatterton:
Ships and Ways of other Days (1924)
The Old East Indiamen (1933)
R. A. Fletcher:
Steamships: The Story of their Development to the Present Day (1910)
W. Fry:
History of North Atlantic Steam Navigation (1896)
A. J. Maginnis:
The Atlantic Ferry (1900)
R. J. Cornewall-Jones:
The British Merchant Service (1898)
W. S. Lindsay:
History of Merchant Shipping and Ancient Commerce (1883)

RICHARD W. VAN ALSTYNE

The American Empire[1]
Its Historical Pattern and Evolution

I. THE CONCEPTION OF AN IMPERIAL REPUBLIC

THE United States, in the minds of its Revolutionary founders, was born an imperial republic. It was a 'nascent empire', to borrow an expression of George Washington's, that is, it was an *imperium*, or sovereign state, and it possessed the ambition and the capacity to expand in population and in territory. The term 'empire' involves a study in historical semantics since, as Dr. Richard Koebner has demonstrated, it has gone through cycles of approval and rejection and has had, even to the Romans, different meanings at different times. It was accepted in England during the eighteenth century as suitably descriptive of the overseas colonies, but at first it was used conservatively and in its original limited sense. Maps and books published in London after 1690 designated the British West Indies and the coastal colonies of the continent as 'the English Empire in America'. But the century was one of constant pressure for territorial expansion; and with the sweeping victories over France in the mid-century, its broader meaning, embracing ideas of conquest and glory, again became general. The frame of reference was the Roman

---

[1] In 1956 I had the honour of presenting the Commonwealth Fund Lectures at University College London on the theme of *The Rising American Empire*, and these, completely revised and rewritten, have been published under the same title by Basil Blackwell. Inasmuch as full documentation appears in the book, it is deemed unnecessary to encumber this essay with footnote citations. The reader, however, will find on the last page a selected list of references.

Empire in the Age of Augustus. Chatham, Shelburne, and the victorious Whigs, determined to keep Canada, so used it; and Washington, Franklin, and other Americans who had participated in this war and who ardently desired to eliminate the French and make North America a British continent, readily accepted the new interpretation. And so, with the coming of the Revolution and with the ambition to weld the Thirteen Colonies into a national, sovereign state, the substitution of the phrase 'American Empire' for British came easily and naturally. 'The Almighty,' declaimed a prominent South Carolinian in 1776, 'has made choice of the present generation to erect the American Empire.' The Revolution also revived and strengthened the ancient Roman conception of patriotism and, through the zeal and passion of this feeling, it breathed life into the American *imperium*. Franklin used the terms 'nation' and 'empire' interchangeably. The imperial state, that is to say, was the national state. But, the Revolution being conducted by thirteen separate colonies loosely joined together, the idea of a centralized state supreme over its component parts was a tender plant which the founders nurtured almost esoterically.

II. THE PRE-REVOLUTION PATTERN

The pattern of American expansion, and the forces pushing it along, can be understood by using the Peace of Utrecht as the point of departure. According to the theory of the Anglo-French treaty of 1713, the British colonies on the mainland were to attain maximum growth when they reached the mountains. The Empire was to be a maritime, rather than a continental, structure. Neutral zones of wilderness and independent Indian nations were to constitute permanent buffers between the coast and the French hinterland. But pressures on the Board of Trade—pressures which came principally from the colonies—brought forth from that body in 1721 a notable report which viewed the mountains as merely a temporary frontier. 'It were to be wished,' the Report proceeded, 'that the British Settlements be extended beyond [the Alleghenies], and some small forts erected on the great Lakes, in proper places. . . .' During the second quarter of the century the frontier changed from a primeval wilderness into an armed frontier, a 'zone of international friction' as Mr. L. H. Gipson had properly characterized it. A pincer movement, the Indian nations its hapless victims, developed and reached a triumphant climax for the British Empire in 1763. American ambitions fed upon the competitive forces of this period and produced a vision of an unlimited inland empire.

A good example of colonial influence on the Board of Trade is to be found in the case of James Logan, a politician, landowner, and fur trader of Pennsylvania who was instrumental in inducing the Board to commit itself in 1721. But Logan continued to clamour for action against the French on the ground that the latter were 'debauching' the Indians and encircling the British dominions. The French, he insisted in a Memorial written in 1732, were seeking control of the headwaters of the rivers that flowed into the sea. And, to drive home his point, he added an argument calculated to appeal more directly to the British sense of security. 'It is manifest,' he wrote, 'that if France could possess itself of those dominions and thereby become masters of all their trade, their sugars, tobacco, rice, timber and naval stores, they [sic] would soon be an overmatch in naval strength to the rest of Europe, and then be in a position to prescribe laws to the whole.'

Logan's Memorial reached the right people in London through Micajah Perry, a well-to-do merchant with an interest in the American trade, especially in Maryland and Virginia tobacco. But it is also of particular interest because of its direct, personal influence upon Benjamin Franklin at a time when Franklin's ideas were in the formative stage. There is only one extant copy of this document, and it is in Franklin's own papers in the handwriting of Benjamin himself. Franklin in the next two decades became one of the Empire's leading advocates. In a pamphlet written in 1751, which he called *Observations Concerning the Increase of Mankind*, he shewed himself both a precursor of T. R. Malthus and a disciple of Machiavelli. Prophesying that the colonial population would double itself every quarter of a century, he demanded more living room and admonished the British that a prince 'that acquires new Territory, if he finds it vacant, or removes the Natives to give his own People Room', deserves to be remembered as the father of his nation. Past gains established the 'duty' that Britain now owed her Colonies. 'What an Accession of Power to the *British* Empire by Sea as well as by Land! What Increase of Trade and Navigation! . . . How important an Affair then to *Britain* . . . and how careful should she be to secure Room enough since on the Room depends so much the increase of her People.' At the Albany Congress in 1754 Franklin had ready a plan for a federal type of empire; and at the close of the great war he sided with Pitt in the controversy over the retention of Canada, which was of course the key to the Mississippi valley. Moreover he was now dreaming of new worlds to conquer: the valley, he asserted, could be used for 'raising a strength . . . which, on occasions of a future war, might easily be poured down the Mississippi upon the lower country [Florida, a Spanish possession] and into the Bay of Mexico, to be used against Cuba, the French islands, or Mexico itself'.

Franklin ranks with Pitt as the Empire's leading philosopher. But there were many others, such as Thomas Pownall and William Shirley, both of them influential ex-governors of Massachusetts and distinguished advocates of British expansion into Canada. Shirley, who had in 1745 sent his Massachusetts soldiers to capture the French fortress of Louisbourg guarding the sea route to Quebec, was quick to seize the opportunity in 1755 to remove the Acadian French. His was a decisive voice in bringing about the deportation of those people from their homes; and an emigrating farming population from New England was stimulated to go thither to fill the vacuum. This colonizing movement from New England, which occupied the years 1760-8, was actually the first English-speaking settlement of a land which both history and geography misrepresent as Nova Scotia (New Scotland).

Literary influences were also at work in the Colonies to foster an imperial sentiment and to bring about a final showdown with the French. William Douglass, an immigrant Scot who in 1716 had made Boston his permanent home, is a good illustration. Douglass was a physician with a flair for travel and writing. After extensive tours through the British Colonies, both on the mainland and in the West Indies, he came back to Boston to publish, beginning in 1747, a two-volume *History of the British Settlements in North America*. Douglass shared the New England desire to come to blows with the French, but he never became a parochial Yankee. His History treated the Empire as a whole, and he shewed a comprehension of imperial inter-relationships to which nationalist-minded American historians of the nineteenth century were blind. The great 'imperial' historians of recent times—Herbert L. Osgood, Charles MacLean Andrews, Lawrence Henry Gipson, and others—have restored this tradition and this perspective to the field of American historiography.

III. THE PATTERN OF REVOLUTIONARY CONQUEST

Post-war periods have certain recognizable elements in common: disillusionment and dissatisfaction with the victory won; confusion and disunity in governmental policies; class or sectional animosities and grievances; popular demands for scapegoats. These and other forces of disintegration are familiar to all of our great post-war periods. The popular stereotype of the 1920s, 'We won the war, but lost the peace,' may not have been current in so many words in the post-1763 years; but its substance was there. The Revolution was the *aftermath* of the great war; it broke up the solidarity of the Empire for which that war had been fought. Historical distortions and misrepresentations come easily in an atmosphere of recrimination. Even

Franklin distorted the picture of the war only three years after it was over. Of all people, he denied that the Americans had had territorial ambitions and asserted that, until a British army arrived, they had been 'in perfect peace with both French and Indians'. This statement, so contrary to fact, became one of the enduring legends of the Revolution. With a flourish Tom Paine in 1776 blamed England for all of the past wars of the Americans, and promised eternal peace as one of the rewards of independence. And somehow or other the succession of wars between 1689 and 1763, in all of which American territorial questions had been major issues, went down in American history books as private wars of the kings of England. Such a nomenclature as 'King William's War', 'Queen Anne's War', 'King George's War', and even 'The French and Indian War' does not make for good history. The origins of these names remain to this day an unsolved historical puzzle. I put the question rhetorically: were they not the property of the Revolutionary, anti-British propaganda that made its way in the post-war period? Were the very names of these wars a product of post-Revolution bitterness? However that may be, the distortion they represent is as great as would be the case if the two world wars of the twentieth century were stamped respectively 'Woodrow Wilson's War' and 'Franklin Roosevelt's War'.

The point is, of course, that the rebellious spirits of the post-1763 period wished to blot out the imperial past. They wished to forget the dimly-formed principle of empire solidarity for which both Pitt and Franklin stood in 1761, and to chart a new course of empire unhampered by a distant government. During the ensuing War of Independence belated efforts were made on both sides of the Atlantic to save the principle of British Empire solidarity. The Galloway Plan, which lost in the Continental Congress by a single vote, was the outstanding attempt on the American side. In Parliament a brilliant minority led by David Hartley, former Governor Pownall, Charles James Fox, Chatham, Shelburne, the Duke of Richmond, and others developed the theme of a federalized British Empire. The conciliatory bills passed by Parliament in March 1778 rested on this principle, but hopes for a peace of this kind were dashed by the intervention of France.

Meanwhile the pattern of a North American empire, woven largely by the Americans themselves in the pre-Revolutionary years, drew their attention again with the outbreak of the War for Independence. At a time when the American army was scarcely organized, and when ammunition and heavy artillery were exceedingly scarce, Congress with Washington's full support launched an offensive against Canada. The object was permanent conquest, not a mere diversion. The expedition captured and temporarily held both

Montreal and Quebec, but fundamentally the campaign failed through the unfriendliness of the *Canadiens* and through lack of logistical support. 'We shall lose Canada,' wrote General Schuyler to Washington in May 1776, and the loss 'will be attended with many disagreeable consequences'. Stationed at Albany, the southern gateway to the St. Lawrence, Schuyler had been charged with the duty of forwarding reinforcements, powder, and heavy cannon to the army under General Arnold. The outcome was a bad blow, on which an aggressive British military command in Canada might well have capitalized. Promises of aid received concurrently from France helped soften this disappointment, but these were not enough: the Americans now were obliged to go earnestly in quest of foreign alliances. When in February 1778, after elaborate preparations for war, the French finally agreed to an alliance, the Americans looked to them for support in a second and stronger offensive. 'We are apt to wish for peace,' wrote George Mason to his fellow Virginian, Richard Henry Lee, in July 1778, 'altho I am clearly of opinion that war is the present interest of these United States; the union is yet incomplete, & will be so, until the inhabitants of all the territory from Cape Breton to the Mississippi are included in it. . . .'

But France did not see her interest in aiding the Americans to subjugate Canada. The treaty of alliance, to be sure, gave the United States permission to conquer the British dominions on the mainland, but it contained no pledge of French help and furnished no real foundation for the enthusiastic hopes for all-out aid. Washington's plan of campaign against Canada called for a combined naval and land assault on Quebec, the French to send a fleet capable of seizing control of North American waters. But France had other ideas, and the plan had to be dropped. Franklin in 1782 tried diplomatic pressure to the same end, but the Shelburne ministry ruled this out of the peace negotiations. Still it is the intention that counts. The successive attempts, military and diplomatic, establish the continuity of purpose inherited from the earlier wars of the century. Annexation of Britain's remaining North American colonies was regarded as something to be consummated later.

Jedediah Morse, a Congregational minister of Boston who published in 1789 a book which he entitled *American Geography*, justified his work on the ground that now that the United States 'have risen into Empire', its citizens should not rely upon Europeans for knowledge of its geography. Proceeding in this book, we learn that 'it is well known that empire has been travelling from east to west. Probably her last and broadest seat will be in America . . . the largest empire that ever existed. . . . We cannot but anticipate the period, as not far distant, when the AMERICAN EMPIRE will comprehend millions of souls, west of the Mississippi. . . . Europe begins to look forward with anxiety to her West India Islands, which are the natural legacy of this continent, and will doubtless be claimed as such when America shall have arrived at an age which will enable her to maintain her right.'

Now at this point two ideas, inseparable from each other, emerge and find expression in the single term *empire*. One is the idea of the national, sovereign state—the Leviathan of Hobbes as conceived at the Constitutional Convention of 1787 and created in the form of a perpetual union with a powerful central government. The other is the idea of growth without end, in territory and in power. 'However unimportant America may be considered at present', Washington wrote, conservatively enough, in 1786, 'there will assuredly come a day, when this country will have some weight in the scale of Empires. . . .' More concretely Alexander Hamilton talked in terms of securing control of the Caribbean Sea and of becoming 'the arbiter of Europe in America'. To both of the political parties— Federalists and Republicans—the new federal union was an empire. The two terms were equivalents in the vocabularies of Washington, Adams, Hamilton, and Jefferson. But words very commonly change in meaning, sometimes becoming archaic or obsolete. The substance which they represent, of course, need not change. Thus until the Civil War the phrase 'our federal union' was given preference. This was the language of Daniel Webster, Andrew Jackson, and Abraham Lincoln. But after the Civil War the term 'American nation' began to supplant it. That war was unitary, national, and imperial in its objective. It wiped out the doubt that had hung over the country regarding the nature of the union. It made a reality of the Leviathan State. The term 'expansion', applied to the territorial growth of the United States, has long been given preference over its eighteenth-century equivalent, although the older term 'empire' persisted in the vocabularies of nineteenth-century politicians, statesmen and writers. Historians have seized upon the expression 'manifest destiny' as a medium for describing the expansionist urge of the nineteenth century. This is a catch phrase which has been attributed to John L. O'Sullivan, an Irish-American editor writing in 1845. But O'Sullivan's better known contemporaries, such as Thomas Hart Benton and William H. Seward, continued to speak and write of the American empire. Semantically the change took place at the time of the Civil War, eighteenth-century usage falling from favour. But by all the tests of pragmatism the United States emerged from that war more than ever an imperial state. It entered its period of consolidation and centralization, it began developing its internal economy intensively, and abroad it soon joined in the international scramble for material wealth and power. 'Empire' and its confusing derivative 'imperialism', which was coined at this time, fell afoul of an intellectual and an emotional bias, but the flattering expression 'great power' appeared as a ready equivalent and was pridefully applied by Americans to their nation. But to revert to fundamentals: the United States is by its very essence an imperial power. It is a creature of the classical Roman-British tradition. It was conceived as an empire; and its evolution from a weak state, strung out on a long exposed coastline in 1789, to a world state, with commitments that are truly Roman in their universality, has been a characteristically imperial type of growth.

IV. THE NINETEENTH-CENTURY PATTERN OF EXPANSION

Is this growth of which I speak—whether it be called empire-building, imperialism, manifest destiny, or simply by the pedestrian word 'expansion'—distinguishable by a certain geographical and historical pattern? To be sure it is, and if it can be presented in its broadest outlines, we shall have a comprehensive view of the evolution of the American world state. Let me begin with a few observations on the so-called 'westward movement', a concept of American history handed down from the frontier hypothesis of Frederick Jackson Turner. In its simplest form, this version builds up a picture of a steadily moving frontier of settlers which took about a century to advance across the continent. The 'frontier' is said to have come to an end in 1890. Then, and then only, we commonly read, the United States 'left the frontier behind and entered upon an era of overseas expansion'. A natural conclusion drawn from this version—one that is widely believed—is that until 1898 or thereabouts, the United States had little, if any, interest in the outside world. From this arises the highly imaginative picture of the United States marching slowly across the continent and then, equipped with seven-league boots fitted to its unwilling feet by Theodore Roosevelt, making a sudden long jump to the Philippines and the Orient. 'Imperialism', it is declared dogmatically, came to the United States only when it acquired island possessions and then only by 'accident'. With the appearance of protest and criticism against the island conquests of 1898 and against the alleged 'big stick' policies of Theodore Roosevelt, 'imperialism' became an epithet applied indiscriminately to various nations but to the United States only for the years 1898 to 1912. This period is torn out of context and given a unique frame of reference, leading to the profound historical fallacy that the United States under the influence of Theodore Roosevelt suffered an unfortunate, temporary 'aberration' from its hallowed republican (or

128

democratic) traditions, from which it subsequently recovered, under Woodrow Wilson, as from a sickness. From this arose the curious belief that only nations with island possessions are empires, and the denial that the United States, in developing continental ambitions, was an imperial nation. A moment spent with a dictionary should dispel this illusion.

But to return to the frontier hypothesis, which rivets attention upon the continental United States and makes 'the West', or 'the westward movement', its exclusive frame of reference. Propounded for the first time in 1893, Mr. Turner's theory in due course established its ascendancy over American historical thought and provided a remarkable stimulus to the teaching and writing of American history for a whole generation. Under its influence, the pattern of American expansion becomes much less complex than it really is, and this perhaps is the principal weakness of the theory. In his later writings Mr. Turner shewed that he recognized the United States as historically an empire, and he grasped the geopolitical significance of the Mississippi heartland. But he made no attempt to develop this conception. His mind, for instance, seems not to have strayed northward past the artificial Canadian-American boundary. He seems to have been utterly oblivious to the northern neighbour, whose own 'West' was growing substantially even as he was writing. And the Canadian West was quite different from Mr. Turner's West. The alleged uniqueness of the American frontier loses much of its vitality when viewed comparatively with Canada's history. Furthermore, it is a commentary upon how spellbound even a brilliant intellect can become when it is remarked that Mr. Turner, living in Wisconsin within a few miles of the Canadian border and placidly deciding that 'the fronter' had 'closed', failed to observe the veritable flood of migrants moving northwards from the United States into the prairie provinces. Actually between 1896 and 1914 occurred one of the greatest folk-wanderings in the history of North America, leading to the colonization of the Canadian West; and in the decade 1901–11 the number of persons emigrating from the United States averaged a hundred thousand a year.

The growth pattern of the American Leviathan is not confined to Turner's West, nor is it merely continental. The agrarian influence has been over-stressed, for historically the United States is a commercial no less than an agricultural state. American expansion has been maritime, global in its reach, and has consisted of multiple thrusts, seaward as well as landward, carried on simultaneously in many directions. Thomas Jefferson and John Quincy Adams, both of them children of the eighteenth century, cut out the first designs. Jefferson's design in particular shows the influence of tradition. It called for a parent state whose territorial domain should follow closely the boundaries of the British Empire in North America in 1763: i.e. a western boundary at the Mississippi, a northern boundary that would take in the Canadian provinces, and a southern boundary that would embrace the Floridas and their appendage, Cuba. These were, to Jefferson's mind, the natural limits of the federal republic. Infiltration of American settlers into the British and Spanish borderlands would lead to annexation. It was already going on at a substantial pace when Jefferson was President, and the war of 1812 was expected to finish this process of rounding out the American frontiers. Jefferson must have been disappointed at the failure in that war to 'liberate' Canada—he was a hold-out even in 1814 for annexation—but he lived to see the Floridas absorbed. Cuba, he is said to have exclaimed, would 'be ours in the first moment of the first war'.

Louisiana—the vast country to the west of the Mississippi and its capital city of New Orleans on the east bank near the river's mouth —was Jefferson's diplomatic windfall of 1803. A shrewd concession by Napoleon, this acquisition meant undisputed possession of the continental heartland only twenty years after the formalities of independence had been concluded. It gave the United States a position of independence *vis à vis* the European powers so strong that it was almost ready to jump on to the same stage with them. Jefferson looked upon Louisiana as a bridge for colonizing movements that would set up new, independent republics in the south-west and north-west corners of the continent respectively. The Pacific North-west had been the object of his attentions ever since 1783, when he made his first attempt to get someone to find a route. He probably first learned of the Northwest from reading of the voyages of Captain Cook, but at any rate he was even then uneasy lest Britain colonize the Northwest first. And when, tardily, an American outpost was finally planted on the Columbia River, Jefferson bubbled over with enthusiasm. 'I view it [Astoria]', he exclaimed, 'as the germ of a great, free, and independent empire on that side of our continent, and that liberty and self-government, spreading from that as well as this side, will insure their complete establishment over the whole.' In other words, a Pacific Northwest Republic was to develop and to stand to the United States, its mother country, as Virginia had stood to Britain. The trans-Mississippi desert, as the western prairies were long regarded, was, like the Atlantic Ocean, too wide and too formidable a barrier to make unification with the mother country practicable. Independence, the catchword of the American Revolution, would be an even more fitting objective for the Northwest: it would carry out the ideological mission of the American Republic. As for the south-west, it may be that, when the Jefferson record is complete, we shall find him expressing a similar sentiment concerning Texas. For Texas in its early history is a perfect illustration of the Jeffersonian pattern filling out: a colony of free American emigrants appropriating for its own use a valuable piece of territory and winning its independence from an alien and far-distant government. 'Our confederacy', Jefferson had once said, 'must be viewed as the nest, from which all America, North and South, is to be peopled.'

John Quincy Adams was more of an empire-builder in the tradition of William Pitt. 'Our proper dominion', he asserted in 1819, 'is the continent of North America'; and Adams's diplomacy during the next decade aimed at rounding out the continental domain. He would bargain Mexico out of the south-west, Britain out of the north-west as far as the sixty-first parallel if possible. The Monroe doctrine (which Adams inspired) is commonly interpreted as aimed at Russia so far as the Northwest was concerned. But there is better ground for believing that Britain was the principal rival, for she, not Russia, possessed an interest in, and a capacity for, colonizing this region. The point, however, is that Adams meant to have, or at least to pave the way for the United States to have, *all* of the habitable portions of North America. With his trading New England background, Adams meant to possess all of the good ports of the continent. And he did not think in terms of separate republics loosely allied with the mother country. He conceived of the parent state keeping pace with the colonists whom it sent out, appealing to their nationalism and bringing them directly under its dominion. The Monroe doctrine, so-called, has the qualities of a powerful negative: it proposes to circumscribe freedom of action on the part of European powers in the political and in the ideological field; it erects a fence around the imaginary area of the western hemisphere; and in time it turned into a potent psychological weapon in the stimulation of American nationalism. But it is not the negatives of the Monroe doctrine that really count: it is the hidden positives to the effect that the United States shall be the only colonizing power in North America and that it shall be the directing power in both North and South America. This is imperialism preached in the grand manner, for the only restrictions placed upon the directing power are those which it imposes upon itself. The Monroe doctrine would be better described as 'the Monroe manifesto'.

This Adams concept of dominion over all North America found a niche in the American mind plainly visible for a hundred years thereafter. The forces which justified this belief had been forming as far back as the seventeenth century, and there is a continuity in the expression of purpose until the age of Theodore Roosevelt and Woodrow Wilson. There was a thrust to the north—a *Drang nach*

Norden—a thrust to the south, and a thrust to the west. Seward, Adams's greatest successor, made bold to complete the thrust to the north: his purchase of Alaska in 1867 was a stroke of policy comparable to Jefferson's in 1803. He had outflanked the British and believed that he had found the means of ousting them from the continent. British North America was now partially encircled. And Russia, like France in 1803, believed she was serving her own interests in strengthening the American rival to the British Empire. But the American *Drang nach Norden*, begun by the New Englanders and the New Yorkers in the seventeenth century, had been checked repeatedly by opposing forces; and these forces finally crystallized, late in the nineteenth century, in the new nationalism of the 'maple leaf'. Canada is the other colonizing power in North America. But as late as 1911 the American mind was reluctant to admit defeat in this direction. Recognition of the permanency of Canada came in fact only in consequence of World War I.

The American *Drang nach Süden* has equally remote origins, being an outgrowth of the British seventeenth-century push into the Spanish Caribbean. The New England Yankees shared in the commercial benefits of this push, and in the eighteenth century gained the lead. Candid recognition of this pull to the south came from Benjamin Franklin in 1761, when he suggested Cuba and Mexico as the next objects of aggression. This, incidentally, was about the same time as Russia commenced her quest for the Turkish Straits. For nearly a century after this date war was regarded as a possible means of capturing control of the Caribbean. The Mexican War of 1846–8 was partly a Caribbean war: it was brought to its triumphant conclusion by an amphibious expedition sailing from New Orleans, which attacked and invaded the heart of Mexico. And it whetted the appetite for further conquest. Filibustering bands staged repeated incursions into Mexico, Cuba, and Central America; and the most notorious of the filibusterers, William Walker, made himself the ruler of Nicaragua. Walker's rule was comparatively short, but not so short as to discourage the thought of a personal empire that would eventually take in Cuba. The governments of James K. Polk and Franklin Pierce made this 'Pearl of the Antilles' their own special object of interest and made successive attempts at its acquisition. Except for the inter-sectional dissension within the United States, which worsened after 1854, it seems probable that a pretext for a war with Spain would have been found, with the conquest of Cuba as its object. The war of 1898 was in fact a long deferred contest, and it meant fulfilment for the American *Drang nach Süden*. Cuba was converted into a protectorate, and the Caribbean became an American lake.

The pull to the West—or, as it is commonly called, the westward movement—was part of an all-embracing programme of building an empire in North America. Once the Mississippi heartland was in American possession, the process of completing this thrust moved rapidly along. There were four correlative movements occupying roughly the second quarter of the nineteenth century: the advance into the south-west, culminating in the annexation of Texas in 1845; the advance north-westward into the Columbia River country, pointed at the annexation of the entire Pacific Northwest, but stopping in 1846 with a partition agreement with Britain which saved a portion of the sea coast for the future Dominion of Canada; the advance due west to California, related to an approach to that province by sea and resulting in the expulsion of Mexico from all of the present American West; and finally a fourth prong northward through the valley of the Red River, forestalled, however, by British and Canadian collaboration in firming up the boundary at the 49th Parallel.

Meanwhile there was a rapidly advancing maritime frontier in the Pacific, invisible in a sense but no less real than Turner's frontier on the continent, possessing many of the same attributes and recognizing no geographical limits. Again we must go back to the eighteenth century if we would comprehend not merely the origins, but the immense sweep of this thrust. The voyages of the English mariner, Captain Cook, aroused intense interest in the seaboard United States. Cook's third voyage coincided with some of the bitterest years of the War of Independence, 1776–80; but in spite of the hostilities, Yankee naval vessels had orders that, should they happen upon the English explorer, they were to pay him all honour and respect. The first complete account of the voyage appeared in London in 1781, and an American edition followed two years later. Furthermore, the success of Cook's men in selling to the Chinese the pelts of sea otters which they had procured from the Indians of the Pacific Northwest attracted the attention of New England merchants. The new China trade, begun by the latter in the 1780s, marked out the path of empire to the Pacific.

We must not, however, make the mistake of narrowing this movement to the dimensions of a path. Merchants, missionaries, adventurers, sea captains, naval officers, and consular officials crowded into the Pacific during the nineteenth century and spun a web whose strands extended to every part of the ocean. The history of this movement has yet to be written. Historical research has hardly scratched the surface. There is an epic story still to be told of this American penetration of the Pacific basin, and when properly described it will rank equally in importance with the transcontinental movement which it paralleled in time. The process of building an empire in the Pacific is not in any sense *in sequence* to continental expansion. It was correlative, contemporaneous, and like its British counterpart, global in pattern.

How rapidly the American imagination began taking in the whole Pacific basin can be appreciated by recalling a letter written by Captain David Porter in 1815 to President Madison. 'We border on Russia, on Japan, on China,' Porter insisted. 'We border on islands which bear the same relation to the N.W. Coast as those of the West Indies bear to the Atlantic States. . . . The important trade of Japan has been shut to every nation except the Dutch. . . . [It is for us], a nation of only forty years standing, to beat down their rooted prejudices, secure to ourselves a valuable trade, and make the people known to the world.' For a nation that had just emerged from, at best, an indecisive war in which it had realized none of its declared objectives, this expression of a desire to perform a public relations service for the Japanese seems a bit extravagant. Porter's communication went into the Presidential pigeonhole, but it was not long before others took up the same plea. In 1828 J. N. Reynolds of New York reported to the secretary of the navy on information he had gathered first-hand from the whaling captains of New London, Newport, New Bedford, Nantucket, and other New England towns. These navigators, he said, know more about the Pacific and the South Seas than those of any other country. At least two hundred ships were employed in whaling and sealing. Reynolds's object was to learn all he could concerning the navigation, geography, and topography of the whole range of seas from the Pacific to the Indian and Chinese oceans. The navy department, he declared, was now better informed than any other admiralty, 'for those seas are truly our field of fame. Too much credit cannot be given to our whalers, sealers, and traffickers for the information they have acquired. . . .'

Ten years of pressure from New England finally brought about the United States Exploring Expedition, commanded by Captain Charles Wilkes. The expedition was to blanket the Pacific, sailing from Valparaiso to the Society Islands and thence to the Fijis where, it was hoped, a safe harbour could be selected. It was to take in Hawaii and the Pacific Coast, where it was to make surveys with special attention paid to San Francisco Bay. From the Northwest Coast it was to sail by the great circle route to Japan and thence south to the Straits of Sunda and the port of Singapore. Wilkes has told the story of his expedition in his five volume *Narrative*, published in 1845. We need a study that will show the impact of this work on the reading public and on governmental policy. One conclusion to be drawn from it, because it is supported by considerable other evidence, concerns the interest in the Pacific Coast, including California and Oregon. It is commonly supposed that agrarian, colonizing interests brought about the acquisition of these coastal provinces, that they belong exclusively to the 'westward movement'. But the New England mercantile community was on the coast many years before there was any colonization, and it was supplemented by visits from the navy. The mercantile and naval interest was in the ports and in the trans-Pacific trade. Daniel Webster and George Bancroft, Polk's secretary of the navy, both desired San Francisco. Bancroft got his knowledge of the Northwest from William Sturgis, a Boston merchant who had lived both on the Columbia and in Monterey, California, as well as in Macao. And the navy under Bancroft had something to do with precipitating the war with Mexico, of which California was the prize. The conquest of the province came first from the sea, not from the land. This war, as I have said, was a demonstration of sea power. Indicative of the frame of mind in which the navy had long been accustomed to view the Pacific coast is the official language it used in 1829 referring to the different harbours *belonging* to the United States. And in instructing Wilkes in 1838 the secretary mentioned 'the territory of the United States on the seaboard'. The sceptical historian should be pardoned for pointing out the premature character of these claims.

After Wilkes comes the expedition of Commodore Matthew C. Perry with its determined thrust against Japan. Perry had acquired a background of first-hand knowledge of the Orient, and he intended to employ force, if necessary, to open up the island kingdom, as the British had done with the Chinese. Basic to his purpose was his appraisal of the strategy of the Pacific Ocean, and his belief that Britain and the United States, the two leading commercial powers, were fated to have a war over the Pacific. Perry had plans for converting the island of Okinawa into a depot for American commerce and for initiating treaty relations with Japan equivalent to those previously imposed upon China. But he did not persist in his intentions, strangely enough, and the net result of his expedition was a mere 'shipwreck convention' which opened two small Japanese ports for the purchase of provisions.

Less familiar to history, but perhaps more important, was the United States Surveying Expedition to the North Pacific Ocean, 1853-6. This expedition started out under the command of Lieutenant Cadwallader Ringgold, who had sailed with Wilkes; but Ringgold broke down of a fever and was replaced, at Perry's direction, by Lieutenant John Rodgers. The mission of this expedition was to explore the waters of Japan and North China which, it was explained, were of 'uncommon interest to the United States'. These waters would 'soon become the preferred route of the immense commerce that is now anticipated to grow up between the eastern coasts of Asia and the western coast of Australia'. Rodgers performed his task with consummate tact and ability, but he left the secretary in Washington in no doubt over the attitude of the Japanese. In Porpoise Sound (near Hakodate), he reported, 'we asked for water, and the authorities sent off about five gallons. We asked for provisions, and they gave us a bunch of turnips. The people are jealous, and timid, and very poor. They regret doubtless that the world has found them.' From the north of Japan Rodgers proposed to sail for San Francisco via the Arctic; and from San Francisco he would survey a route to Shanghai, 'because interesting points lie on the route, and because opinion points to that as the Chinese Emporium of American Commerce'. Then, after outlining his homeward course from Shanghai, Rodgers closed his dispatch with an evaluation of his cruise. 'It will devote our labours,' he said, 'to the Ocean upon which we have important possessions, and are the only powerful race; to the Ocean in which we of all the world have the deepest interest.'

Unfortunately, Rodgers was not permitted to complete his survey. He was notified, when he reached San Francisco, that his funds were exhausted. But he clung to his conviction that the survey should be made. 'I think that the Pacific Railroad, and Steamers to China, will turn the tide of commerce this way,' he declared in a final dispatch in January 1856. 'We shall carry to Europe their teas and silks from New York. I believe that this result is inevitable; and I also think the time of its attainment will be shortened by accelerating as far as possible the passage to China. The results are so vast as to dazzle sober calculation. . . .' Rodgers, of course, could not have foreseen the Suez Canal, Europe's answer to this bid for supremacy in the China trade. Still, one of the most remarkable coincidences of the nineteenth century occurred in the year 1869: the opening of Suez was matched by the completion of the Union Pacific-Central Pacific Railroad, the first American transcontinental. Beyond Sacramento, the first western terminal of the Railroad, lay San Francisco and the trade of the Orient.

This expectation of a North American route to the Orient, first acted upon by Jefferson, we recall, in 1783, was widely held by the middle of the nineteenth century. The railroad was under serious consideration after 1845, and always it was associated with the China trade. In the flowery oratory of the senate, William Henry Seward of New York permitted his imagination free play, but his language was not really different from Rodgers'. 'The world,' declared Seward, 'contains no seat of empire so magnificent as this, which . . . offers supplies on the Atlantic shores to the over-crowded nations of

Europe, while on the Pacific coast it intercepts the commerce of the Indies. The nation thus situated . . . must command the empire of the seas, which alone is real empire.'

Seward is the central figure of nineteenth-century American imperialism. He understood the nature and the directions which American expansion historically strove to follow—the effort to absorb British North America, which was to come to a head between 1867 and 1871; the drive southward into the Caribbean; and the trans-Pacific thrust into North-east Asia. With the suppression of the Southern rebellion in 1865 Seward acted adroitly to set these forces again in motion. Alaska was his masterpiece: it is the north star of the American empire, shedding its light on two continents. It was the backdoor to the British Northwest, a hint that the Hudson's Bay Company would do well to allow its vast holdings in Rupert's Land to go by default to the advancing Americans. But Seward and his contemporaries overlooked the potentialities of the new Canadian Federation, consummated in the same year that the United States purchased Alaska from the Russians; and the speed with which the Canadian leaders acted, in co-operation with Her Majesty's Government to buy out the Bay Company and to annex the Crown Colony of British Columbia on the coast, meant that by 1871 the United States was confronted with an accomplished fact.

But Seward also meant that Alaska and its dependent island chain, the Aleutians, should be the finger pointed at North-east Asia; and the demogogic Senator Nathaniel P. Banks of Massachusetts undertook to make the finger wag. Alaska, declaimed Banks, was the key to the Pacific. Through it 'we have in our grasp the control of the Pacific ocean, and may make this great theater of action for the future whatever we may choose it shall be'. Seward, meanwhile, had made a futile gesture at annexing Hawaii, long since Americanized by New England merchants and missionaries; but he got Midway Island farther out, thus registering the trend toward Asia. In the Caribbean he manœuvred to get possession of Santo Domingo and the Virgin Islands, thus trying to revive the historic pull to the south. But here too he fell short of his goal. In these post-war years the currents of American imperialism flowed temporarily underground, to surface again during the 1890's.

V. THE PHILOSOPHICAL IMPERIALISM OF THE 1890S AND THE WAR WITH SPAIN. THE LIMITS OF THE TRANS-PACIFIC THRUST

Now it is evident that these older American expansionists were not without their creed. Jefferson and Adams, for instance, delighted in waging ideological warfare against European monarchies. And

Adams, the doughty New England Puritan, waxed indignant against the Chinese in 1842 for the 'enormous outrage' they had committed in trying to bar the Christian, commercial nations from their doors. During the first Anglo-Chinese War Adams cast himself in the unaccustomed role of an Anglophile praying that Britain 'will extend her liberating arm to the farthest bounds of Asia'. Even Seward, the empiricist, was not without his sentimental side. But it remained for the philosophical and religious imperialists and the economic determinists of the 1890s to formulate and lay emphasis upon an ideological system as justification for promoting an American empire on a world scale. John Fiske, the New England historian, and Josiah Strong, a Congregational clergyman of Ohio, can be paired off for study. Strong in his book *Our Country* synthesizes Anglo-Saxonry, Protestant Christianity, the teachings of Darwin, and economic acquisitiveness into a rationale for the United States virtually taking over the world. 'If I read not amiss,' he declared, 'this powerful race will move down upon Mexico, down upon Central and South America, out upon the islands of the sea, over upon Africa and beyond. . . .' Then there is the fascinating record of Horace N. Allen, the Presbyterian minister, in Korea between 1884 and 1905. Allen's personality was a remarkable blend of the missionary, the politician, the trader, the entrepreneur, and the strategist. Given a free rein, Allen unquestionably would have made an American protectorate out of Korea by 1895; but Japan stood in his way and Theodore Roosevelt was on her side. In the fierce international rivalry that converted North-east Asia at this time into one of the world's great storm centres Roosevelt played the part of a moderate.

No sooner had war been declared against Spain on 21 April 1898, than the excitable Albert Beveridge of Indiana rose in Boston, Massachusetts, to make himself the mouthpiece of the imperialists. He declaimed:

'American factories are making more than the American people can use; American soil is producing more than they can consume. Fate has written our policy for us; the trade of the world must and shall be ours. . . . We will cover the ocean with our merchant marine. We will build a navy to the measure of our greatness. . . .'

Beveridge may well have known, at the moment he spoke, that an American squadron under Commodore Dewey was on its way from Hong Kong to strike the first blow at the Spaniards in Manila bay. There has never been a satisfactory explanation as to why this attack took place. The direct order to attack is attributed to Theodore Roosevelt, who was temporarily occupying the secretary of the navy's chair in Washington. But Dewey's squadron had been previously prepared for war, and Manila, its only possible objective, was peculiarly located to serve American designs in the Far East. American naval forces on duty in the Far East had always been obliged to make use of British facilities, although there had been a desire to have a separate American base ever since 1850. Manila was a natural choice, and therefore the conclusion is inescapable that it was selected in advance, the coming war with Spain over Cuba to furnish the opportunity. Furthermore, the Americans were not content with the mere destruction of the Spanish squadron. An expeditionary force was soon thereafter dispatched, with the capture of Manila its objective. Incidental to this expedition, but determined upon in advance, was the occupation of the vacant island of Wake and of the Spanish-owned island of Guam, nicely spaced on the shipping lane between Honolulu and Manila; and during the same summer months of 1898 the long deferred annexation of the Hawaiian islands was engineered. The naval life-line between San Francisco and Manila was thus completed, although the acquisitive spirit was by no means appeased. In November 1900 Secretary of State John Hay started a negotiation for a base and territorial concession at Samsah bay in Fukien province, opposite Formosa; and the navy, disappointed there, continued to look for a base in Korean waters. These moves, however, remained unfinished, partly because of Japanese opposition.

The question of how far the American thrust across the Pacific should go—whether it should stop short of Japan or whether it should override that country and penetrate the Asiatic mainland—comes now into view for the first time. The vaguely defined programme of the middle century seemed to point at penetration of the mainland. But the rise of Japan and the concomitant injection of European rivalries into this area introduced new factors which men like Theodore Roosevelt recognized.

In Alfred Thayer Mahan and Brooks Adams, the two ablest of the American philosophical imperialists of this generation, we have the two opposite answers to this question. Mahan's great works, of course, were his histories. But his didactic interpretations and generalizations are to be found in his collected essays that appeared in book form in 1898 and 1900. Unlike Josiah Strong and Albert J. Beveridge, Mahan never let himself go over the effusive cults of race, religion, and superior civilization. He recognized that the United States was a member of the complex of national states, and he saw its survival in terms of sea power. Except for Hawaii, he refrained from advocating the acquisition of islands or other dependent territories, he was no advocate of an American conquest of Asia. He accepted the conquest of the Philippines only after the accomplished fact; and in China he would, in co-operation with Britain, hold the door of the Yangtze valley open for commerce, but would not support the Celestial Empire with political guarantees. Mahan's ultimate hope lay in a close community of interests with Britain, functioning through joint command of the seas. We have, I believe, much still to learn about this celebrated author of *The Influence of Sea Power on History*. He was a contemporary of Turner, but outside of professional naval circles his writings and his theories have been, by comparison, strangely overlooked.

Brooks Adams, on his part, was an avowed pessimist. His *Law of Civilization and Decay* taught that economic competition would eventually reach the breaking point and bring about the collapse of society. Yet he used his pen to prod his countrymen into seeking empire in Asia. 'Our geographical position, our wealth, and our energy pre-eminently fit us to enter upon the development of eastern Asia,' he declared, 'and to reduce it to a part of our economic system. . . . The Chinese question must therefore be accepted as the great problem of the future, as a problem from which there can be no escape; and as these great struggles for supremacy sometimes involve an appeal to force, safety lies in being armed and organized against all emergencies.' In 1900 Brooks published a book on this theme, which he entitled *America's Economic Supremacy*. 'For upwards of a thousand years,' he wrote, 'the tendency of the economic center of the world has been to move westward, and the Spanish War has only been the shock caused by its passing the Atlantic. Probably, within two generations, the United States will have faced about, and its great interests will cover the Pacific, which it will hold like an inland sea. The natural focus of such a Pacific system would be Manila. Lying where all the paths of trade converge, from north and south, east and west, it is the military and commercial key to eastern Asia. Entrenched there, and backing on Europe, with force enough to prevent our competitors from closing the Chinese mainland against us by discrimination, there is no reason why the United States should not become a greater seat of wealth and power than ever was England, Rome, or Constantinople.'

Brooks ignored Japan in this book which was written at least five years before the Russo-Japanese War. Economic pressures from within the United States had meanwhile compelled the McKinley administration to declare for the open door, followed by a circular letter demanding recognition of the independence and integrity of China. Adam's books reflected both the fears and the ambitions of many interests in business and in politics—fears of a saturated market at home, ambitions to dominate the vast market which

China, it was fancied, could provide. These interests found ready use for the popular stereotype 'open door', which seemed merely to mean the right to compete on equal terms; but, as Adams, Beveridge, and others candidly announced, they expected to come out on top in the scramble for the economic domination of the Orient. The construction of the Panama Canal, the laying of a cable across the Pacific, the annexation of Hawaii, and the retention of the Philippines were related moves designed to give the United States the needed advantage in this competition.

Nevertheless, the advantage was more apparent than real. The sailing was far rougher than Brooks Adams, for example, could imagine. To venture into the storm waters of the twentieth century in East Asia would be to attempt the impossible in an essay of this nature. Nor is it necessary. Trying to navigate these waters, the United States entered a long period of vacillation, the first phase of which ended in 1941 in the war with Japan. It finished that war in 1945 by obtaining supremacy over the Pacific Ocean, but except for the small and costly keyhole of Korea, it encountered a tightly shut door on the mainland.

VI. CONCLUSION

In the foregoing pages I have tried to convey a sense of direction and unbroken continuity in the history of the United States. The nation did not just grow in 'a state of absence of mind', nor was its expansion confined to a single direction westward. The process involved a number of thrusts extending like spokes of a wheel from the coastal hub, thrusts intelligently conceived and consistently pursued. Even in the infant stage as scattered British colonies, the Americans developed imperial ambitions and began moving seaward as well as landward beyond their borders. The pattern of future expansion was visible even in the seventeenth century, and became clear and unmistakable in the Revolutionary period of the eighteenth when the United States started on its career as an independent nation state.

Much has been written about the United States in the spirit of isolation. In historical usage this word carries certain overtones and symbolizes a complex concept which has never been placed in perspective and critically explored. It has been, I think, a red herring, leading to the belief that the United States historically stands apart from (and, by implication, above) other nations. Isolationism, the ideology or the body of doctrine emanating from the original and deeply rooted belief, not really shaken until 1941, in the geographical remoteness and security of the country, is the underlying expression of American nationalism. Indeed it *is* nationalism, and like the nationalisms of other countries (or perhaps even more) it is a coat of many colours. If, by some miracle, historians could be persuaded to adjust their thinking to the point of blotting out even the term 'isolation' and then of treating the United States as a national state possessing nationalist urges, they would be in a position to make a tremendous new advance toward comprehending the inner meaning of American history. For, like South African nationalism, American isolationism is apartheidism, though only in isolated cases does it assume such crude expression.

This essay rests on the assumption that the United States is a national state, so conceived and so dedicated by its eighteenth-century founders, and as such it possesses the attributes and the drives which have made it in fact a typically ambitious and expanding national state. In its energies, which never seem to slacken, and in its thrusts outward, it is the Germany of the American continents; though geography and other considerations have given it far more freedom of movement than the German Reich ever possessed. Not until the coming of the Second World War did the United States find itself blocked in the pursuit of its national 'mission' by strong opposing forces. This means that, in the second quarter of the twentieth century, one era of history came to an end and a new one, compelled to think in different terms and to develop new patterns, has begun. An important part of this new and inadequately grasped compulsion is the abandonment of the traditional approach to American history and the courage to create a new frame of reference.

This new frame of reference is, I am convinced, international. Whatever international history is—and it is still something of an intellectual novelty—it concerns the inter-actions and inter-relationships of the national states. But it is certainly not old-style diplomatic history, nor is it to be regarded as another name for the history of 'civilization'. The United States is a member of the complex of the national state system, and therefore its history is not to be interpreted according to the assumptions of the Monroe doctrine, which is exclusionist by nature and which perpetuates a geographical and historical fallacy. For the historian to assume that the Monroe doctrine (and other well worn stereotypes) is 'truth' in the sense of eternal verity is to help in the promotion of the national myth. Mythology and history are almost like twins, whom it is difficult to tell apart. Indeed, many prefer to keep the national myth sacred, and to them essays like this can only be disturbing.

Finally, if I may be indulged in quoting myself, I would say again that the United States is one of the oldest of the national states, that its history is coterminous with the history of nationalism.[1] Yet, only the fringes of American nationalism have been touched, and then only very gingerly. Since the Revolution, which was the first of the upheavals in the Euro-American 'world' to generate this mass emotion, history has been conceived and written in terms of the national state, presumed to be the ultimate in political society. For each nation the myth is gospel, and the body of beliefs the prison from which escape is hazardous. Nevertheless, escape must be attempted. New wine must be poured, even if old bottles be broken.

[1] Cf. my article, 'American Nationalism and its Mythology', *Queen's Quarterly*, Kingston, Ontario, LXV, No. 3 (1958), 423–36.

SHORT BIBLIOGRAPHY

H. C. Allen: *Great Britain and the United States: A History of Anglo-American Relations (1783–1952)*. N. Y., 1955.

Clarence W. Alvord: *The Mississippi Valley in British Politics*. 2 vols., Cleveland, O., 1917.

Howard K. Beale: *Theodore Roosevelt and the Rise of America to World Power*. Baltimore, 1956.

Charles S. Campbell, Jr.: *Anglo-American Understanding, 1898–1903*. Baltimore, 1957.

Charles S. Campbell, Jr.: *Special Business Interests and the Open Door Policy*. New Haven, Conn., 1951.

Lawrence Henry Gipson: *The British Empire before the American Revolution*. 9 vols., N.Y., 1936–56.

Norman C. Graebner: *Empire and the Pacific: A Study in American Continental Expansion*. N.Y., 1955.

Gerald S. Graham: *Empire of the North Atlantic: The Maritime Struggle for North America*. Toronto, 1950.

Frederick Merk: *Albert Gallatin and the Oregon Problem*. Cambridge, Mass., 1950.

Julius W. Pratt: *Expansionists of 1898. The Acquisition of Hawaii and the Spanish Islands*. Baltimore, 1936.

Gerald Stourzh: *Benjamin Franklin and American Foreign Policy*. Chicago, 1954.

Richard W. Van Alstyne: *American Diplomacy in Action*. Stanford, California, 1947.

Richard W. Van Alstyne: *The American Empire: Its Historical Pattern and Evolution*. London, 1960.

Albert K. Weinberg: *Manifest Destiny. A Study of Nationalist Expansionism in American History*. Baltimore, 1935.

William Appleman Williams: *American-Russian Relations, 1781–1947*. N.Y., 1952.

Edward H. Zabriskie: *American-Russian Rivalry in the Far East: A Study in Diplomacy and Power Politics, 1895–1914*. Philadelphia, 1946.

R. A. HUMPHREYS

Latin American History[1]

I. INTRODUCTION

AMERICAN history, in this country, in so far as it has been recognized at all, is commonly taken to mean the history of the United States. It is true that we are not alone in this provincialism. 'There is need,' wrote Professor Herbert Bolton, as President of the American Historical Association in 1933, 'of a broader treatment of American history, to supplement the purely nationalistic presentation to which we are accustomed,' and Professor Bolton chose for his theme, in addressing the Association, 'The Epic of Greater America'.[2] For nearly 400 years America, not the United States alone, but the New World as a whole, was a European frontier, a trade, an immigration, and an investment frontier. For nearly 300 not New York or Boston but Mexico City and Lima were its foremost cities; and American history as seen from those capitals has a very different aspect from

---

[1] This essay was written in 1943. I have thought it right to leave the text unchanged, except for a few minor emendations. But the notes enclosed in square brackets are new, and these are designed both as a guide to further reading and to enable the reader to correct or amplify judgments which I formed nearly twenty years ago. R.A.H.

[2] *American Historical Review*, xxxviii (1933), pp. 448–74. [In 1943 there were only two Chairs of American History in Great Britain, at London and Oxford, and the attention given to the subject in schools and universities was slight indeed. Twelve years later Professor H. C. Allen could rejoice that 'it is no longer true, as it once was, that, for a young university teacher in this country, to embrace the study of American History is a kind of academic kiss of death'. *American History in Britain* (London, H. K. Lewis, 1956), p. 22. The study of Latin American history, on the other hand, remained almost completely excluded from the history schools.]

the conventional interpretation in terms of the expansion of the thirteen mainland English colonies westwards from the Atlantic to the Pacific. Nor was there merely one 'American Revolution'. Between 1776 and 1826 the map of the New World was redrawn. Not the thirteen seaboard English colonies alone, but almost all the mainland colonies of the European powers achieved their political emancipation. Since then no other American country has rivalled the United States[1] in its swift and impressive rise to power. But the emancipation of Spanish and Portuguese America, like the emancipation of what it is convenient but inaccurate to term 'Anglo-Saxon' America, was one of the formative events in modern history. It marked a further stage in the shift from a Mediterranean to an Atlantic civilization. It opened a vast area, hitherto legally reserved for Spain and Portugal, to trade and immigration. It brought into existence a galaxy of new States. And in politics, in strategy, and in commerce it was destined to have far-reaching effects on the balance of world affairs.

II. THE ORIGIN OF THE LATIN AMERICAN STATES

The Latin American states are new nations but old lands. It was not till 1902 that Cuba attained to self-government and not till 1903 that Panama, the youngest of the twenty-one American republics, achieved independence from Colombia. But Cuba was discovered by Columbus on his first voyage in 1492. 'I found it to be so extensive,' he wrote, 'that I thought that it must be the mainland, the province of Cathay';[2] for it was the Orient he sought and America lay in the way. And the project of a canal between the Atlantic and the Pacific on the isthmus of Panama was discussed as early as 1529, almost four hundred years before it was realized. Spain built her empire in the New World, moreover, at least in the more populous parts, on the ruins of old civilizations. Mexico City, rising from the foundations of the Aztec city of Tenochtitlán, is at once a monument to two empires that have passed away and a symbol of a new civilization that has come into being.

The Pilgrim Fathers (it has been remarked) fell first upon their

---

[1] Citizens of the United States of Mexico, the United States of Brazil, or the United States of Venezuela are sometimes inclined to take this designation amiss. But there is no other which is convenient.

[2] E. G. R. Taylor, 'Idée Fixe: The Mind of Christopher Columbus', *Hispanic American Historical Review*, xi (1931), p. 292. [The quotation is from Columbus's letter of 15 Feb. 1493, written on his homeward voyage. See the excellent revised translation of Cecil Jane's *The Journal of Christopher Columbus* by L. A. Vigneras (London, Anthony Blond and The Orion Press, 1960).]

knees and then upon the aborigines. Apologists for Spain, anxious to defend her against the charges of cruelty and tyranny with which she has been reproached from the days of Bartolomé de las Casas, the Apostle of the Indians, onwards, are in danger of replacing a *leyenda negra* by a *leyenda blanca*. But it is a striking fact that today of the Spanish-speaking countries in Latin America, there are only three—Argentina, Uruguay, and Costa Rica—whose population is almost wholly white; and it is to the credit of Spain as a colonizing power that she sought not the extermination of the Indians, but their conversion and civilization. Not the Indian but the mestizo is the true American man. There was indeed a wide gap between the benevolent promises of the Spanish crown and the performance of the Spanish colonists. 'Obedezco pero no cumplo' ('I obey but I do not carry out')—the phrase is not a complimentary commentary on the Spanish colonial system. But if the Spaniards exploited the Indians, they also tried to save their souls. The colonizing, the religious, and the acquisitive impulses were equally strong; and Spanish civilization is deeply imprinted upon Spanish America. Cuzco, Lima, Bogotá, Quito, Mexico City, there were no English cities in the New World to compare with these. 'What Rome did for Spain,' Edward Gaylorn Bourne has remarked, 'Spain in turn did for Spanish America.'[1]

For three hundred years, moreover, Spain gave her empire peace. In the face of bitter colonial rivalries (for where Spain led others sought to follow) she maintained her sway from California to Cape Horn. Nor was it till the end of the eighteenth century that she was compelled to abandon her exclusive claims to the north-west coast of North America and parted also with the ill-defined area of Louisiana. It was less choice than necessity that confined English, Dutch, and French colonization to the seaboard of North America, to such islands as could be obtained in the West Indies and to the Guianas.[2] Only Portugal rivalled Spain in the extent of her territorial acquisition in the Americas. Her achievement was less spectacular, and for a time both Portugal and Brazil fell under the dominion of the Spanish crown. But it was through the action of Portuguese colonists and their relentless pressure on the outposts of Spain that the line of

[1] E. G. Bourne, *Spain in America, 1450–1580* (New York and London, Harper, 1904), p. 202. [On Spanish concern for the welfare of the Indian peoples see Lewis Hanke, *The Spanish Struggle for Justice in the Conquest of America* (Univ. of Pennsylvania Press, 1949), and his *Aristotle and the American Indians* (London, Hollis and Carter, 1959); on royal government in general, C. H. Haring, *The Spanish Empire in America* (rev. ed., New York, Oxford Univ. Press, 1952).]

[2] [French penetration to the heart of the North American continent began, however, from two bases, Canada and the Caribbean, in the late seventeenth century, and Louisiana, erected into a royal province in 1731, was only ceded to Spain in 1762–3.]

demarcation between the Portuguese and Spanish dominions, first fixed by Pope Alexander VI and then superseded by private treaty between the two crowns, was bent and pushed westwards, so that today Brazil occupies an area larger than that of the continental United States (excluding Alaska) and more than half of the total area of South America.

But, to a degree unequalled by their rivals, Spain and Portugal subjected their colonies to a rigid monopolistic system and imposed upon them a paternal autocracy. Spaniards born in America were almost, if not completely, excluded from the work of government. There was little real comparison between the New England town meeting and the Spanish *cabildo abierto*.[1] There was none at all between the government of an English colony and the organization of a Spanish viceroyalty. And while there was little relaxation from this tutelage, the colonists were also restrained within a double trading monopoly. Trade was rigidly restricted and controlled in the interests of a few favoured centres and groups in the Americas and in those of the privileged merchants of the mother country. As Lima was dependent on Seville, so Buenos Aires was dependent on Lima. It is a striking fact that the first struggle for independence on the part of Buenos Aires was directed not against Spain but against economic and political subordination to Peru.[2]

It is true that in the eighteenth century these commercial restrictions were to some extent relaxed, and natural trading routes opened up. The age of Charles III was an age of reform. But these reforms came too late, and did not go far enough. Already the foundations of Spain's economic monopoly had been undermined. Insufficient as a source of supply, her own economic organization incapable of adaptation to the needs of her empire, unable to share in the commercial expansion of Europe, she had attempted in vain to combat a vast system of contraband trade. The greater her debility, the greater the contraband trade, the weaker her empire. Significantly enough, Mexico and Lima, the strongholds of the monopolists, were the last parts of the empire to fall; from Caracas and Buenos Aires, where foreign trade and foreign influence had most deeply penetrated, the

---

[1] The *cabildo* is the town council. A *cabildo abierto* was a meeting of the town council reinforced by the principal citizens. The representative character of the colonial *cabildo* has sometimes been much exaggerated, as by Cecil Jane, *Liberty and Despotism in Spanish America* (Oxford, 1929), though *cabildos abiertos* did, on occasion, play an important rôle.

[2] R. A. Humphreys, ed., *British Consular Reports on the Trade and Politics of Latin America, 1824–1826* (Camden Third Series, lxiii, Royal Historical Society, 1940), p. 28. [See also John Lynch, *Spanish Colonial Administration, 1782–1810. The Intendant System in the Viceroyalty of the Río de la Plata* (London, Athlone Press, 1958), pp. 36–45.]

revolutions for Spanish American independence took their rise and drew their strength.[1]

The revolt of the English colonies in America provided the first example of freedom in the New World; and to the achievement of their independence both France and Spain lent their aid. The French revolution provided a similar example from the Old. It was Spain's turn next to reap the whirlwind, faced, as she was, by the commercial expansion and sea-power of England on the one hand, and threatened on the northern border lands of her empire, on the other, by the territorial expansion of the United States. For though the Latin American peoples, under the leadership of such men as Bolívar, Sucre, O'Higgins, and San Martín, won their own independence, external no less than internal influences played their part in creating a revolutionary frame of mind. It was inevitable that when Napoleon destroyed the power of Spain at home, overthrew her government and left her colonies to their own resources, the first feeling of loyal indignation should have merged into the desire for independence; and what chance Spain might still have had of appealing to that not-forgotten loyalty her own incompetence and folly destroyed.

The area affected by the Spanish American wars of independence was far greater than that affected by the war of North American independence. The peoples involved were far more numerous and the struggle lasted twice as long. And while the thirteen English colonies emerged as one United States, by 1830 thirteen separate states replaced the empires of Spain and Portugal. In South America the Spanish Viceroyalty of the Río de la Plata split, along the lines of old administrative divisions, into the United Provinces of the Río de la Plata (modern Argentina), Paraguay, and Bolivia. Uruguay (with the aid of British diplomacy) was also carved from its territory as a buffer state between Argentina and Brazil. On the west coast the republics of Chile and Peru replaced the former Spanish Captaincy-General and Viceroyalty, respectively. Farther north, Bolívar's creation of Great Colombia, formed from the Viceroyalty of New Granada, dissolved into the three states of Ecuador, Colombia, and Venezuela. What are now the five states of Central America established in 1823 the Confederation of the United Provinces of Central America, which survived only till 1838. Mexico passed rapidly from colony to empire

[1] Humphreys, *op. cit.*, p. ix. [Cf. A. P. Whitaker, 'The Commerce of Louisiana and the Floridas at the End of the Eighteenth Century', *Hispanic American Historical Review*, viii (1928), p. 202. On the importance of the reforms of Charles III, which the above paragraph tends to underestimate, see in particular Lynch, *op. cit.*, Richard Herr, *The Eighteenth-Century Revolution in Spain* (Princeton, 1958), and R. J. Shafer, *The Economic Societies in the Spanish World (1763–1821)* (Syracuse Univ. Press, 1958).]

and from empire to republic. Haiti, which declared its independence from France in 1804, established its rule over the Spanish colony of Santo Domingo; and Brazil, whither the Portuguese Court had fled in 1807-8, became in 1822, by an almost bloodless revolution, an independent empire, and, an empire amid republics, so survived till 1889.

III. THE RISE OF THE NEW STATES

The emancipation of Latin America involved a political revolution; to some extent it involved an economic revolution. But, like the earlier revolution in North America, it stopped short at the point at which it might have involved a social revolution. Essentially, the structure of colonial society, the feudal hierarchy inherited from mediæval Spain, remained unchanged, with the sole exception that Spaniards born in America now stood in the shoes of Spaniards born in Spain. In rural society the hacienda, the great landed estate which had become so characteristic an institution in the days of colonial rule, remained the characteristic institution in the twentieth century. And while the fathers of the new Spanish American states attempted to establish a pattern of freedom in constitutions which combined the Declaration of the Rights of Man with the machinery of the Constitution of the United States, for long the new states remained between two worlds, the one dead the other yet unborn. They had achieved statehood but not nationhood; their peoples were independent, but they had yet to learn the meaning and discipline of freedom. 'This country,' declared Bolívar, 'will inevitably fall into the hands of the unbridled multitude and pass afterwards under the sway of little tyrants. . . . If it were possible for a part of the world to return to primitive chaos, this would be the fate of America.'[1]

The task of political organization was indeed formidable. Throughout the whole of Latin America the white population was no greater than that of the thirteen original United States at the close of the eighteenth century; probably indeed it was less.[2] The masses were poor and illiterate; many belonged to native or mixed races, burdened by a heritage of oppression; the centres of population were

---

[1] [Simón Bolívar, *Obras Completas*, ed. Vicente Lecuna and Esther Barret de Nazaris (2 vols., La Habana, Cuba, 1947), ii, 959-60.]

[2] Alexander von Humboldt, *Personal Narrative of Travels to the Equinoctial Regions of the New Continent, during the years 1799-1804* (translated by Helen Maria Williams, 7 vols., London, 1814-29), iii, 438, supposed that at the beginning of the nineteenth century, out of a total population of 14 or 15 millions in Spanish America, there were some 3 million creoles (Spaniards born in America) and 200,000 Europeans. At the time of the first census of the United States in 1790 the European population was just under four millions.

remote from each other and the means of communication painfully difficult; regional and sectional rivalries added to the disabilities which geography imposed; there was no organized public opinion and no middle class to give stability to politics; finally, all the new Spanish American states emerged from their struggle for liberation not only underpopulated but financially and economically exhausted and with the inherent tendency of the Spaniard to personalize politics intensified by the experience of long and devastating wars.

It followed that, during the nineteenth century, government was in the hands of small minorities. Indeed in most Latin American states government is still the business of the few and politics is a way of life —and of making a living—remote from the control of the masses. And while this division between the governors and the governed, between the technical work of administration and the broad interests of the people, is still inimical to the development and functioning of representative democracy, it played, in the nineteenth century, into the hands of military chieftains and professional armies. Democracy obtained in theory, dictatorship in practice. Constitutions followed constitutions and Presidents followed Presidents in bewildering succession. In the first seventy-five years of their independent life Bolivia experienced more than sixty military risings and Colombia ten national civil wars as well as a variety of lesser conflicts.[1]

Yet while parties tended to represent the personal following of rival chieftains rather than divisions of principle, the sum of politics was not contained simply in an alliance of the landowners, the Church, and the military to maintain an antiquated social system and in rivalries among the ruling caste to establish a monopoly of power. The Latin American area was not closed to ideas, just as it was no longer closed to trade and immigration. In most Latin American states there was a vague distinction between Conservative and Liberal, the one standing for a strong central power and the rights of the Church, the other upholding the virtues of federalism and denouncing the vices of clericalism. 'Reformers' challenged the old order; and the old order fought to maintain its privileges. Revolution was endemic; yet revolution frequently meant little more than an accepted extra-legal method of changing the government. Dictators, such as Francia of Paraguay (who aroused the admiration of Carlyle), Rosas of Argentina (who died in exile near Southampton), Díaz of Mexico, and Gómez of Venezuela, were ruthless and cruel; yet dictatorship was often the sole alternative to anarchy; and capricious and arbitrary as the dictators may have been, their rule

[1] [J. F. Rippy, *Historical Evolution of Hispanic America* (New York, Crofts, 1932; Oxford, Blackwell), p. 200; C. H. Haring, *South American Progress* (Harvard Univ. Press, 1934), p. 185.]

was not wholly bad; they bent and moulded lesser caudillos (chieftains) to their will, and so doing they helped to substitute a larger conception of the state as a nation for the agglomeration of personal and local loyalties which had hindered its action and restrained its growth.

From these conditions some countries emerged more quickly than others; some have not yet emerged or are only just emerging. Three, Argentina, Brazil, and Chile, had already won for themselves by the late nineteenth century a position of decisive superiority; and of these Brazil, under the rule of her scholar-emperor, Pedro II, presented in her imperial form, in her 'peculiar institution' of slavery, and in her relatively peaceful evolution, a marked contrast to her neighbours:[1] nor was it till 1889 that a bloodless revolution prepared the way for the Federal Republic. The last half-century, however, has witnessed a remarkable transformation not only in these three countries, but elsewhere in Latin America. The development of industry, immigration and the growth of population, the rise of the cities, the improvement of communications, all these have resulted in the advent of a new commercial and industrial governing class, a middle class, an artisan class and, in Mexico, Chile, and Argentina in particular, of organized labour.[2] In Latin America generally the cruder forms of militarism have gone, and in all, or almost all, the states there has appeared a greater sense of social responsibility and an increasing approximation between political theory and political practice. Nationalism, as a political force, has grown with the growth of a middle class, with the increasing spread of literacy and with the development of industrialization; and while democracy is still a label which covers very different governmental systems, new social forces challenge old social orders. What direction these forces will take, it is not easy to foresee. It is possible that the experience of Mexico may be repeated in some at least of the other republics, and that suppressed social discontents will burst into conflagration. It is possible also, as recent events in Brazil have suggested, that the modern state may assume new forms in the New World.[3] No Pro-

[1] [Among the Spanish American states the 'aristocratic republic' of Chile alone experienced a comparable evolution.]

[2] [On these developments and the effects of the rise of 'middle groups' in Mexico, Chile, Argentina, Brazil, and Uruguay in particular see J. J. Johnson, *Political Change in Latin America. The Emergence of the Middle Sectors* (Stanford Univ. Press, 1958).]

[3] [The 'recent events' in Brazil were the creation of the *Estado Novo*, or *Estado Nacional*, as it was later known, of President Getulio Vargas, who fell from power in 1945 after a dictatorship which had lasted for fifteen years, returned to the presidency in 1950, and committed suicide in 1954. Since 1943 both Bolivia and Cuba have experienced social upheavals, and the régime of President Juan Perón initiated something in the nature of an economic and social revolution in Argentina.]

crustean classification fits the Latin American states and the transformation which is in progress is only in its beginnings.

IV. FRONTIER AND SETTLEMENT

In Latin American politics persons have mattered more than programmes and, in the political framework in which most Latin American governments operate, it would be obviously unwise to ignore the danger to the stability of existing institutions or to the future of representative democracy arising from what has been termed the 'extremist fringe',[1] exemplified in particular in so-called 'nationalist' groups. Nor is this the only danger. If Professor Preston James is right in defining the central theme of Latin American development as the task of imposing order on diverse and discordant elements, that task is still far from complete.[2] Nevertheless, in their political life the countries of Latin America (though in this, as in other respects, there are great differences between them) display an increasing maturity. There is nothing to show that the mestizo, given the opportunity, cannot become the equal of the white. Whatever the moral, Colombia, which is predominantly a mestizo country, is one of the more genuinely democratic of Latin American states.[3] Mexico, which is mestizo and Indian, has attacked, in the last quarter of a century, a task of social regeneration of extraordinary complexity. The existence, especially in the Andean countries of Bolivia, Ecuador, and Peru, of great numbers of Indians, illiterate and politically and economically inert, gravely hampers the attainment of national unity and political and social coherence. But the student of Latin American history, when faced with the problems of political disorder and social disunity, should beware of calling racial explanations to his aid. They are too easily an excuse for lack of accurate observation.

It is primarily to the operation of economic and social forces that the increasing stability and maturity of the Latin American countries is due; just as political instability, where it occurs, reflects a failure to achieve social and economic integration.[4] At this point, however,

---

[1] [On the left and on the right.]

[2] Preston E. James, *Latin America* (London, Cassell, 1943), p. 35.

[3] [But the structure of democratic government crumbled in Colombia in the late nineteen-forties, and, for several years, the country abandoned the constitutional path in 1953.]

[4] [But so strong is the revolutionary tradition that since the end of the Second World War there are only four of the twenty republics—Mexico, Chile, Uruguay, and Nicaragua—in which a *de facto* régime has not succumbed at one time or another to military force or armed rebellion, and five heads of government have been assassinated.]

the question must be asked, even if it is only partially answered, why it is that the material development of the United States and of the Latin American states during the first century of their independence present so striking a contrast?

In the nineteenth century the Latin American area, like the Mississippi Valley, was a European frontier, an immigration and an investment area. The movements of peoples and of capital to Argentina and Brazil and to the Mississippi Valley were part and parcel of the same great process, the rise of the Atlantic basin. But, despite these apparent similarities, north and south, with their very different distribution of natural resources, underwent a very dissimilar evolution. Whereas the population of the United States has multiplied more than thirty times since 1780, that of Latin America has multiplied less than eight times since 1823 (though there is now a more rapid rate of increase).[1] In the United States the relentless movement of westward expansion carried the frontier from the Alleghanies to the Pacific, so that in a hundred years the exploration and occupation of the continent were relatively complete. There was no comparable movement in Latin America. Its average population density is still between fourteen and sixteen persons to the square mile. Brazil, which occupies an area larger than that of the United States, contains a population smaller than that of the British Isles. Argentina, which is more than four times the size of France, has less than a third of its population. Moreover, in South America as a whole, some three-quarters of the total population lives in a quarter of the total area.[1] It is true that there have been frontier movements in Latin America which resemble the westward movement of the frontier in the United States; yet in the main these frontiers have been, to cite Professor James again, 'hollow frontiers'.[3] As the frontier has rolled forward, it has left behind a depopulated, sometimes a devastated, area. It has rarely been a true frontier of expanding settlement.

In part, of course, political and economic insecurity, and social and physical conditions, the serious disabilities imposed by nature as well

---

[1] [As of 1943. The rate of population growth in 1960 was nearly 2½ per cent a year as compared with 0·8 per cent for Europe, 1·6 per cent for Asia and 1·7 per cent for North America and for Africa, and the population as a whole was then roughly equal to that of the United States and Canada combined. It is estimated that it will rise to nearly 600 millions by the year 2,000. See F. Benham and H. A. Holley, *A Short Introduction to the Economy of Latin America* (Oxford Univ. Press, 1960), pp. 4–5.]

[2] [Though these statements were true in 1943, the population of Brazil had risen to an estimated 65 millions in 1960, that of Argentina to an estimated 20 millions. The population density for Latin America as a whole in 1960 was 25 to the square mile.]

[3] James, *op. cit.*, p. 5.

as man, diminished the attractive pull of Latin America for the European immigrant. In part also the United States, with its positive promise of assistance to the immigrant, remained pre-eminently the land of opportunity. There was in the Latin American states no legislation genuinely comparable to the homestead legislation which set the pattern of rural expansion in the United States; nor was there an equal demand for labour. On the contrary, the system of large landed estates still prevalent in most Latin American countries restricted the possibilities of settlement and depressed the conditions of the agricultural labourer. In Chile, for example, even in 1925, 98 per cent of the farm land in the province of Aconcagua, in the rich Central Valley, was comprised in 3 per cent of the rural properties. In Brazil, in 1920, 90 per cent of the occupied agricultural population were wage earners, and in Argentina in the nineteen-thirties, some 2,000 families still owned one-fifth of the total area of the republic.[1] Only in a few areas in Latin America (Costa Rica is a notable example) has landownership taken the form of small holdings.

Landownership in Latin America, moreover, has meant control of the major instrument of production in a quite special way. The hacienda, the great landed estate, has, no doubt, in some areas and some instances, an economic justification. But it has led to a stratification of society based on birth and a plantation system; it has been accompanied by the maintenance of the status of the agricultural labourer at a level far below that which prevails in most civilized countries; and, at the same time, it has concentrated political power in the hands of small minorities. Latin America thus reproduced on a wider scale the conditions which in fact existed in a part of the United States, the southern plantation states; and here, despite the contrast between the material development of the Latin American states and that of the United States, as a whole, there is also a comparison. The traveller who leaves the highroad in Mississippi or Alabama will find indeed that the comparison is more impressive than the contrast. If the raising of the standard of living of the rural and urban worker is one of the most urgent and most difficult of the problems facing the Latin American states in the field of social policy, it is no less urgent and no less difficult in the southern states of the United States.

[1] G. M. McBride, *Chile: Land and Society* (American Geographical Society, New York, 1936), p. 124; R. Paula Lopes, 'Social Problems and Legislation in Brazil', *International Labour Review*, xliv (1941), p. 505. For the situation in Argentina see Enrique Siewers, 'Openings for Settlers in Argentina', *ibid*, xxx (1934), p. 457, and Mark Jefferson, *Peopling the Argentine Pampa* (American Geographical Society, New York, 1926). [A redistribution of the large estates took place in Mexico, of course, as a result of the revolution which began in 1910 and has been carried out also in Bolivia.]

Nevertheless, foreign immigration, foreign capital, and foreign trade contributed decisively to the rise of the Latin American states and to their increasing political and economic stability. In parts of Argentina, in southern Brazil, and in southern Chile, foreign agricultural communities—especially German communities—survived the difficulties of trans-Atlantic migration, and, as in Missouri and Texas, grew and flourished. While the German, Swiss, and Polish elements were important, Italians, Spaniards, and Portuguese, however, constituted the major elements in the immigration stream. In the seventy years before 1930 six million immigrants entered Argentina (though not all of them remained); nearly four and a half millions entered Brazil in the first century of its independence. It was the continuous influx of European farmers that made Argentina one of the granaries of the world; foreign immigrants made possible the great development of the coffee industry in Brazil.[1]

In Argentina, in southern Brazil, and to a lesser extent in Uruguay and Chile, immigration has played something of the part that it has played in the development of the United States. Yet it is only to a few favoured regions that immigration has taken place on any considerable scale, and large parts of the continent remain relatively untouched by immigration.

The migration of capital, however, has been, perhaps, still more significant than the migration of people. At this point it behoves the student to be wary. In the eyes of many of the representatives of the Latin American countries foreign capital has been synonymous with foreign exploitation, and exploitation is a word coloured by emotions. The Spaniards no doubt exploited their overseas colonies. Economically they regarded them primarily as a source of gold and silver. The amount of the precious metals which they extracted was huge. But the action of Spain in America was not limited to the extraction of the precious metals; Spain transplanted a civilization.

The myth of El Dorado, the Golden Man of Raleigh's dreams, survived the fall of the Spanish empire. The boom in Mexican and South American mines in the eighteen-twenties was only one manifestation of its vitality. Under the expansive economy of the nineteenth century, Latin America was a fair and fertile field for foreign investments, and European capital played much the same part in the development of Latin America as it played in the United States. British, and later United States, capital (as well as Dutch, French, and Belgian) built the railways and ports and opened the mines, developed the public utilities, the plantations and the oilfields, and established the banks and insurance companies. Without this capital the deve-

[1] [On the coming of the immigrant see my *Evolution of Modern Latin America* (Clarendon Press, 1946), pp. 51–77.]

lopment of the Latin American area would have been gravely retarded. But there were three important differences in the rôle played by foreign capital in Latin America and in the United States. In the United States native capital itself accumulated and, by the end of the nineteenth century, sought outlets abroad. Indeed, in the twentieth century United States capital entered Latin America as the effective rival of British capital.[1] Secondly, in the management of foreign enterprises in the United States, United States citizens took a controlling part. Thirdly, foreign capital promoted the growth of industrialization.

In Latin America a very different situation prevailed. Foreign capital increased rather than decreased the dependence of the various countries on one or two staple products, mineral or pastoral; it was rarely associated with native capital; and, in the nineteenth century at least, few Latin Americans possessed either the requisite training or the desire to be associated with the management of foreign enterprises. Latin America in short was the perfect example of what it is now fashionable to term a 'colonial' area; its prosperity was dependent on the exchange of raw materials and foodstuffs for manufactured articles; and the development of its domestic industry was negligible.

V. LATIN AMERICA BETWEEN THE TWO WARS

Since 1914 this situation has been subjected to a radical change. This is not to say that the economy of Latin America is not still primarily an agricultural and extractive economy. It is still dependent for its prosperity on the exchange of raw materials for manufactured products. One of the richest raw material producing areas in the world, it still requires foreign capital and foreign skill to further the development of its resources. It will need and is capable of absorbing large numbers of immigrants, provided immigration policy is adapted to local needs and is a planned and not a haphazard immigration. Even should the Latin American states undergo an industrial revolution remotely comparable to that experienced by the United States, it is a significant fact that it was not till 1917 that the United States, with its far more intensive exploitation of its natural resources and its enormous industrial development, ceased to be a debtor and became a creditor nation.

[1] [United States' investments in Latin America achieved a rough equality with British by 1930, and while, between the two world wars, the United States replaced the United Kingdom as chief lender, the nominal value of British investments in the area fell, during and after the Second World War, from £754 millions in 1938 to £245 millions in 1951. See Benham and Holley, op. cit., pp. 72–3.]

Nevertheless in the inter-war period there has been a persistent attempt to reduce the dependence of the Latin American nations on the fluctuating fortunes of international trade, to develop manufacturing industries, to diversify the basis of the Latin American economies, and to achieve what is commonly (though not altogether accurately) described as a greater degree of 'economic independence'. It is associated with a spirit of economic nationalism (whose roots are political as well as economic), which has been reflected in persistent attacks on foreign investments and foreign-controlled enterprises; and it is associated also, in more liberal quarters, with an urgent desire to raise standards of living.

These movements were first stimulated by the war of 1914–18 which displayed the dangers for the Latin American countries of too great a dependence on overseas markets and sources of supply. They received a still greater stimulus by the advent of the Great Depression, and the effects of the depression years, unlike those of the war years, were far-reaching and permanent. The prices of the principal Latin American exports fell catastrophically. Purchasing power was drastically reduced. The flow of capital to Latin America ceased. And rising tariff barriers and autarkic policies in the world at large forced the Latin American states into an attempt to produce a larger proportion of their own needs. Nor was this all. The combination of an acute shortage of foreign exchange together with the emergence of a new sense of nationalism resulted in a new attitude to foreign influence in commerce and industry generally. Tariffs went up, interest payments went down. The familiar machinery of exchange control appeared. A wave of nationalistic and restrictive legislation swept the Latin American countries. Even the labour legislation of the period was used as an instrument against the dominance of foreign capital. The expropriations of the foreign-owned oil companies in Bolivia and Mexico were only the most spectacular examples of the prevalent hostility to the foreign-controlled export and extractive industries, the foreign-owned public utility enterprises, and the foreign-controlled insurance and banking institutions.[1]

Meanwhile the Latin American countries turned to industrialization with the manufacture of consumption goods. What began as a movement of national defence became a permanent economic aspiration. Brazil, Argentina, Chile, and Mexico are now the major manufacturing countries of Latin America, and though in large parts of Latin America industrial development is hampered by local insuffi-

[1] See the essay by Richard F. Behrendt, *Economic Nationalism in Latin America* (Univ. of New Mexico Press, 1941), and Dana G. Munro's study under the same title in *Latin America in World Affairs, 1914–1940*, by L. S. Rowe, C. H. Haring, S. Duggan and D. G. Munro (Univ. of Pennsylvania Press, 1941.)

ciencies in coal and iron and by transport difficulties, as well as by restricted purchasing power and a relatively small population, the movement thus begun will inevitably continue.

The present war [of 1939 to 1945] has, in fact, given a decided impetus both to industrial development and to agricultural diversification, and these movements have received the powerful support of the United States. While surpluses of old staple crops, such as maize and coffee, have piled high on Latin American shores, new agricultural products have been developed or old ones revived to replace Far Eastern sources of supply; mineral production has been increased; and industrial progress (though hampered by import shortages) has made rapid strides. In Brazil and Chile, as well as in Mexico and Peru, efforts are now being made to develop heavy as well as light industries; and while Mexicans are apt to look upon the expropriation of the foreign-owned oil companies in 1938 as a symbol of national sovereignty and national independence, Brazilians regard the great iron and steel plant now rising at Volta Redonda as symbolic of the 'economic independence' of Brazil and its industrial future.[1]

VI. LATIN AMERICA IN WORLD AFFAIRS

The economic structure of Latin America is thus basically changing, and with it the pattern of its foreign trade. But what the present war has emphasized, more even than the last war or the Great Depression, is not the economic independence of Latin America but its interdependence, political, economic, and strategic, with the rest of the world.

At this point it is pertinent to examine briefly the conditions which have shaped the international evolution of the Latin American states. For it is only in the present century, with enhanced political and economic stature, that these countries have begun to play, *proprio motu*, any significant part in international affairs, and, till the war of 1914–18, they remained on the margin of international life. At the first Hague Peace Conference in 1899, only one Latin American country, Mexico, was represented; and though, at the second conference, in 1907, all were invited to be present, the attitude of the great powers towards them (it was well said) was that of 'parents of

[1] [The Volta Redonda steel plant began production in 1946 and is the largest integrated steelworks in Latin America. Other plants are operating in Mexico, Chile, Argentina, Colombia, Peru, and Venezuela. In Latin America as a whole the volume of industrial output increased by about 30 per cent between 1945 and 1950, by 28 per cent between 1950 and 1955, and by 8 per cent between 1955 and 1957. Benham and Holley, *op. cit.*, p. 51.]

the old régime: children at the international table should be "seen and not heard" '.[1]

(i) Great Britain, the Monroe Doctrine, and Latin America

The reasons for this past position of inferiority have been made sufficiently plain. Retarded in their political and economic development and too poor to build up powerful armies and navies, the Latin American states had no military significance outside their own borders; they were junior, not equal partners in a society of nations.

Why was it, however, that in an age of acute colonial rivalries Latin America should have escaped the fate of Africa? The process of recognition, indeed, by Spain of her former colonies was not completed till 1895, shortly before the Spanish American war swept away the last vestiges of the Spanish Empire in the New World. In the eighteen-forties Spain toyed with the idea of the establishment of a Bourbon monarchy in Mexico and she engaged, in the sixties, in a little-known war with Chile and Peru. France, also, though she sought no territorial acquisitions in Latin America, intervened in Mexico, at a time when the United States was convulsed in civil war, to establish the brief and ill-fated empire of Maximilian. Early in the present century there were strong suspicions of German designs in the Caribbean, and President Theodore Roosevelt has left a highly-coloured and tendentious account of his own counteractions in the celebrated Venezuelan controversy of 1901–3. But the only territorial losses (except to each other) which the Latin American states have suffered since their independence is the loss by Mexico of a half of its territory to the United States, and that loss, given the conditions of the time and the 'manifest destiny' of the United States in its march from the Atlantic to the Pacific, is one of the few historical events which can rightly be termed inevitable. As for Great Britain, while she retained her title to the Falkland Islands and their dependencies, to British Guiana and to British Honduras, she abandoned any shadowy intentions she might at one time have entertained in Central America.

While, therefore, in the nineteenth century, Latin America was torn by internal strife (there were three major wars in South America besides a number of lesser conflicts and boundary disputes) and presented at least the appearance of a disintegrating area, the conflicts of the great powers in the western hemisphere were limited to rivalries in trade. There was no 'grab' for South America. A British peace succeeded to a Spanish peace; and, sheltered behind the British Navy and the Monroe Doctrine, the Latin American states preserved their territorial integrity unimpaired.

[1] *Latin America in World Affairs*, p. 7.

The Monroe Doctrine is a prohibition on the part of the United States against the extension of European power and influence to the New World.[1] Dictated by the unique position of the United States in the western hemisphere, it was, in its origin, partly the expression of a 'good neighbour' policy, partly an expression of national self-interest, partly a measure of national security. But, for the major part of the nineteenth century, such respect as it obtained in Europe was due to the silent support of British naval power. Protective, it was also mainly passive. And if, at the end of the nineteenth century, the United States occupied, in relation to Latin America, a special position, at its beginning that position was occupied by Great Britain.

The British Government did not, it is true, actively promote the political independence of Latin America, though the sympathies of the growing liberal movement and the interests of British trade were early enlisted in its cause. But Great Britain played a larger part in Latin American emancipation than any other foreign power.[2] The United States took the lead, in 1822, in according recognition to the new states; President Monroe's famous message followed a year later; and it was not till 1825 that Great Britain accorded recognition through the negotiation of commercial treaties,[3] though she had, in 1822, recognized the flags of South American vessels. But the resources of British merchants and bankers and the services of British volunteers on land and sea afforded invaluable aid to the insurgents, and the action of Castlereagh in 1817 in intimating to the European courts that force should not be employed against the Spanish colonies by any other power than Spain made any designs of European intervention in Latin America illusory.[4] With that resolve on the part of the world's greatest naval power, the independence of Latin America was assured. The stand which Castlereagh took Canning supported, and while, in 1823, there were genuine fears of intervention, historians are now generally agreed that these were groundless.

Because of the actions of Castlereagh and Canning, the two greatest of British Foreign Secretaries,[5] at the close of the wars of independence Great Britain enjoyed in Latin America a position of

[1] Dexter Perkins, *Hands Off. A History of the Monroe Doctrine* (Boston, Little, Brown and Co., 1941), p. 4.
[2] C. K. Webster, ed., *Britain and the Independence of Latin America, 1812-30. Select Documents from the Foreign Office Archives* (2 vols., Oxford Univ. Press, 1938), i, p. v.
[3] With Argentina and Colombia. A treaty with Mexico was negotiated but not ratified [and was replaced by a new treaty in 1826].
[4] Webster, *op. cit.*, i, 14; ii, 352-8.
[5] [And because, also, it should be added, of the resources of British merchants and bankers, and of British naval power.]

unrivalled prestige. That position she never attempted to employ for political dominion or control, nor was she willing to permit other European powers to acquire territory in Latin America; and there was, in the nineteenth century, a remarkable parallel between British and United States policy in Latin America. Each feared the territorial expansion of the other. To the desire of Great Britain to link the new states to Europe, the United States opposed the idea of an American and republican system. The preservation of the principle of monarchy in Brazil was the culminating point of Canning's grand design to oppose the theory of the two spheres on which the Monroe Doctrine was founded. There was, moreover, a growing commercial rivalry between the two nations and sometimes acute jealousy between their diplomatic representatives. But both also were conscious of a certain community of interest. Both pursued in Latin America a policy that was commercial rather than imperial. Though for a time Great Britain maintained special commercial privileges in Brazil, these grew progressively less important, were subordinated to the abolition of the slave trade, and finally vanished, and, with this exception, both upheld the principle of the open door. Both were resolved to prevent the partition of Latin America by other powers. Finally, though it was not till the end of the century that Great Britain, faced with the alternative either of challenging or of accepting the interpretation of the Monroe Doctrine current in the United States, gave to it positive encouragement and support, there was behind British and United States policy, despite occasional sharp conflicts and even disagreements in principle, an essential conformity of outlook.

The Monroe Doctrine itself, however, grew with the growth of the American nation and, with the rising strength and power of the United States, it experienced at the end of the nineteenth century a remarkable extension. Formerly protective but passive, it now became both active and aggressive. For reasons partly political, partly strategic, and partly economic, it was used to justify the exercise by the United States of a police power in the Caribbean, and it led the United States into a series of repeated interventions in that area. This expanded interpretation, indeed, stopped short in the Caribbean; it reflected a Caribbean rather than a Latin American policy on the part of the United States; and on the whole the United States employed its coercive powers with restraint and moderation. But it led also to bitter criticism of the United States in Latin America, and even violent antagonism; it undermined, or at least gravely retarded, the attempt of the United States to link the American nations together in a Pan American movement whose purposes were, it is true, at that time more commercial than political; and it coincided with the discovery among the Latin American states themselves of a new-found independence of judgment and with their entry on to the larger field of world affairs.

(ii) *The International Relations of Latin America*

The association of some of the Latin American states in the First World War and in the Paris Peace Conference, and the eventual participation of all of them in the League of Nations gave them, indeed, a new international status. The League not only appealed to Latin American idealism; it seemed to provide a counterpoise to the power and influence of the United States at a time when feeling towards the United States was becoming increasingly embittered; above all it afforded a platform on which the Latin American states could make their voices heard in world affairs. Some Latin American states, no doubt, joined the League with special ends in view; the degree of enthusiasm varied; and some of the states ceased to participate or formally withdrew when their special demands failed to win acceptance. Argentina absented herself after the opening session of the League and did not resume participation until after the withdrawal of Brazil, offended by her failure to obtain a permanent seat on the Council. But from first to last Latin American membership in the League was an important fact; for some Latin American states it had much the same emancipating effect as it had for the British Dominions; and though the degree of interest in Geneva diminished as the prestige of the League declined and in the late thirties withdrawals became numerous, on more than one occasion Latin American loyalty to the League had important consequences. Moreover, the Latin American states showed an increasing interest in the work of the International Labour Office, and while the political action of the League in Latin America was embarrassed by the absence of the United States from Geneva, the work of its technical organs met with a considerable degree of success in that area.

The League of Nations, then, stimulated the self-reliance of the Latin American states; but in the nineteen-thirties membership for them had become more a liability than an asset. The contrast now was not between the bright promise of the League and the stagnation of the Pan American movement, but between the failing vitality of the League and a Pan American movement clothed with new vigour. Already before the nineteen-thirties the United States had begun the process of retreat from the expanded interpretation of the Monroe Doctrine current in the early years of the present century. The change was slow but sure. It had been anticipated by President Wilson. It was initiated under Presidents Coolidge and Hoover. But it remained for President Roosevelt to transform the negative process of withdrawal into the positive process of actively seeking the co-operation of the Latin American states in the affairs of the western hemisphere. The 'Good Neighbour' policy, first proclaimed by President Roosevelt on 4 March 1933, was not merely a recognition that the previous policy of the United States had outlived its usefulness and was in fact menacing the political and economic relations of the United States with the Latin American states. Nor was it merely an expression of the idealism which is always a fundamental element in United States policy. It was a recognition that the Latin American states had come of age and that, in the world in which we now live, they have an active political and economic importance.

The Latin American policy of the United States today is based upon the idea of partnership among the nations of the New World.[1] But it is not and cannot be a partnership in isolation. While the Old World needs the assistance of the New, the New World, in the words of Mr. Sumner Welles, 'can never attain that measure of security and well-being to which it aspires except in collaboration' with other States and other regions. The cycle of four hundred and fifty years is complete. In policy, in strategy, and in commerce, it leaves the peoples of the New World intimately associated with the peoples of the Old. We need indeed that 'broader treatment of American history', perhaps better of Atlantic history, to supplement the nationalistic interpretations to which we are accustomed.

[1] [On developments in the Latin American policy of the United States since 1945 see T. W. Palmer, *Search for a Latin American Policy* (Univ. of Florida Press, 1957), and two articles by S. G. Hanson, 'The Good Partner Policy', *Inter-American Economic Affairs*, x, No. 2 (1956), pp. 45–96, and 'The End of the Good-Partner Policy', *ibid.*, xiv, No. 1 (1960), pp. 65–92, together with the documents published by the Pan American Union (Washington, D.C., 1961), under the title *Alliance for Progress*, and 'The Alliance for Progress', *Inter-American Economic Affairs*, xvi, No. 1 (1962), pp. 3–95.]

ERICH EYCK

Bismarck

'THAT world history has to be rewritten from time to time, about that there remains no doubt in our day. This necessity exists, not because much about what has passed has been discovered since, but because new points of view arise, because the contemporary of an advanced age is led into a position from which the past can be surveyed and assessed anew.'

Thus wrote Goethe over a century and a half ago. The wisdom of his words is shown by the changes in the assessment of the personality and the achievements of one of the greatest men of world history, Otto von Bismarck. When the ex-Chancellor of the German Empire died on 30 July 1898, his creation, the German Empire, stood splendid in all its strength and power, and the bearer of the German Imperial Crown, which Bismarck himself had called into existence, was considered one of the most powerful and brilliant rulers of the world. Nobody was bold enough to imagine that he would live to see all this changed. Bismarck's glory was then at its zenith. Although his deeds in the last years of his life, as for instance the disclosure of the Reinsurance Treaty with Russia, were open to the very strongest censure, his spell over the German people was almost boundless and no name filled a gathering of German students more quickly with enthusiasm than the name of Bismarck. A whole generation of German historians grew up under the influence of his personality and his enormous prestige, and even the most scholarly and exact among them touched only lightly upon the undeniable faults of his character and the mistakes of his policy: they faded away almost completely behind his glorious achievements.

Twenty-five years later, in 1923, Germany presented quite another spectacle. The formerly victorious German Army, which everyone had considered invincible after Sedan, had been defeated in the greatest of all wars and reduced to a mere token army; the German Emperor had been dethroned and exiled; Alsace and Lorraine, the gain in the war against France, had been lost once more; the government of the Reich, now a republic, was in the hands of the parties which Bismarck had stigmatized as 'Reichsfeinde', had hated with all his heart and persecuted with all his vigour, the Democrats, the Zentrum, nay, the Social Democrats. A reassessment of the great founder of the Reich was thus unavoidable, and it is understandable that Erich Marcks, who in 1909 had brought out the splendid first volume of his Bismarck biography, never brought out a second. It is not quite so easy to see why not one of the German professors of history who, year in year out, produced detailed studies on this or that aspect of the Iron Chancellor, undertook the task of giving a picture of the whole man, by making use of the masses of new material which had come to light since 1919 from the archives of Europe.[1] These included the German publications,

Die Grosse Politik der Europäischen Kabinette, 1871–1914. *Sammlung der Diplomatischen Akten des Auswärtigen Amtes* (hgg. von Thimme, Lepsius, Mendelssohn. 1922 ff. vol. 1–6).

Die Auswärtige Politik Preussens, 1858–71 (Dipl. Aktenstücke, hgg. von der Historischen Reichskommission, 1930 ff.).

Quellen zur Deutschen Politik Oesterreichs (hgg. v. H. von Srbik).

Die Gesammelten Werke Bismarcks (Friedrichsruher Ausgabe, hgg. von Thimme, Andreas, u.a. 1926 ff.).[2]

[1] In 1949 appeared a biography by the late Professor Arnold O. Meyer, *ob.* 1944 (*Bismarck, der Mensch und der Staatsmann*, Leipzig, Koehler und Amelang). Although Meyer draws on many, and even on unprinted, sources, his biography is written in the old-fashioned style of hero-worship, mixed with sentimentality. Many things which would put the hero in an unfavourable light are not mentioned (cf. Walter Goetz, *Historiker in meiner Zeit*, Köln, Böhlau 1957, p. 381). Otto Becker's *Bismarcks Ringen um Deutschlands Gestaltung* (Heidelberg, Quelle und Meyer 1958) is not a biography and ends with the foundation of the German Empire of 1871 (cf. my review in *Deutsche Literatur Zeitung*, June 1961, p. 546).

[2] The latest publication from the archives is *Bismarck and the Hohenzollern Candidature for the Spanish Throne*, edited with an introduction by Georges Bonnin, and with a foreword by Dr. G. P. Gooch (London, 1957). It contains the secret documents from the German Foreign Ministry Archives from February to July 1870, and throws new light on the question of Bismarck's responsibility for the outbreak of the German-French war (see below p. 169). In my view it only strengthens the opinion expressed here (cf. the review by Professor Medlicott in *History* 1959, p. 84, and my essay 'Bismarck, Wilhelm I und die Spanische Thron Kandidatur' in *Deutsche Rundschau*, August 1958, p. 723). Different interpretations are given in J. Dietrich, *Bismarck, Frankreich und die Thronkanditatur des Hohenzollern* (Munich, Oldenbourg, 1962, with new material from

and the French publications,

> Les Origines Diplomatiques de la Guerre de 1870. (Recueil de Documents publié par le Ministère des Affaires Etrangères, 1909 ff.).
>
> Documents Diplomatiques Français, 1871–1914. (1929 ff.)

and the innumerable books of memoirs of German, French, English, and Russian statesmen and diplomatists.

Fifty years after Bismarck's death there was nothing left of his creation. German unity had been destroyed, at any rate for the time being, and was the object of bitter and fruitless haggling among the powers whose armies were in occupation of German soil. Even if some form of German unity should in the end be restored, it would never be the whole Germany: the eastern part of it, at least partly, was lost, and Konigsberg, the cradle of the Royal Crown of Prussia, where Bismarck was a spectator at the coronation of his king, William I, in 1861, was destined to be a Russian town. Even the State of Prussia, which Bismarck had led from success to success and raised to the apex of its power, authority, and size, had ceased to exist. And the 'Führer', whom the Germans had made their absolute ruler for a dozen years, who had embodied their hope for victory and world-rule? This Austrian agitator who had never done one honest day's work stood for all that Bismarck despised and hated most. When we read today his famous speech on colonial policy of 13 March 1885, with the often-quoted peroration about the 'blind elector Hödur who is unable to judge the bearing and consequences of things and allows himself to be misled into slaying his own fatherland' (iii, 419),[1] we must think of the millions of irresponsible voters who followed Hitler's drum, intoxicated by his grandiloquent promises and his bombastic rhetoric. How had Bismarck thundered against rhetoricians (iii, 363), meaning men like Eugen Richter, the Progressive leader, who in his sense of responsibility, capacity for thinking things through to their logical conclusions, the extent of his knowledge and sobriety of judgment, differed as much from Hitler as Odysseus from Thersites! In the jubilant Germany of 1940 Bis-

---

[1] This and subsequent page references given in brackets in the text are to Erich Eyck, *Bismarck: Leben und Werk* (Eugen Rentsch Verlag, Erlenbach-Zurich, three vols., 1941, 1943, 1944).

the Sigmaringen archives), and D. Steefel, *Bismarck, the Hohenzollern Candidacy and the Origins of the Franco-German War of 1870* (Harvard, 1962). Much material about Bismarck's personality and politics is contained in the *Holstein Papers,* edited since 1955 by N. Rich and M. A. Fisher (Cambridge University Press), but on account of the problematic character of Holstein it is to be used only with much criticism and caution (cf. my essay 'Holstein as Bismarck's Critic' in *Studies in Diplomatic History* in honour of G. P. Gooch, edited by A. O. Sarkissian, London, Longmans, 1961).

marck would have felt as much a stranger as a Liberal who preferred to leave his fatherland to bowing before the swastika.

Thus it is in a fundamentally changed world and in view of a fundamentally changed Germany that we try to appraise anew the figure of the first Chancellor of the German Empire in the light not only of an enormous mass of new material, but also of the political experience of half a century.

Let us take as an example of both these factors in our current judgment the Franco-German war of 1870. The German victory over France was then considered Bismarck's greatest and most glorious achievement, and indeed not only by Germans. Carlyle called it 'the hopefullest fact that has occurred in my time'. Gladstone's apprehension, that the 'violent transfer' of Alsace and Lorraine 'is to lead us from bad to worse and to the beginning of a new series of European complications',[1] would then have been repudiated even by most of his fellow countrymen. Our generation, which has seen Gladstone's prophecy come true, is bound to ask many questions. Was a war against France really the only method of achieving German unity? Who was responsible for the war? Was Bismarck right in yielding to the popular clamour for Alsace and Lorraine?

The question whether German unity could have been achieved peacefully can, of course, never be answered with certainty. But one thing we can say: the strongest obstacle to a peaceful unification was the dominating position which Bismarck had given to the Prussian Crown in the Constitution of the North German Federation of 1867, and against which turned the opposition of the majority of the southern Germans, not least because they were afraid that it would lead to a militarization of the united nation (ii, 483). Now this prominence and power given to the Prussian Crown is the focus of Bismarck's German programme. In August 1869, he writes to his most important collaborator, the Minister of War, von Roon: 'The form in which the King (of Prussia) exercises his rule in Germany, was never of special importance to me. But I have put the whole strength that God has given me to the effective establishment of this rule' (ii, 422). The full significance of this programme becomes clear, when we contrast it with the famous phrase, which Ludwig Uhland, Germany's most popular poet, uttered in the National Assembly of the Paulskirche, in January 1849: 'No head will shine forth over Germany that is not anointed by a full drop of democratic oil.' That is what Bismarck was resolved to prevent and succeeded in preventing. The German Emperor, who was his creation, was completely free from any democratic contamination. True, Bismarck gave the

---

[1] Erich Eyck, *Gladstone* (Allen and Unwin, 1938), p. 220.

Germans universal franchise in the North German Constitution, from which it was transferred to the Constitution of the Empire (*Reichsverfassung*). But he did that only in order to outbid Austrian competition, not at all in order to give the German people a share in the government (ii, 152). By taking from the defunct German Bund the old 'Bundestag', and transforming it, under the slightly changed name of 'Bundesrat' into a council of delegates bound by the instructions of the governments of the single federal states, he counterbalanced the Reichstag elected by universal franchise and nipped in the bud the development of parliamentarism. This became clear in the so-called 'Liberal Era' (1867–78), for instance, in his peremptory refusal of the liberal motion asking for responsible 'Reichsminister' (Motion Twesten-Münster, 1869) (ii, 417). Many South Germans who read this debate of the North German Reichstag could not help feeling that the rule of the Prussian King over Germany, upon which Bismarck insisted, was not at all the system they wanted for a united Germany.

All this was changed by the common victory over France. So far Bismarck's policy was justified by events. But the question remains whether another constitutional policy would not have made possible a peaceful solution of the problem of German unification.

That brings us to the second question, the responsibility for the outbreak of the war. The great majority of contemporaries had no doubt that this responsibility rested with the Emperor Napoleon III and his ministers. That was not only the opinion of *The Times*, expressed in a thundering leader after the declaration of war, but even of Gladstone. This version was so commonly accepted that Bismarck could venture to say in the Reichstag debate about the military *Septennat* of 1887, that Napoleon had 'launched into the war against Germany only because he believed that it would strengthen his rule at home'.

Now, even today, nobody can deny that Napoleon and his government made the silliest and most fateful blunder after Prince Leopold of Hohenzollern's withdrawal of his candidature for the throne of Spain, and that they have to bear the responsibility for its dreadful consequences in common with the French journalists and parliamentarians, who pushed them along the road to ruin. But that is not the whole story. The story does not begin with July 1870, when the Hohenzollern candidature became manifest, but in the spring of 1869, when Bismarck sent a confidant into Spain in order to prepare the candidature in strictest secrecy (ii, 442). This story will never be known in all its details. But we know much more of it than Bismarck's contemporaries, since the archives have revealed many secrets. We can see now that Bismarck was the moving spirit of the whole intrigue, and we can hardly refrain from agreeing with his most intimate collaborator, Lothar Bucher, that it was 'a trap for Napoleon', putting deliberately before him the alternatives of either ruining his dynasty or making war. Can Bismarck's admirers plead that in acting thus he only forestalled an offensive prepared by Napoleon and Francis Joseph's minister, Beust? Even that is more than doubtful. There was no French-Austrian-Italian Triple Alliance in 1870, and Napoleon could not hope to conclude it because the surrender of Rome to the Italian Kingdom was the condition *sine qua non* of Victor Emanuel's collaboration and Napoleon did not want to, and could not, sacrifice the Pope (ii, 408). Before the storm broke over the Hohenzollern candidature, French policy was more peace-loving than ever, for the leader of the French government, Ollivier, recognized frankly and publicly the right to unification of the German nation.

Therefore, without absolving Napoleon, we must hold Bismarck mainly responsible for the war.

It is different with the annexation of Alsace and Lorraine. Here Bismarck was not the prime mover. He only yielded to a popular movement, the romantic motives of which he derided, and to the pressure of the king and the generals. While he himself was in favour of the annexation of Strassburg, the population of which spoke German, he was against the annexation of the completely French Metz (ii, 571). But he did not uphold his objection with the same tenacity with which he had opposed the wishes of the king at Nikols-burg in 1866, when the latter wanted to annex Austrian territory. That was a mistake he not only confessed in later years to the French ambassador; he knew it even at the time. It had indeed the most fateful consequences. Bismarck's ideal was always to be able to dis-pose freely of all the squares of the diplomatic chessboard. He was never able to dispose of the French square, much as he wished it in the eighties, because the French could never forget and forgive Strassburg and Metz.

Looking back over three-quarters of a century, we see that Bis-marck is primarily responsible for the most dangerous and fateful wound to the peace of Europe and not free from responsibility for its incurability. But that should not blind us to the quite incompar-able statesmanlike qualities by which he conceived his policy and carried it through: the greatness of his conception, his courage and patience, the richness and superiority of his intellect, his almost marvellous understanding of all the persons with whom he had to deal, whether opponents or allies, kings or subordinates, his never failing adroitness in finding a way out of the most difficult and complicated situations. No contemporary statesman could compare himself with him in these aspects, neither Palmerston nor Gorchakov, Gladstone nor Disraeli, let alone Napoleon III. Nothing can match his achievement in 1870, except one of his earlier career, the Prussian solution of the Schleswig-Holstein question against all conceivable objections and handicaps: the opposition of his king, of the Prussian Chamber of Deputies, of the German Bund and—the great powers (i, 578). All this was, of course, secret diplomacy, and we know what is to be said against it. But in a world in which secret diplomacy was the order of the day, Bismarck's achievements stand out as incomparably the most clever, daring, and reckless, as well as the most successful.

Whether the same tribute can be paid to his foreign policy after the victory over France and the foundation of the German Empire, is less certain. It was undoubtedly in the best interest not only of Germany but of Europe that he upheld the peace in the last twenty years of his régime (1871–90). That does not mean that his ideas about war as an instrument of policy had changed, or that he denied himself the use of the threat of war as an instrument of policy, as, for instance, in the war scare of 1875 (iii,149) or the struggle for the *Septennat* of 1887 (iii, 459). But he saw quite clearly that the German Empire was 'satiated', i.e. that it had nothing to gain by a war and that its position among the great powers left nothing to be desired, as every statesman in Europe wished nothing more than to be on good terms with its masterful ruler. Even if he came into antagonism to another power he always knew how far he could go without driving it to extremities. But in reaching conclusions about Bismarck's foreign policy we must never forget its connexion with his home policy, which was much closer than earlier historians supposed. An example is his colonial policy, which was an instrument to checkmate his parliamentary opponents, who were very strong in the first half of the eighties, and the Crown Prince, whose imminent succession to the throne was an incessant nightmare to the Chancellor in view of the advanced age of the Emperor (born 1797) (iii, 418).

The most debatable point in Bismarck's foreign policy in this period is his alliance with the Austro-Hungarian Monarchy in 1879 (iii, 315). There can be no doubt that he was right in declaring that the preservation of Austria's position as a great power was a vital German interest. But did it follow that Germany had to make an alliance with her which must necessarily antagonize Russia? We know today that this alliance involved Germany in the end in the catastrophe of 1914, which proved fatal to both empires. Bismarck's admirers assert that he would never have allowed Austria to take Germany in tow, that under his leadership Germany would always have remained in the saddle of the Austro-Hungarian horse. That was certainly Bismarck's own idea, and nobody can doubt that he was the man to carry it through. But alliances sometimes outlive even the greatest statesmen who conclude them, and it is in their nature that they are invoked by each partner in his own specific interests. That Bismarck himself developed some doubts about the value of this alliance is shown not only by his very guarded comments in his *Reflections and Reminiscences*, but more still by his conclusion of the Reinsurance Treaty with Russia in 1887, less than eight years after the ratification of the Austrian alliance.

The Reinsurance Treaty of 18 June 1887 was for a long time applauded as Bismarck's diplomatic masterstroke (iii, 477). Even now many historians call it the key-stone of the system of treaties which he concluded in the second half of the eighties in order to strengthen Germany's position in any emergency. But it is not only open to very serious criticism from the point of view of public morality and of the law of nations; it was ineffective and did not in fact help to improve Russo-German relations. That it was secret diplomacy with a vengeance, nobody can deny. It had to be kept secret, because one partner, Bismarck, had to hide it from his allies, Austria-Hungary, Italy, and Rumania, and the other partner, the Czar, had to hide it from his people. In order to conclude this treaty, Bismarck was compelled to betray the Emperor of Austria and to reveal the secret treaty of the Austrian alliance to the Russian ambassador, Paul Shuvalov. He gave to international diplomacy an example of double-dealing which others did not scruple to follow. When the Italians concluded, in 1902, a reinsurance treaty with France, in spite of their partnership in the Triple Alliance, they cited Bismarck's Reinsurance Treaty as a welcome precedent.[1]

As to the effectiveness of the treaty, its admirers claim that it pre-vented an alliance between Russia and France. This alliance was, indeed, only concluded after Caprivi had refused to renew the secret treaty with Russia in 1890. But would the Reinsurance Treaty have prevented the Czar from concluding an alliance with France? Not more than the alliance with Austria had hindered Bismarck from concluding the Reinsurance Treaty. More important still is the fact that the relation between Russia and Germany were hardly at any time less satisfactory and the Czar's mistrust of Bismarck never greater than during the three years, 1887–90, when the Reinsurance Treaty was in force. In the year 1888 Germany increased her army enormously. In his famous speech of 6 February 1888, for this army bill, Bismarck declared before the Reichstag and the whole world (iii, 491): 'We do not court for love, neither in France *nor in Russia*.

[1] Erich Eyck, *Das Persönliche Regiment Wilhelms II* (Eugen Rentsch Verlag, Erlenbach-Zurich, 1948), p. 369.

The Russian press, the Russian public opinion have shown the door to an old, powerful and reliable friend, which we have been; we do not obtrude ourselves on anybody. We have tried to reconstitute the old confidential relations, but we run after nobody.' This was six months after the conclusion of the secret treaty with Russia. At the same time Bismarck conducted his campaign against the Russian public funds (by a decree of 10 November 1887 forbidding the Reichsbank to accept Russian securities as collateral for loans), and this drove Russia, urgently in need of capital, into the arms of France, which was well provided with it. The high esteem in which the Reinsurance Treaty is held is explicable only by the fact that it was never put to the test. One can suppose that even Bismarck was not certain whether it would stand it. For in the same Reichstag speech he proclaimed: 'No great power can stick permanently to the text of a treaty in opposition to the interest of its own people'.

But the worst was still to come. In October 1896, six years after his dismissal, the former Chancellor of the Empire revealed to the world the secret of the Reinsurance Treaty (iii, 626). He did not give the exact facts, so that it was generally supposed to have been concluded in 1884. But he revealed enough to let the world know that he had concluded this treaty behind the back of his allies and while the alliance with Austria was in full force, and he reproached his successor, Caprivi, with having dropped 'the wire to St. Petersburg'. He offended not only against public morality, but even against the written law of the Empire he himself had created. In the whole of modern history there is no statesman of equal importance who has been guilty of a similar betrayal. That the government of the day nevertheless declined to institute proceedings against Bismarck, is completely understandable; not even his most embittered opponents would have liked to see Bismarck as a defendant in a criminal trial. But the whole episode had very deplorable consequences for the political morality of the German people, which we see now much more clearly than did former generations. It learned to consider lack of morality as a quality of a great statesman. The machiavellian doctrine of the *raison d'état*, which justifies every infringement of written and unwritten law, began to spread and to take deeper roots until even Hitler's broken treaties and brutal cruelties were accepted not only as excusable, but as proofs of his greatness. There was no Lord Acton among German historians to warn the German people of these consequences of uncritical hero-worship.

Unfortunately, the real wisdom of Bismarck's foreign policy was neither understood nor followed by his successors. How sane and reasonable appears to us now his policy of limited liability in comparison with the world-wide aims of William II and the conquering madness of Hitler. What he knew and they did not know was that the aims of the foreign policy of a state must never exceed its power of maintaining them. However highly he rated Germany's strength, he never considered it overwhelming enough to challenge a combination of the other great powers. He was careful not to antagonize them in points which were to them a matter of life and death. He did not hesitate to oppose them in certain concrete questions, where he knew they were able to give way without permanently losing their position. Even his colonial policy shows that. He did not disdain exacerbating in a quite unnecessary way the dispute with the British government, because it was the government of the hated Gladstone; he did so both in his dispatches and in his Reichstag speech against Lord Granville (2 March 1885). But he knew when it was time to come round, and on the day after this speech he sent his son Herbert to London, to bring about an amicable arrangement. From reasons of party politics he went so far as to foment anti-English feeling in Germany. But he knew that the momentary weakness of Great Britain was only a passing phase due to the occupation of Egypt (1882); a few years later he offered an alliance to Lord Salisbury (1889). He would never have consented to the naval policy of William II. For he would have seen that a powerful fleet of battleships a few hundred miles from the English coast was bound to be viewed by the English as a grave threat to their existence, which they could tolerate under no circumstances in the long run and which would make Anglo-German friendship impossible. At least he would have inferred from this situation that Germany was the more compelled to be complacent about Russian susceptibilities and not to cross her path in the Near and Middle East. The difference between Bismarck's and William's policy comes quite clearly to light in the question of the Bagdad Railway. It was, for instance, clear to Baron von Marschall, the German ambassador in Constantinople and the foremost advocate of this policy, when he wrote in 1899; 'Bismarck's famous words, that the whole Orient is not worth the bones of one Pomeranian grenadier, may become an interesting historical reminiscence, but cease to be an actual reality.'[1] At this time many Germans would have been disposed to agree with Marschall. The following decades have shown that Bismarck was right and Marschall was wrong.

It was formerly usual to praise Bismarck's foreign policy because of its alleged independence of home policy and to call it the realization of Ranke's doctrine of the 'Primat der Aussenpolitik'. This assessment is bound to be qualified to a considerable extent today. True, in the period of his great struggles against France and Austria

[1] *Ibid*, p. 244.

(1864–70) he had not the smallest scruples about winning supporters for his foreign policy wherever he could find them. While he fought in Prussia for the king's rights and the monarchical idea against the Progressive Prussian Landtag, he incited the Hungarian revolutionaries against their king. In 1870 he tried to win the support of Garibaldi and Mazzini, and—most characteristically—he used for his confidential communications with them Karl Blind, the stepfather of the young man who had attempted to murder him in May 1866.

But, on the other hand, Bismarck's home policy frequently influenced his foreign policy, particularly in the period after the foundation of the German Empire. He himself shows this quite clearly in the twenty-ninth chapter of his *Reflections and Reminiscences*. Here he writes that his foreign policy was influenced decisively by his belief in the idea that a struggle between 'the system of order on the basis of Monarchy' and the 'social (socialistic) Republics' was bound to come. That is not at variance with his policy of supporting the republican form of state in France and with his conflict with the ambassador in Paris, Count Harry Arnim, whom he reproached with having opposed this policy (1874) (iii, 135). For his reason for this policy was his conviction that France would not be able to find an ally so long as she was a republic. Moreover in many cases his policy was influenced by his concern about a possible strengthening of the liberal movement in Germany. This concern is expressed by his fear that a German 'Gladstone Cabinet' was waiting for a chance to overthrow him, presumably with the help of the heir to the throne and his wife, the Crown Princess Victoria. During the *Septennat* crisis of 1887 he compelled the German ambassador in Paris, Count Münster, to withdraw a report to the Kaiser (*Immediatbericht*) which denied the danger of French aggression, because it would make it impossible for his government to proceed with the *Septennat* Bill, which was motivated by this alleged aggression (iii, 455). Here it is not the foreign, but the home policy, which has the *Primat*.

Bismarck's home policy has always been more open to criticism than his foreign policy. Even his most ardent admirers could not help finding fault with some of its acts. For instance, the *Kulturkampf* could not be defended whole-heartedly after Bismarck himself had abandoned it in a manner not at all consistent with his former statements. The irritation which the Vatican Decrees and the declaration of Papal Infallibility (1870) excited in those days is hardly comprehensible to the present generation. Nevertheless, it was quite a real one, deeply felt not only in Germany but in this country, too, as Gladstone's pamphlets about the Vatican Decrees and Lord (John)

Russell's applause for Bismarck's policy show. Bismarck knew to perfection how to exploit this feeling, and when he exclaimed in the Reichstag: 'We shall not go to Canossa!' (*Nach Canossa gehn wir nicht*) he not only aroused reminiscences of Germany's most dramatic past history, he became the unrivalled hero of the whole Protestant world. But in fact he did not care so very much about this great spiritual antagonism. His real aim was to make the Pope pliant, in order to induce him to put the Roman Catholic deputies at the disposal of his government. He was quite willing to discontinue the *Kulturkampf* when he saw that no laurels were to be won by it and when Windthorst, the very clever leader of the Centre Party, was ready to support his new protectionist policy in 1879.

Here we come to the point that must seem to us the most important after the experience of half a century. The lamentable and tragic failure of the Germans to find in the comity of nations a place worthy of their intellectual capacity and unparalleled laboriousness, is intimately connected with their inability to govern themselves. There was a time in German history when the German people was homogeneous enough and rich enough in political talent to learn this most difficult business. After the unification of the German people under Prussian leadership public opinion, particularly among the educated classes, was overwhelmingly liberal, and the National Liberal Party, the representative of this opinion, had a galaxy of first-class parliamentarians in the Reichstag, men like Bennigsen and Forckenbeck, Miquel and Bamberger, Lasker and Stauffenberg. They were quite willing to acknowledge Bismarck's superiority and to leave to him the monopoly of the conduct of foreign policy, and even to acknowledge the exalted position of the Prussian Crown, little as it fitted into their original political conception. An alliance between these Liberals and the Crown, i.e. Bismarck, would have given to the political development a stability which was conspicuously absent, particularly after the fall of Bismarck. It would have produced an élite of German politicians, experienced in the art of government and accustomed to take responsibility.

A development of this kind seemed to be a possibility during the so-called 'Liberal Era' (1867–78), when the National Liberal Party was Bismarck's main support in the German Reichstag and the Prussian Landtag (iii, 41). But the designation, 'Liberal Era', is, in fact, an exaggeration. The influence of the Liberals was restricted to legislation about economic questions, where their help was in any case indispensable to Bismarck, because they represented the commercial and industrial part of the population. It never reached, for instance, the political administration, so important in a country like Prussia. Here Bismarck had always taken good care that it remained in the hands of the Conservatives or of his personal followers. Nor did he at any time allow the Liberals to have their way in military questions.

These questions were, during the whole Bismarck period, intimately connected with the question of parliamentary control over the budget. It was over this question that Bismarck had fought and defeated the Liberals in the era of the Prussian constitutional conflict (1862–6) (i, 458). But the budgetary competence of the Reichstag was not less involved in the period after the unification of Germany. For Bismarck never allowed parliament to vote the military estimates *annually*, as is the case in parliamentary governed countries. He always insisted that the number of men to be called to the colours (*Friedenspräsenz-Stärke*) was to be fixed by law for a longer period, seven years as a rule (*Septennat*). That meant a restriction, almost a negation of the budgetary competence of the Reichstag, as the army budget amounted to about nine-tenths of the whole Reich budget. The Liberals were, therefore, by their constitutional principles, obliged to oppose this form of military legislation. But Bismarck compelled them to give way, even in 1874, when the Liberal Era seemed to be at its zenith (iii, 71). As an intelligent and critical English observer, Sir Robert Morier, saw it, he considered the army as the talisman, the possession of which he wanted to preserve with all his might to the executive, i.e., to the king, or, for his own lifetime, to himself. What the Liberals from their own point of view considered indispensable, Bismarck regarded as a parliamentary infringement of the rights of the king, and therefore absolutely inadmissible. He knew that these questions were much less well understood by the people than by the leading parliamentarians, and he therefore concentrated on these issues to drive a wedge between them. His demagogic master-stroke in this direction belongs to a later period. When the Army Bill of 1887 was before the Reichstag, its majority was quite willing to vote 'every man and every penny'. But that would not do for Bismarck. What he wanted was a dissolution of the Reichstag. He knew that the strong 'Deutsch-Freisinnige Partei' (Radical Liberal Party) was obliged by its programme to oppose a vote for seven years, while it was ready to vote the army estimates for three years. Bismarck insisted on the seven years' period all the more strongly, as his aim was to destroy this party before the ninety-year-old Kaiser William I died and was succeeded by his son, the Crown Prince Frederick William. For the 'Freisinnige Partei' was known as the 'Kronprinzen-Partei' and Bismarck suspected the Crown Prince, and still more the Crown Princess Victoria, of intending to form with the leaders of this party the so-called 'Gladstone Cabinet' that would replace him. He probably considered Prince

Alexander von Battenberg, the former Prince of Bulgaria, whose rule in that country he had done his best to destroy, to be the future Chancellor of Victoria's choice (iii, 447). He knew that Alexander was high in Victoria's favour, and he thought that as a general in the Prussian Army and as the much-acclaimed victor in the Bulgarian defeat of the Serbs at Slivnitza (1885) he would have enough prestige, with the German people, to serve as a figurehead in this abhorred 'Gladstone Cabinet'. These were the dangers which Bismarck wanted to avoid by the dissolution of the Reichstag. Again he succeeded. The 'Freisinnige Partei' was beaten decisively and became completely unable to form the nucleus of a non-Bismarckian government. As a few months later the mortal illness of the Crown Prince became apparent, the last hope of a Liberal German government under the Empire disappeared for ever.

To return to the 'Liberal' Era of the seventies. None of the eminent leaders of the National Liberal Party became a minister as long as Bismarck ruled. Miquel had to wait till Bismarck's dismissal to become the most important minister of finance that Prussia had had for a long time.[1] True, the leader of the party, Rudolf von Bennigsen, was at one time (1877) offered a place in the government by Bismarck (iii, 203). But the negotiations failed, because Bennigsen was unwilling to enter the government alone and insisted on taking two friends, Forckenbeck and Stauffenberg, with him. This condition was declined by Bismarck for reasons which today are quite obvious. Three highly competent National-Liberal ministers would have been a political force and would have developed a will of their own—while Bennigsen alone, surrounded by a majority of obsequious instruments of the Chancellor, would—earlier or later—have been compelled either to follow him or to resign with a considerable loss of prestige. During his negotiations with the liberal leader Bismarck made to a confidant a highly characteristic remark. He reproached the National-Liberals with their lack of 'subordination'. What he wanted was not a partner with independent political views, who took part in the counsel and the responsibilities of the government, but a subordinate, who would be obliged to follow him and, at the same time, be a hostage for the good behaviour of his party, which was then indispensable for a parliamentary majority. When he found that Bennigsen was not ready to play this rôle, but wanted a share of the political power, he coolly turned to the man, whom until then he had fought with the help of the National-Liberals and against whom he had stirred up the fury of the majority of the German people: Ludwig Windthorst, the leader of the Centre Party. When he in-

[1] *Ibid*, p. 48.

augurated his protectionist policy in 1879, he could choose between Bennigsen and Windthorst. Both were ready to support this policy, and each made his support dependent upon certain conditions. Bismarck preferred Windthorst and accepted his conditions. Bennigsen was quite taken aback. But Bismarck's choice was quite logical from his point of view: Windthorst could never have the ambition of being a partner in the government. That was what the National-Liberals had wanted, and this was in Bismarck's eyes a mortal sin, never to be forgiven.

His anti-socialist policy, too, was meant as a blow against the National-Liberals. When he heard about the attempt of Nobiling (2 June 1878), who had wounded the old Emperor by pistol shots, his first words were not a question about the health of his old master, but the cry: 'Now we dissolve the Reichstag!' ('Jetzt lösen wir den Reichstag auf!') (iii, 227). He did not wait to see whether the National-Liberals would now vote for the bill against the socialists, which he had resolved to propose. He wanted to weaken them first, and then to compel them to vote as he wished. This does not mean that he was not in earnest about the suppression of the Social Democrats. But that part of his programme was for him less an end in itself than a means to a higher end, the defeat of parliamentary opposition. In 1890, when he felt his position threatened, he wanted to exploit the question of the anti-socialist law for a *coup d'état* and the abolition of the universal franchise (iii, 570). He himself had given universal franchise to the German people but as its results did not satisfy him he felt no scruple about taking it away. He even considered the dissolution of the Reich by an act of the German monarch as an appropriate and admissible way to achieve this object.

All these facts show that Bismarck was absolutely opposed to a development of German political life in the direction of parliamentary government. He had entered politics in 1847 as a Junker and a Conservative of the most uncompromising reactionary type, and a Junker he remained at heart during the whole of his life. The Revolution of 1848 had in him one of its most bitter enemies, who even played with the idea of an armed counter-revolution. He was, of course, too great a statesman and possessed too independent and critical a mind not to see in the course of time the weakness and limitations of the doctrine of the old Prussian Conservatives. Nor was it in his nature to be bound by any doctrine at all. A born ruler, as he undoubtedly was, he saw in doctrines as well as in persons no ends in themselves, but means for his personal ends. Only two classes of persons existed for him: persons who could be used for his ends, and persons he could not use. It was not very different with political doctrines. He was therefore able to ally one day with one party and the other with the one opposite. He had differences and conflicts also with the Conservatives, for instance, over the German question and during the *Kulturkampf*. As he was never tolerant of opposition and always suspected personal motives, he fought these differences through with his usual vehemence. But nevertheless he always considered the Conservatives as his natural allies and took it as a matter of course, when they returned to their old allegiance in 1879 with his protectionist policy. It was very advantageous to the landed interest, which was in a high degree identical with the interests of the land-owning Junkers, a class to which he himself belonged as the owner of large landed property acquired with the help of the rich gifts (*Dotationen*) with which a grateful king and country had endowed him after his enormous successes in 1866 and 1871. Thus, for the rest of his rule, the Conservatives were the core of his political and parliamentary army. On the other hand, he understood the Liberals much better after 1866 than at the beginning of his political career; but as soon as they aspired to political power they were in his eyes no better than the revolutionaries of 1848. At a time when even the most radical Liberals were true monarchists, he tried to stigmatize them as republicans. The greater his difficulties with the opposition majority of the Reichstag (1881-7) became, the more he proclaimed himself as the champion of the rights of the King and the more he identified his policy with 'the policy of the King and Emperor'. He not only produced time and again personal messages of the old Emperor William I in support of his policy: he even went so far as to declare in the Reichstag that in Prussia the King personally was and remained in fact the real President of the ministry (24 January 1882).

This absurd doctrine proved a boomerang to its author. It was all very well for Bismarck to proclaim it when the king was a very old and tired man who left practically everything to his great Chancellor. But matters looked quite different when a young man ascended the throne, bent on making his own policy, immature and unstable though his ideas were. Only *one* policy could be the 'policy of the Kaiser'. Then one of them had to give way, and as the monarch was immovable, the Chancellor had to go. It is not in order to excuse William II's behaviour that we state the issue of the conflict in these simple terms. It is only to show that Bismarck reaped what he had sown, that the conflict was inevitable just on account of Bismarck's own policy. So long had he preached to the German people that the confidence of the Kaiser was the only basis of his government, so effectively had he destroyed every other possible basis, that his dismissal was unavoidable when he lost this sole basis of his power, the confidence of the Emperor. But his responsibility extends even further. He laid the foundation of the political system that William II practised. Sharply and mercilessly as Bismarck criticized its practice, it was nevertheless his own creation. The young Kaiser would have been quite unable to venture upon his personal régime if Bismarck had not, with his enormous prestige, taught the German people that the German Kaiser and Prussian King alone had to hold the reins of the government in his hands. We now know the fruits of this personal régime: this is one of the principal reasons why we must assess Bismarck's policy differently from observers fifty years ago.

In spite of all this criticism Bismarck remains the greatest and most important figure of his time. If the age in which he lived can be associated with the name of one person, there can be no doubt that it is the Age of Bismarck. There was nobody whose speeches were heard with the same attention by the whole world, or whose despatches were studied with the same care and respect in every Foreign Office of Europe. And they were, indeed, worth this care and attention. No man was able to express and argue his views in such a masterly fashion and to clothe his claims and grievances in such telling words. If we read one of his great dispatches now, when the questions he dealt with have been dead for more than fifty years, we are deeply impressed by his personality and feel that no other man could have written them in quite the same way. The phrases he coined in his speeches and writings became household words (*Geflügelte Worte*) often quoted even by persons who hardly know of his existence. For he was one of the greatest masters of the German language.

We see this not only in his official utterances. His personal letters, particularly those to his wife and sister, are gems of letter-writing. The letters of his earlier years show personal qualities which one would not have expected from his political activity: an intensity of feeling, expressed in a language worthy of a great poet, a wit, a humour and satire, which remind one of Heinrich Heine. True, the longer he held power the weaker this feeling became, and in his later years Lord Acton's famous words come to mind: power tends to corrupt and absolute power corrupts absolutely. This is shown, for instance, in his behaviour to his son Herbert, whom he compelled by every possible, even brutal, means to renounce the marriage with his beloved, because she was related to a family the Chancellor hated.

The outstanding product of his pen is his *Reflections and Reminiscences*. George Gooch puts it 'at the top of the list of political autobiographies, not merely because he is the greatest man who ever wrote a full-length narrative of his life . . . but because its value as a manual of statecraft is unsurpassed'. But he quite rightly warns the reader: 'Every statement of fact has to be verified, every judgment of men and events to be checked.'[1] Bismarck was not able to do justice to an adversary, even if the differences were only slight—and he did not at all care to do so. The passage of years did not mellow his judgment. He had no respect for the majesty of truth, and did not shrink, for instance, from repeating the old lies about the Hohenzollern candidature, although they were already publicly disproved before he wrote his reminiscences. Whoever desires to know what really happened (*wie es eigentlich gewesen ist*, to use Ranke's famous phrase) should not turn to this book. But the critical reader, whose interest is to know the version which Bismarck wished to impress on posterity, will be richly compensated. He will not only find reflections about the duty of the statesman or the problems of Europe which are worthy of the closest attention. He will admire the art of narration, which even the greatest historians, a Macaulay or a Mommsen, have never surpassed, as for example, in his story of his difference with the King at Nikolsburg in 1866, or of the Ems telegram of 1870.

This book will keep Bismarck's memory alive even for a generation which knows the weaknesses and black sides of his personality and has ceased to admire his greatest achievements.

[1] G. P. Gooch, *Studies in Diplomacy and Statecraft* (Longmans, 1942), p. 261.

BERNADOTTE E. SCHMITT

The Origins of the First World War

I

T<small>HE</small> First World War broke out suddenly and unexpectedly in midsummer 1914, following the murder of the Archduke Francis Ferdinand of Habsburg, heir to the throne of Austria-Hungary, at Sarayevo, in Bosnia, on 28 June. Since no war involving the European great powers with each other had occurred since 1871, the possibility of a general war seemed increasingly remote, at least to the man in the street. At the moment, the international atmosphere was calmer than it had been for some time, for while some Balkan problems were threatening to become difficult, there was nothing unusual about that, nothing so dangerous as the questions that had been settled peacefully in the winter of 1912–13. Another crisis would, it was assumed, be resolved by another compromise. Statesmen everywhere professed their devotion to peace and more or less sincerely believed their professions. Only a few persons in any country were psychologically prepared for the catastrophe which in the last two weeks of July 1914 plunged Europe into war. To be sure, there were prophets who had made predictions in English, French, German, Italian, and Russian of impending disaster, all written in the ten or fifteen years before 1914, but, truth to tell, they aroused little attention and only a handful of experts believed these Cassandras.

The belief was widespread, on the contrary, that modern governments were much too enlightened to go to war. A great sensation was produced in 1911 by a book called *The Great Illusion*, by Norman Angell, an American who had lived most of his life in Europe. Angell asserted bluntly that wars did not pay. He did not say, as was sometimes alleged, that for economic reasons governments would not go to war, but he put it to them that if they did, they would lose much more than they could gain, for the complicated mechanism of modern business would be thrown out of gear and economic ruin would result for the victors as well as for the vanquished. Angell's arguments were by no means universally accepted and more than one formal refutation was offered. Nevertheless, the view was often expressed that if governments did try to go to war, financiers would stop them; while still others, chiefly socialists, hoped that the workers would not respond to the order of mobilization. But when on 23 July Austria-Hungary in a formidable note accused its small neighbour Serbia of responsibility for the death of the Archduke and made demands that seemed to portend military action, it was instantly recognized that here was no ordinary crisis which might be overcome by negotiation, but that the whole constellation of European power was at stake. Illusions vanished overnight, and millions who before Sarayevo had had no thought of war accepted it as something which could not be avoided.

Once the shock of war had been absorbed, men asked themselves how it had happened, both the intermediate antecedents and the underlying causes. A popular explanation was that the war had grown out of economic jealousies and rival imperialisms. Cited in proof were the trade competition between Germany and Great Britain for a generation before 1914; the conflicting colonial ambitions of the European powers which had more than once led to the 'brink' (to use the term adopted forty years later); and the intrigues of high finance for concessions in Asia, Africa, and the Near East, concessions for loans, railways, canals, and other profitable enterprises. This interpretation was automatic for socialists, who derived their ideas from Karl Marx, but it was not exclusive with them, for an English radical, H. N. Brailsford, on the very eve of the war published a well-known book entitled *The War of Steel and Gold*, which said much the same thing.

Economic interests and rivalries undoubtedly had much to do with poisoning international relations in the forty-three years from the Treaty of Frankfort in 1871 to the outbreak of war in 1914. Thus, the Austro-Serbian dispute, which in 1914 was to provide the spark for the explosion, became serious only when Austria sought to control Serbia by means of 'pig wars' and harsh commercial treaties. On the colonial side, there were sharp conflicts between Britain and Russia in Persia and the Far East, between France and Italy in Tunisia, between France and Germany in Morocco, between France and Britain in Egypt and Siam, between Britain and Germany in South Africa. More than once war threatened to break out. Likewise, the most famous project of financial imperialism, the Baghdad railway, involved Britain, France, Germany, and Russia in long years of bitter wrangling. These disputes about colonies and the competition for concessions had much to do with the building up of large navies by the western powers, for sea power seemed necessary to guard overseas interests.

Yet economic interests, in the ordinary sense of that term, had little to do, directly at least, with the outbreak of war in August 1914. The most conspicuous trade rivalry of the pre-war years, the competition between Britain and Germany, was ceasing to be a cause of tension because the two countries were developing their markets in different parts of the world, Britain more and more with its own Empire, Germany more and more on the continent of Europe. In July 1914 the loudest protests against war were made by the businessmen in Germany and Britain, who foresaw clearly what war would do to them.

On the colonial side, to the credit of much-abused secret diplomacy, the great powers succeeded in partitioning Africa without recourse to war. To be sure, the British fought the Boers in South Africa, and British, French, Germans, and Italians fought native peoples in Africa, but they did not fight each other. In the spring of 1914 Britain and Germany, sixteen years after they had begun to negotiate, were ready to sign an agreement providing for the ultimate disposition of the Portuguese colonies. Also at this time the western powers arrived at a compromise respecting the Baghdad railway and had divided the Ottoman Empire in Asia into spheres of economic influence for the laudable purpose of avoiding war over the Ottoman succession. Thus by 1914 the economic rivalries that were so troublesome in the first decade of the century had been in large measure adjusted, and they played no part in the hectic negotiations that preceded the war. Finally, it is to be noted that in 1914 the ruling groups in European governments were not men who thought in terms of business and economic advantage. They were usually members of the hereditary aristocracy, who thought in terms of strategy and military power and national prestige and who, in the crisis of 1914, paid little heed to the wails of businessmen.

The primary cause of the war was the conflict over political frontiers and the distribution of peoples, the denial of what is commonly called the right of self-determination (although this term was not ordinarily used before 1914). In 1914, from the Rhine eastwards, political frontiers, as determined by the Congress of Vienna a century before and by the wars of the nineteenth century, everywhere cut across well-recognized lines of nationality. To begin with, Germany held Alsace-Lorraine, taken from France in 1871, where the majority of the population resented having been annexed to Germany, disliked German rule, and wished to return to France. Austria-Hungary contained eleven different racial groups, nine of which were kept in greater or less submission by a ruling clique of the other two (Germans, Magyars). In the Balkans, racial and political frontiers rarely coincided. Finally, the western portion of the Russian Empire was made up of non-Russian regions represented today by Finland, the Baltic States, and Poland. Poland was the most notorious case, for it was still divided between the Austrian, German, and Russian empires which had partitioned it in the eighteenth century.

So Germany was faced with the problem of French, Danish, and Polish minorities, and Austria-Hungary consisted chiefly of minorities. Some minorities were treated more harshly than others, but everywhere they were growing increasingly restless and demanding change. In some cases minorities were able to look across their own frontiers to free kinsmen who, it was hoped, would one day free them from the oppression (as they saw it) under which they suffered. The Yugoslavs in both Austria and Hungary, denied relief by their Habsburg rulers, turned for help to Serbia under King Peter Karageorgevich, and the Rumanians of Transylvania, in south-eastern Hungary, gazed longingly across the Carpathians at independent Rumania under its Hohenzollern king. Neither Yugoslavs nor Rumanians had in the past been united, but if the nineteenth century had seen the unification of Italians and Germans, why should not the twentieth century witness the joining together of Yugoslavs or Rumanians? The Poles, too, dreamed of reunion, even if before 1914 there seemed no prospect of it.

More than any other circumstance, this conflict between existing governments and their unhappy minorities was responsible for the catastrophe of 1914. Germany understood perfectly well that the annexation of Alsace-Lorraine could be maintained only by the sword, and France knew equally well that the provinces could be regained only by the sword. The multi-national Habsburg state depended more and more on force, less and less on the loyalty of its peoples. The partition of Poland was maintained only by force. Since the astonishing victories of Prussia in the wars against Denmark, Austria, and France were attributed to its conscript armies, it was not surprising that the new German Empire established in 1871 continued to recruit its armies by universal service. Inevitably, Germany's neighbours adopted the same system. Not only that, but every increase in strength, every improvement in the weapons of war made by one country, had to be met by all. From 1872 to 1913, this rigorous competition in the building up of armies went on, every government spending as much money as it could persuade its people to pay or the national economy would support (Germany bore this cost easily, but for Italy the burden was ruinous), without, however, any corresponding increase in security being felt. In fact, the proportionate strength of the various armies was not greatly different in 1914 from what it had been in 1872, but the feeling of insecurity was much greater than it had been forty years earlier. The memoirs of General Ludendorff, the most famous German soldier of the war, are eloquent on this point.

Of course, disputed and unstable frontiers were not the exclusive reason for great armies. From time immemorial European governments had maintained armies, partly to keep order at home, partly for use in diplomatic bargaining, and sometimes for aggression and conquest; but certainly the determination of monarchs and governments to preserve their territories intact in the face of growing dissatisfaction with the *status quo*, made the competition in armaments more deadly than it had been in earlier generations.

It was because of the increasing feeling of insecurity that European governments, one after another, sought to strengthen their respective positions by concluding alliances with other governments having similar interests. Germany enjoys the doubtful honour of launching this system of alliances, as it does in the matter of conscript armies, for it was Bismarck, the German chancellor, who in 1879 made an alliance with Austria-Hungary and in 1882 engineered a second alliance, the Triple Alliance between Germany, Austria-Hungary, and Italy. These alliances marked a turning-point in the history of Europe. There had often been alliances in the past, but they were usually concluded for specific purposes and were dissolved when the aim was accomplished. These Bismarckian alliances were destined to be permanent, the Austro-German treaty lasting until it was dissolved by military defeat in October 1918, the Triple Alliance surviving until 1915. Since the principle and the practice of the balance of power were as old as European history, it was to be expected that sooner or later a counterpoise should be created to the Triple Alliance. Bismarck succeeded in staving this off by very clever diplomacy (first by a Three Emperors' League from 1881 to 1887 and then by a 'reinsurance' treaty with Russia from 1887 to 1890) which kept France isolated; but after his fall in 1890, his complicated system was discarded by his successor, and in the early nineties a Franco-Russian alliance—which had been Bismarck's nightmare—came into being. One combination dominated the centre of Europe, the other possessed the periphery.

Both of these continental alliances were originally strictly defensive, providing for the maintenance of the *status quo* and for assistance only if one party were attacked. Gradually, however, each alliance was transformed. The Triple Alliance was modified to permit changes in the *status quo* in the Balkans, in Africa, and even in Europe, for the Italo-German treaty signed in conjunction with the second treaty of the alliance concluded in 1887 contained a promise by Germany to support, in certain conditions, Italian claims to Nice and Savoy (which had been ceded to France in 1860 as payment for French assistance in the war of unification). Likewise, the Franco-Russian alliance was modified in 1899 to provide for 'the maintenance of the balance of power', the words being meant to take care of the situation which would arise when the Habsburg state went to pieces, as it was confidently expected to do when the Emperor Francis Joseph died. Finally, in 1909, the Austro-German alliance was given a new twist when the chief of the German general staff, by an exchange of letters with his Austro-Hungarian opposite number, promised that if Austria invaded Serbia and in consequence Russia intervened on behalf of Serbia, Germany would go to the assistance of Austria-Hungary, a promise that Bismarck had consistently refused to give, for he insisted that Austria must not provoke Russia. Thus the alliances ceased to be the guarantors of the *status quo*, and might instead become instruments of aggression. The terms of the several treaties and commitments were not published, but each side came to suspect the other of sinister intentions.

Down to the turn of the century, Great Britain did not join either of the continental groups, preferring a policy of 'splendid isolation'. The two groups, although directed against each other, were often more concerned, in the nineties, with diplomatic action against Great Britain, and stood, as it were, side by side, rather than face to face. In 1898 and again in 1901, Britain tried to come to an agreement with Germany, but the German terms proved too high: Britain was asked to join the Triple Alliance, which it was unwilling to do because it was reluctant to underwrite the shaky Habsburg state. The German chancellor of the day, Count Bülow, was sure that in the end Britain would come to heel and stood on his terms. When in 1904 Britain adjusted its many old disputes with France and in 1907 compromised its differences with Russia in the Middle East, Germany found itself confronted by a Triple Entente which had been deemed impossible. Europe was not mentioned in any of the several agreements, but the British, French, and Russian governments were all suspicious of Germany, and by settling their own differences they ensured themselves free hands in dealing with Germany. Nevertheless, for years after the formation of the Entente, Germany held on to a policy based on the premiss of irreconcilable hostility between Britain and the Franco-Russian Alliance.

At the beginning of the twentieth century, Germany was the most restless nation in Europe. Its population, its industry, its foreign trade were growing more rapidly than those of any other country, and its future seemed brilliant, at least to other countries. But the Germans themselves were not so sure. As they looked at the world around them, they observed that Britain and France had secured control, in one form or another, of the most desirable parts of Africa, held large possessions in Asia, and ruled the ocean lanes from innumerable islands in the seven seas, which provided naval bases and coaling stations. In comparison, the German colonies in Africa and Asia and the German islands in the Pacific were pitifully inadequate. Even the colonial nations of the past, Spain, Portugal, the Netherlands were better off than Germany. In the current view colonial possessions were considered necessary for an industrial nation, in order to supply raw materials needed in industry and to furnish markets for manufactured goods and opportunities for the investment of capital, and Germany, not having rich, productive, and populous colonies, felt discriminated against. So there arose a tremendous agitation and a loud cry for 'a place in the sun', and along with it, the charge was heard that Germany's rivals, principally Britain and France, were standing in the way of Germany's acquiring what was its just due. The Pan-German League, a small but noisy and influential association, proclaimed what needed to be done in Europe to achieve the unification of the German people, and innumerable books and pamphlets set forth in considerable detail what was wanted elsewhere in the world. Since these programmes were to be realized at the expense of other nations and the view was often expressed that if necessary Germany would use force to accomplish its ends, it was not surprising that the countries most affected should draw together, as Britain, France, and Russia did in the Triple Entente.

The German government never associated itself with the specific demands of the expansionist agitation, but it resorted to methods of diplomacy which gave great offence. Thus, it took advantage of the Boer War in South Africa to force concessions from Britain in Samoa; it used the opportunity offered by the Russo-Japanese War to secure a tariff treaty from Russia that was unduly advantageous to Germany; and when Russia, France's ally, was being defeated in the Far East, Germany compelled France to get rid of its foreign minister and to change its policy in Morocco. The resistance which Britain, France, and Russia offered to this policy, which they regarded as blackmail, was denounced by Germany as 'encirclement', and Germany reacted to it by giving unqualified support to the action of Austria-Hungary when that power proclaimed the annexation of Bosnia in 1908, which caused great irritation in Russia.

In addition, the German government, from 1900 onwards, began the construction of a navy which was intended to be second only to that of Great Britain. This was a pet project of the Emperor William II, and he declined all suggestions from Britain for a limitation of naval armaments. The faster the German fleet grew, the more alarmed the British became, the closer they drew to the French and the Russians—and the more the Germans complained of 'encirclement'. As the years passed, the more clearly did Europe appear to be divided between the Triple Alliance and the Triple Entente.

Actually, things were not so simple. In 1902 Italy made a secret agreement with France by which it promised to remain neutral if France went to war with Germany in consequence of a German attack on Russia. In 1909 Italy concluded a secret agreement with Russia by which both parties recognized each other's interests in the Balkans and promised support for each other's policies. Thus the Triple Alliance was for some years a broken reed. But in the Balkan wars of 1912–13 Italy worked with Austria-Hungary to establish an independent Albania, and in the winter of 1913–14 negotiated new military and naval conventions with Germany and Austria-Hungary which seemed to bring the wavering ally back into the fold. The chief of the German general staff, General von Moltke, became convinced that Italy's loyalty was 'not open to doubt' and he acted on that assumption in the crisis of July 1914.

The Triple Entente never became so closely-knit as the Triple Alliance, for the British government refused to commit itself to go to the help of France, in spite of French arguments that an Anglo-French alliance would be the most effective means of discouraging Germany from going to war. The most that Britain would concede was a promise, made in 1912, that if either Britain or France had grave reason to expect attack by a third party or a threat to the general peace, they would consult with each other and if they should decide to take common action, they would put into effect the plans which their general staffs had drawn up.

These plans, elaborated from 1906 on, provided for the sending of a British army of 160,000 troops to fight in France alongside the French Army, and for the deploying of the French Navy in the Mediterranean while the British fleet guarded the North Sea and the Channel. The French had to be satisfied (as of course they were not!) with this 'half-alliance', which left the British free to decide whether to intervene—a freedom of which they took full advantage in 1914.

Anglo-Russian relations never reached the degree of intimacy of those between Britain and France. Russian interests in the Near East were not regarded in Britain as something Britain might have to fight for, and Russian activity in Persia was much disliked. In the spring of 1914 the Russian foreign minister, Sazonov, proposed that the Triple Entente should be converted into a Triple Alliance, but this was rejected by the British foreign secretary, Sir Edward Grey. Grey agreed, however, to the Russians being informed of the Anglo-French notes exchanged in 1912 and to the opening of conversations between the British and Russian admiralties, so that, as he said to the German ambassador, although Britain was not allied with France and Russia, it 'did from time to time talk with them as intimately as allies'.

Thus in July 1914 the two groups, Triple Alliance and Triple Entente, were at long last ranged face to face, three on each side. Was war the inevitable consequence of this schism of Europe? At the moment there was no immediate prospect of it. Relations between Britain and Germany had improved considerably since 1912. An informal agreement had been reached for the construction of battleships in the ratio of 16:10. During the crisis of the Balkan wars (1912–13) Britain and Germany had co-operated to restrain Russia and Austria respectively, and in 1914 they had negotiated and were ready to sign two agreements regarding the future of the Portuguese colonies and settling their differences about the Baghdad railway. This led the British to expect that in the event of another Balkan crisis they could count on German help to deal with it; on the other hand, the Germans drew the conclusion that Britain would no longer necessarily take the side of France in the event of war.

After the great crises of 1905 and 1911 over Morocco, during which Germany seemed ready for war with France, the relations between those two countries had also taken a turn for the better. In February 1914 an agreement was reached concerning railway schemes and spheres of economic interest in Turkey, and the president of the Republic, Poincaré, who was later to be denounced as a warmonger, had dined at the German embassy, breaking a tradition of forty years. If Alsace-Lorraine had not been forgotten, there was practically no sentiment for a 'war of revenge' (as the German ambassador recognized), and the elections of May 1914 gave a majority to the parties of the Left, who wished to abolish the three-years' military service restored in 1913.

In the midsummer of 1914, then, neither Anglo-German nor Franco-German relations involved any threat to peace. On the other hand, there was plenty of explosive material lying around in the Near East. At the end of 1913 such tension was produced between Russia and Germany by the despatch of a German military mission to Constantinople for the rehabilitation of the Turkish Army that Sazonov toyed with the idea of seizing the Straits by force (an idea rejected by his colleagues and the Russian general staff); a compromise was patched up, but public opinion in both countries remained excited. Austria and Italy were intriguing against each other in Albania, Bulgaria was sullenly nursing its defeat the year before at the hands of Serbia, Greece, and Rumania, Greece and Turkey were at loggerheads about certain islands in the Ægean. As it happened, however, the spark that touched off the explosion was a completely unexpected incident, the murder of the Archduke Francis Ferdinand of Habsburg at Sarayevo on 28 June.

The tragedy at Sarayevo was the culmination of an antagonism between Austria-Hungary and Serbia that had been growing for a generation. In 1859 the Habsburgs had faced the question of Italian unification, and had been driven out of Italy; in 1866 they faced the same problem in Germany, and with the same result. From 1903, when the pro-Austrian king of Serbia, Alexander Obrenovich, was assassinated, they were confronted with the Yugoslav problem. At the beginning of the century, the Yugoslavs were widely disunited in Austria, Hungary, Bosnia, Serbia, Montenegro, and Turkey. In the decade before 1914 it became evident that a national movement was gaining headway because of the rather shabby treatment of the Yugoslavs within the Habsburg monarchy, and one of two things seemed likely to happen: either Austria-Hungary must bring the Yugoslavs outside the Monarchy (those in Serbia, Montenegro, and Turkey) under Habsburg rule, or the Serbs, the most energetic group among the Yugoslavs and the possessors of an independent state, would detach their kinsmen from Habsburg rule and establish a unified independent Yugoslav state. If Habsburg experience with the Italians and the Germans provided any guide, the second contingency was the more likely.

Naturally the ruling groups in Austria-Hungary favoured the first course. The military party, led by the chief of the general staff, General Conrad von Hötzendorf, made no secret of its desire for war against Serbia, which would lead to direct annexation of the troublesome little neighbour. The political leadership was more cautious, thinking in terms of a customs union or a change of dynasty, which might be accomplished by diplomacy, but it was just as eager as the soldiers to put an end to Serbian independence and thus extinguish the restlessness of its Yugoslav peoples. The first step in this direction was the annexation of Bosnia-Herzegovina, two provinces with a mixed population of Serbs and Croats which had been under Habsburg administration since 1878 but were nominally still part of the Ottoman Empire. This action precipitated a six months' crisis (October 1908–March 1909), which almost ended in an Austrian attack on Serbia and was settled only after Germany had sent a near-ultimatum to Russia requiring the cabinet of St. Petersburg to recognize the annexation without reference to a European conference. The Russian foreign minister of the time, Izvolsky, accused his Austro-Hungarian opposite number, Aehrenthal, of tricking him, and he bitterly resented the intervention of Germany at the last minute. The echoes of this conflict had not died away in 1914.

In the plans of the Austro-Hungarian government to deal with the Yugoslav problem, the Archduke Francis Ferdinand played a peculiar rôle. He had come to the conclusion that the existing Dual system, by which the Germans ruled in Austria, the Magyars in Hungary, although both were minorities, was driving the Monarchy to destruction, and he hated the Magyar clique and was determined to clip its power. He proposed to solve the Yugoslav problem by granting to the Yugoslavs within the Monarchy full autonomy (which would destroy the Dual system) and then bring Serbia into some kind of connexion with the Monarchy. Whether Francis Ferdinand would have been able to accomplish this is anybody's guess. He was a rather hot-headed, bigoted, avaricious man who was heartily disliked by the great majority of his future subjects, and any attempt to carry out his plan, had he lived to succeed his uncle Francis Joseph, would have met with determined resistance by the Germans and Magyars. But his violent death at the hands of a man of Serbian race (who, however, was a Habsburg subject) provided the forward party with an excuse for action against Serbia that was too tempting to be neglected.

The full circumstances of the crime at Sarayevo have never been cleared up. That the conspirators were fitted out with arms in Belgrade and secretly passed across the frontier into Bosnia became known in 1914 and was used by the Austro-Hungarian government as justification for the demands made on Serbia. But precisely who inspired the crime,[1] how much the Serbian government knew about the plot in advance, what steps it took to prevent the crime's execution—either by warning Vienna or by attempting to stop the assassins from crossing into Bosnia, whether also the authorities in Sarayevo took proper precautions to protect their heir to the throne, are questions to which precise answers are still not possible. Actually the answers did not really matter, for an official sent from Vienna to Sarayevo reported that the responsibility of the Serbian government was not established; yet Austro-Hungarian policy could hardly have been more drastic if Serbian official complicity had been proved.

The situation in 1914 cannot, however, be judged exclusively in terms of Austro-Serbian relations, for Serbia, a small nation of

[1] The person most often credited was the chief of the intelligence section of the Serbian general staff, Colonel Dragutin Dimitriyevich, but the evidence is not conclusive.

5,000,000 people, occupied a key position in Europe. Rumania was the ally of Austria-Hungary; Bulgaria was anxious to be taken into the Triple Alliance; in Turkey German influence was stronger than that of any other power. If Serbia were brought under Austrian control, then German-Austrian influence would prevail from Berlin to Baghdad. If, on the other hand, Serbia were maintained as an independent state, a wedge would be driven into the German-Austrian-Turkish combination, and Constantinople would be susceptible to Russian, French, and British pressure. So the crisis of July 1914 was concerned with more than the question whether, as Austria-Hungary demanded, Austrian officials should go into Serbia and investigate the *minutiœ* of the crime at Sarayevo. The fundamental issue was a test of strength between the Triple Alliance and the Triple Entente, the outcome of which would affect the balance of power in Europe for an incalculable time to come.

II

All the governments were responsible, in greater or less degree, for building up the system of alliances and for the great accumulation of armaments. To that extent they all contributed to the tension that came to a head in July 1914. But they were not equally responsible for the fatal turn of events, the course of which can be followed in microscopic detail. When the crisis culminated in war, the governments began to issue collections of diplomatic documents in coloured (White, Blue, Orange, Red, Yellow, Grey, from the colour of the cover) 'Books', in which each set forth its case and laid the blame for the war on the other side. Not only was it essential to convince its own people of the rightness of its conduct, but it was deemed equally important to gain the good will of neutrals, notably of the United States. For years endless debate raged throughout the world over this question of 'war guilt'; a book by James M. Beck, an eminent American lawyer, *The Evidence in the Case*, enjoyed a wide circulation. After the war, much fuller collections of documents were published which were selected by historians rather than by politicians and propagandists, and it became evident that the documents put out in 1914 had been chosen to prove a case and had often been 'edited', that is, tampered with; that awkward documents had been suppressed and still others invented. From the fairly complete diplomatic files available for July 1914, together with the memoirs of politicians, diplomatists, and military men, a dispassionate and accurate account can now be written of the action of European diplomacy from the murder at Sarayevo on 28 June to the outbreak of the general European war in August.

The Austro-Hungarian government quickly decided that the heaven-sent opportunity for a reckoning with Serbia should not be lost. But since action against Serbia was likely to bring about the intervention of Russia, it was essential for the cabinet of Vienna to know what Germany would do in such a situation. To be sure, the German general staff had declared in 1909, during the Bosnian crisis, that Russian intervention on behalf of Serbia would cause Germany to mobilize, which, in German terminology, was the prelude to war. But, during the crisis of the Balkan wars of 1912–13, the German government had consistently restrained the war party in Vienna, and furthermore, the German Emperor, William II, was supposed to entertain considerable partiality for Serbia. In order to discover the state of mind of Berlin, the Austro-Hungarian foreign minister, Count Berchtold, sent both an official note and a private emissary to the German capital; also Francis Joseph wrote a letter to William II. The letter stated that Austria-Hungary must aim at 'the isolation and diminution of Serbia', which must be 'eliminated as a political factor in the Balkans'. The emissary, Berchtold's *chef de cabinet*, Count Hoyos, explained that the Austrian plan was to 'march into Serbia' without any warning and to partition Serbia between the Monarchy, Albania, and Bulgaria.

Only two weeks before the German chancellor, Bethmann Hollweg, had said that in the event of a new crisis arising in the Balkans, 'whether . . . it would come to a general European conflagration would depend exclusively on the attitude of Germany and England'. But when Hoyos appeared in the German capital on 5 July, this caution was laid aside. The Austrian plan to invade and partition Serbia was cordially received by the German Emperor and the German government, and immediate action was urged on the cabinet of Vienna. Because a royal personage had been murdered, William II professed to believe that Czar Nicholas II would be loath to go to the help of Serbia, but if he did, Germany was ready to support its ally and to wage war against Russia and France. This decision was not a matter of Germany putting its head into a noose (as is sometimes asserted) and signing away its freedom of action; both emperor and government knew exactly what they were doing. They made their decision on the assumption that Great Britain would remain neutral (in spite of the fact that the German ambassador in London, Prince Lichnowsky, had been reporting for eighteen months that in the event of war between Germany and France, Britain would join France). The general staff was confident that Germany and Austria-Hungary could defeat Russia and France, and, assuming war to be inevitable, it now welcomed the prospect of war, for victory would be easier in 1914 than later, when French and Russian military plans would be nearer completion. Some conservative elements in Germany looked upon war as a good means of dealing with the menace of socialism, which seemed to be steadily increasing. The emperor and the chancellor took their decision without reference to the foreign minister, a cautious man who happened to be away on his honeymoon and who had hitherto worked to restrain Austria, and without any formal consultation of the highest military authorities of the Empire; furthermore, the decision was taken instantly, without reflexion. William II and Bethmann accepted the risk of war with unbelievable nonchalance; it was they who put the system of European alliances to the test. Without this German action, it is unlikely that a European war would have broken out in the summer of 1914.

For twenty-odd years German policy had vacillated between East and West. From 1890 to 1914, that is, the period after the fall of Bismarck during which William II was the ruler of Germany, the German government pursued its policy of expansion in both directions. Admiral Tirpitz and the navy people thought Britain the enemy and concentrated on building a fleet, although the more they built the more they alarmed Britain. The general staff thought in terms of French enmity and demanded as much money as possible for the army. Business men were divided, some wishing to go into Africa, others into the Near East. Neither the emperor nor any of his chancellors could make up their minds where the fundamental interest of Germany lay; in one sense they thought that Germany was strong enough to move in both directions. In 1914, however, they were seriously concerned about the stability of Austria-Hungary, the one sure ally, and they persuaded themselves that only a successful military demonstration against Serbia could stop the process of Habsburg decay. The decision of July 1914 to support Austria-Hungary against Russia, in the calculation that Britain would remain neutral, may be interpreted as meaning that the long indecision had, at least for the moment, been resolved by a decision to go East.

The Austro-Hungarian government could now act. But because of the opposition of the Hungarian premier, Count Tisza, the plan to 'march into Serbia' without warning was abandoned. At a ministerial council held on 7 July, in its place a forty-eight hour ultimatum was decided upon which theoretically would provide Serbia with a chance to submit. Actually, seven supposedly unacceptable demands were included, in order to ensure the rejection of the ultimatum and pave the way for military action. In the minds of the Austro-Hungarian ministers the treatment to be meted out to Serbia after the war included 'rectifications of frontier' for the benefit of the

Monarchy, while other parts of its territory were to be apportioned to other Balkan states; what was left might be attached to the Monarchy by a military convention to be signed by a new dynasty. These designs were of course not mentioned when the Austro-Hungarian government assured the other powers that it did not intend to take Serbian territory for itself.

The ultimatum was presented to the Serbian government on 23 July. It contained ten demands, the most important of which required Serbia to admit Austrian officials into Serbia for the suppression of the agitation against the Monarchy and to take action against the persons involved in the murder of Sarayevo. Outside of Austria and Germany, the ultimatum was regarded as a monstrous document which no independent state could accept. To the intense surprise and annoyance of Vienna, the Serbian reply, delivered a few minutes before the expiry of the ultimatum on 25 July, was conciliatory and to a large extent appeared to accept the Austrian demands, as was later stated by both William II and Bethmann Hollweg. Nevertheless, diplomatic relations were broken off, partial mobilization of the Austrian Army was ordered, and on 28 July war was declared against Serbia. The military chiefs would have preferred to wait until mobilization had been completed, but insistent German pressure forced immediate action, which began with the bombardment of the Serbian capital on 29 July.

This action precipitated the intervention of Russia. For generations the principal Russian interest in the Near East had been the question of the Straits: how to break through the barrier of the Bosphorus and the Dardanelles and secure free access to the Mediterranean for Russian merchantmen and men-of-war. Although various plans for accomplishing this had been devised since 1798, no plan existed in 1914, for the Russian generals had rejected a suggestion of the foreign minister for seizing the Straits. The other facet of Russia's Near Eastern policy was the defence of the Slav peoples of the Balkans against Turkish misrule or German pressure. Ever since the Bosnian crisis of 1908, Serbia had looked to Russia for help against Austrian action, but Russia was weak after the war against Japan and the abortive revolution of 1905, so successive foreign ministers kept putting off the importunate Serbs with promises for the future. The Russian government probably did not want war in 1914, for its army was still in process of reorganization and revolutionary symptoms were again in evidence, but, this time, it had to help Serbia or see that country be crushed by Austria. The German argument that the Austro-Serbian conflict could be 'localized' was completely unrealistic, all the more so since the Austrian assurances of disinterestedness were equivocal. The Russian foreign minister, Sazonov, vainly tried to get the terms of the Austrian ultimatum modified; at the same time, by ordering partial mobilization, he sought to make clear that if Austria attacked Serbia, Russia would act. This calculation misfired for two reasons. First, the news of the partial Russian mobilization did not deter Vienna and Berlin from the course they had charted. Second, the Russian general staff was aghast (it had not been consulted!) for it had no plan for a partial mobilization, so the generals persuaded first Sazonov and then the Czar that partial mobilization was impracticable and general mobilization inevitable. The Czar wavered, giving his consent on 29 July and then withdrawing it; but on 30 July he agreed, and on 31 July the order was published.

Russian general mobilization was ordered in the sure knowledge that it would be followed by German mobilization, which, according to the German view, 'meant war'. In a sense, then, Russia 'willed the war', as the Germans were fond of saying; the Italian historian Albertini thinks that the mobilization was premature, for by 30 July Sir Edward Grey had come forward with an idea that might have led to compromise and peace. But inasmuch as Austria had attacked Serbia and Germany had forbidden even the Russian partial mobilization, Russia, as the Russian government saw it, had to mobilize or abdicate as a great power. The Czar promised that his armies would not attack so long as negotiations continued—but these assurances seemed as flimsy to Germany as the Austrian assurances about the integrity of Serbia did to Russia.

From the beginning of the crisis precipitated by the Austrian ultimatum to Serbia, Germany had declined to restrain its ally and had urged it to act quickly. But by 28 July, the day on which Austria declared war on Serbia, the German Emperor had had a change of heart. Reversing his attitude of 5 July when he urged immediate action, he now sensed that the conciliatory Serbian reply had removed 'every reason for war'; he therefore suggested that Austria should stop with the occupation of Belgrade and offer to negotiate. On the following day it began to seem likely that, contrary to German calculations, Britain would be drawn into the war. So the German government shifted its ground and advised Vienna to accept a British proposal, practically identical with that of William II, that after occupying Belgrade, it should offer to negotiate. Before the Austrian government had replied, rumours of Russian mobilization began to reach Berlin. The chief of the general staff, Moltke, now pressed for war (as is admitted by the two most objective German students of the crisis).[1] On the evening of 30 July he persuaded the

[1] Hermann Lutz, *Die europäische Politik in der Julikrise 1914* (1930), and Alfred von Wegerer, *Der Ausbruch des Weltkrieges* (1939).

Chancellor to relax the pressure on Berchtold to accept Grey's proposal, and he himself telegraphed to Conrad urging rejection of this proposal and promising full German support if war resulted. Vienna did as Moltke desired and ordered Austrian general mobilization—before news had been received of the Russian general mobilization.

When the official news of the Russian general mobilization reached Berlin on the morning of 31 July, Moltke, with the help of William II, secured the consent of Bethmann, who had been holding out against the pressure of the generals, to the proclamation of a 'state of danger of war', which was the necessary preliminary to formal mobilization, the order for which was issued on the following day, 1 August. Whether, without the intervention of Moltke, Austria would have accepted the British proposal, whether a compromise with Russia could have been worked out, no one can say; but it is clear that the interference of Moltke prevented any last-minute attempt to keep the peace.

Because Germany expected to have to fight a two-front war against Russia and France, the general staff had persuaded itself that the only chance of victory lay in a headlong attack on France that was expected to defeat the French in six weeks, after which the German armies would be transferred to the eastern front to meet the more slowly mobilizing Russians. In 1914 there was no plan for an attack first on Russia and a defensive action against France. Yet in 1914 Germany had no quarrel with France. In order to have an excuse for attacking France, the German general staff had to make the Russian mobilization a *casus belli* and then ask France if it would remain neutral; since France would, because of its alliance with Russia, reply in the negative, Germany would then have justification for war against France. But the Prussian minister of war, Falkenhayn, was of the opinion that Germany could wait for several days before responding to the Russian general mobilization; Moltke, however, was so eager for war that the German government did not wait to see if Grey's efforts for peace might be successful.

Germany declared war on Russia on 1 August, which enabled the Russian government to say that it had been attacked while it was ready and anxious to negotiate. The German action required France, according to the Franco-Russian treaty of alliance, to attack Germany, but the French government, in reply to the German ultimatum, instead of replying that it would march with Russia (as expected and desired by Germany), said that it would consult its interests. This reply did not stop the German armies from invading France, and on 3 August Germany declared war on France, alleging, wrongly, that French planes had bombarded Nuremberg. Thus France also appeared to be the victim of brutal aggression, a circumstance of great value to France in consolidating sentiment at home and winning help abroad.

France played little part in the crisis of 1914. It had no direct interest in Serbia, but it was the ally of Russia, and if it did not support Russia in this crisis, the alliance would be broken and France would be left isolated. It happened that at the moment when the Austrian ultimatum was presented in Belgrade, the president of the Republic, Poincaré, and the president of the council of ministers, Viviani, were paying a state visit to Russia, and they gave the Czar and his ministers the assurance that France would support Russia in resisting Austria-Hungary and Germany, an assurance that certainly strengthened the determination of Sazonov. During the crisis, the French government advised its ally to do nothing that would provide Germany with an excuse for war, but it did not object to any step taken by Russia. This attitude was firmly supported by all shades of French public opinion, and the government did not feel it necessary to reveal the secret terms of the alliance. It will be noted that both Germany and France supported their allies on an issue—Serbia—not of direct concern to themselves, and thus is was that a quarrel between Austria-Hungary and Serbia became transformed, in the interest of the balance of power, into a general European war.

The role of Great Britain was not easy. The crisis found the Liberal government facing the prospect of civil war in Ireland over the question of Home Rule, which may have helped to convince the German government that Britain would remain neutral. Actually, in view of the European situation, the Irish controversy was adjourned, and both the Irish parties supported the government in its efforts to preserve peace. Grey made various proposals for delay, discussion, and compromise, all of which were rejected by Austria-Hungary and Germany.

Britain was urged by Germany to accept the principle that the Austro-Serbian conflict should be localized, in other words, to proclaim its neutrality, and by Russia and France to declare its solidarity with them as the only means of stopping Germany from war. Grey, together with the Prime Minister, Asquith, and some other members of the cabinet, believed that Russia could not be expected to stand aside and abandon Serbia, and Grey, attaching great importance to British relations with Russia, refused to exert pressure on Russia to do so or to advise Russia against mobilization. They also believed that an Austro-German victory in the approaching struggle would establish a German ascendancy in Europe which would be dangerous for Britain. On the other hand they could not announce British solidarity with Russia and France because this would have been rejected by the majority of the cabinet and no doubt by both parliament and the country. At the moment, even the limited commitment of 1912 made to France (p. 190) was still secret, as were also the military and naval conversations begun in 1906. Whatever Grey and his group might desire, and they were sure that in its own interests Britain must range itself with France, the temper of the country, at the beginning of the crisis, was predominantly for abstention from the war that seemed likely. Grey privately told the German ambassador that, in the event of war, Britain would be drawn in, but he apparently did not inform the cabinet that he had done so. It was not until Germany had declared war on Russia and sent an ultimatum to France that a promise was given that Britain would defend the northern coast of France against German attack, and even this was made dependent upon the approval of parliament and could be given only because the Conservative opposition promised to support it. As Germany promised not to attack the French coast, the British promise might never have been put to the test had Germany not violated the neutrality of Belgium.

This changed the situation immediately, for the German action persuaded cabinet, parliament, and country of the necessity for Britain to join the war. Grey was later reproached for not making clear to Germany much earlier than he did that the violation of Belgium would be a *casus belli*. This would probably have been useless. The German general staff had only *one* plan for fighting the war, a plan which involved going through Belgium, and Moltke was not alarmed by the prospect of British intervention, which he expected; he was confident that his armies would defeat the French before British help arrived or, if the British did manage to land a small army, that it would be easily beaten. It is quite true, as Germans have often asserted, that for Grey the German violation of Belgium was not the reason for British participation in the war, which he advocated on general grounds, but it is equally true that without the Belgian issue, the British government could probably not have persuaded the British people to accept intervention in the war in August 1914. Ever since 1914 the question has been endlessly debated whether a clear-cut declaration of British solidarity with France and Russia would have prevented the war, but there is no agreement among the publicists, diplomatists, and historians who have written on this question. All that can be said with any assurance is that Grey thought it impossible to make such a declaration and never asked it of the cabinet. Mindful of this controversy, the British government of 1939 did make such a declaration, but it did not stop Hitler from making war on Poland.

Italy, the sixth great power, disapproved of the Austrian action from the beginning. In the light of its own history, it did not think it possible for Habsburg power to suppress the Yugoslav national movement by force; but if it did succeed, Italian interests in the Adriatic would be prejudiced. Furthermore, Italy was unwilling to expose its long coastline to the British fleet. The Italian government therefore took advantage of the failure of Austria, in violation of Article VII of the treaty of the Triple Alliance, to inform its ally in advance of its intended action and to arrange compensation, to declare that Germany and Austria were waging a war of aggression and to proclaim its neutrality—which permitted France to withdraw troops from the Italian frontier and send them against Germany.

Previous international crises were long-drawn-out affairs— Morocco 1905, 1911; Near East, 1908-9, 1912-13—during which diplomacy had time to function. In 1914 only thirteen days elapsed from the presentation of the Austrian ultimatum on 23 July to the declaration of war against Germany by Great Britain on 4 August. Austria-Hungary and Germany hoped to force the other powers into accepting their violent programme. To meet this situation, which clearly caught them by surprise, Russia, France, and Britain were forced to improvise, with not too happy results. Sazonov and Grey kept making new suggestions almost daily, before their previous proposals had made the rounds of the chanceries and been considered, so that the diplomatic situation grew more and more confused. The confusion reached its height on 1 August, when Germany declared war on Russia, at the very moment when both Austria and Russia seemed at last to be willing to negotiate. A little time was needed to determine what the situation was in fact, but the military men, thinking in terms of mobilization time-tables, had begun to take over from the diplomatists. The three emperors, Francis Joseph, Nicholas II, William II, all hesitated long before they consented to the irrevocable measures of mobilization and declaration of war; unhappily, the first was almost senile, the second a weak character, the third volatile and impetuous. Also, among the numerous men who had to make decisions, there was no outstanding personality— no Cavour, Bismarck, or Disraeli—who could dominate the situation.

From 1871 to 1914 the peace of Europe was maintained by the combination of alliances and armaments. In the crises before 1914 governments did not take the plunge because they were not ready for war, were not assured of support from their allies, or did not consider the issue worth fighting for. In 1914 what was at stake was the balance of power in Europe for an indefinite time ahead, and the governments were nearer ready for war than they had been in any previous crisis. Austria-Hungary and Germany insisted on a military solution of the Serbian problem, and clearly wished to upset the *status quo*; Russia, France, and Britain were ready to tolerate a diplomatic humiliation of Serbia but not its military subjugation, and while they were not committed to the *status quo*, they were unwilling to see it altered without their consent. Thus the alliances, which had originally served the cause of peace, when put to the final test, almost mechanically operated to convert a local conflict into a general war.

Likewise the great armaments helped to keep the peace—so long as they were not used. But as soon as one power, in order to reinforce its diplomacy, began to mobilize, its action made military men everywhere jittery, for no general staff was willing to allow a rival to get a start. 'Once the dice were set rolling,' as the German chancellor said, nothing could stop them.

SHORT BIBLIOGRAPHY

Since the end of the First World War, many thousands of diplomatic documents have been published from the archives of Austria, France, Germany, Great Britain, Italy, and Russia, and the work is still proceeding; the Italian papers began with 1861, the French and German with 1871, the British with 1898, the Austrian with 1908, the Russian with 1911. The complete files for the crisis of 1914 are said to have been published. There are also innumerable volumes of memoirs by the principal politicians, diplomatists, and military men which often supplement the documents.

These materials have been used in hundreds of volumes, of greatly varying quality, by publicists, propagandists, and historians; several specialized periodicals, which did not survive the Second World War, were devoted to the causes of the first war and the war itself. Practically all of these books were written before the publication of sources was completed, and so they are all 'dated'. This is true of the present author's three books on which this pamphlet is based: *Triple Alliance and Triple Entente* (1934), *The Annexation of Bosnia, 1908–1909* (1937), *The Coming of the War 1914* (1930). His article 'July 1914: Thirty Years After', in the *Journal of Modern History*, for September 1944 (reprinted in Herman Ausubel, *The Making of Modern Europe* (1951), II, 942–991) is a condensation of his book on the July crisis revised in the light of later materials.

The reader is therefore referred to two books written since the Second World War for the most up-to-date discussion of the years 1871–1914: A. J. P. Taylor, *The Struggle for Mastery in Europe, 1848–1918* (1954), and Pierre Renouvin, *Histoire des Relations Internationales*, Vol. VI, *Le XIXe Siècle:* II, *De 1871 à 1914, L'Apogée de l'Europe* (1955). Each volume contains a full and critical bibliography, from which students may easily select books in practically all important languages. For the crisis of July 1914 Luigi Albertini, *The Origins of the War of 1914*, Vols. II and III (1953, 1957), replaces all previous accounts; ironically enough, the Italian documents for July 1914 had not been released when Albertini wrote.

A. J. RYDER

The German Revolution
1918—19

LIKE other revolutions the German revolution of November 1918 was a product of different causes, some of which formed part of the events immediately preceding it, while others belonged to the less recent past. The revolution began as the improvised revolt of an exhausted and disillusioned population against an authoritarian régime which had brought the country to the verge of defeat. Though it never entirely lost the spontaneous character with which it began, the revolution's further course, after its initial success, was shaped by the attempt of the Left wing of the German socialists to transform it into the classic Marxist revolution to which they had long looked forward. It soon became clear to the Left that the victory of 9 November was largely illusory, but its attempt to extend the revolution was resisted by the Right wing socialists, who had the support of the rest of the population. If the first stage of the revolution was marked by the apparently complete collapse of the old order, its second stage was characterized by an internecine conflict between the two socialist parties which developed into a form of civil war. The Left's attempt to seize power was defeated, but in defeating it the Right had to use means (the Freikorps) which weakened its position and reduced the gains of November. In one sense the failure of the revolution was already evident in January 1919; in a more general sense its failure was not complete till Hitler's accession to power in 1933 destroyed what remained of German democracy. The half-completed revolution left a legacy of unsolved problems to the Weimar Republic, and there came into existence an uneasy balance of forces between the

Right wing socialists and their allies, who were concerned to defend and consolidate what had been gained; the revolutionaries, who, though temporarily defeated, still believed in the victory of their cause; and the counter-revolutionaries, whose efforts to undermine the Republic began as early as the summer of 1919.

The three main strands in the German revolution may be described as democratization, socialization, and demilitarization. Democratization was the task which fell to German democrats, Left-wing liberals as well as socialists, as the result of the failure of the 1848 revolution and of Bismarck's defeat of liberalism. But the desire of the German middle-class parties for a democratic régime was, to say the least, lukewarm; the struggle for democracy therefore had to be waged by the Social Democrats with little outside help. Closely connected with democracy, in the minds of socialists, was socialism. If democracy meant little to them without socialism, they realized that socialism was obtainable only through democracy, for the Social Democratic party (S.P.D.) could put its programme of socialization into effect only if it commanded the majority in a Reichstag that had real power. Both democracy and socialism were contained, implicitly or explicitly, in the S.P.D.'s programme of 1891, which was known as the Erfurt programme from the scene of the conference where it was adopted and which remained the party's official programme till 1921. Demilitarization, the third strand in the German revolution, was of a rather different character. Though it was implied, briefly, in the Erfurt programme, and though it followed logically from the desire to abolish the semi-absolutist state in which the army was not subordinate to the civilian power, it did not possess the same ideological importance as democratization and socialization. In practice, however, the desire for thorough-going reform of the army and for the abolition of all military privilege was one of the strongest impulses in the German revolution. But it was not until the old régime had been discredited by losing the war and presenting the country with the consequences of total defeat that the forces of revolt were strong enough to defy it openly; and even then enough of the old régime survived to make the November revolution a less far-reaching change than appeared on the surface.

I. THE PRELUDE TO THE REVOLUTION

The Russian revolution of March 1917 was interpreted in Germany, especially on the Left, as a warning signal. The government's reaction was to make gestures in favour of constitutional reform, but the measures were half-measures and were pursued half-heartedly. The Emperor's Easter message in April 1917 announced a modest liberalization of the three-class Prussian franchise; this was generally felt, by liberals as well as socialists, to be the very minimum required by the situation. Even this cautious and overdue attempt at reform was blocked by the opposition of the Prussian conservatives, whose sudden changes (of tactics, not of heart), in October 1918, came too late to save the Prussian Landtag, which in its existing form was swept away by the revolution. The success of the Russian revolutionaries was felt as an encouragement by the socialists, especially those of the Left. The German socialist movement, which had been united until the war, was divided after April 1917 into two parties: besides the S.P.D. or majority socialists, as they were now called, there was an Independent Social Democratic party (U.S.P.D.) which consisted of the older party's former Left wing. The reason for the split was a difference over war aims. The S.P.D. voted for war credits, supporting, with some misgivings, the government's claim that Germany was fighting a defensive war, while the U.S.P.D. held that the war was not defensive for Germany since its government had annexationist ambitions. The Independents' ideal was peace without victors or vanquished, but they were in no position to enforce this policy on the German government or generals. Loosely attached to the Independents were the Spartacists, whose main leaders, Karl Liebknecht and Rosa Luxemburg, were in prison after 1916 and remained there till October 1918. The Spartacists, like Lenin, wanted to turn the war into a revolutionary civil war and were completely internationalist in outlook. Their strictly logical and theoretical interpretation of Marxism had little influence among the masses, who disliked the war but could not deny the principle of national defence. Yet the masses were becoming more impatient. In the winter of 1916-17, the full harshness of the blockade was felt for the first time. A cut in the bread ration in April 1917 provoked a strike in Berlin and other cities, among them Leipzig. In Leipzig the strike was led by a workers' council which presented political as well as economic demands. This was the first time such a council had been formed or such demands presented. It showed the influence of the Russian revolution on the German working class.

Another result of the Russian revolution was the Stockholm peace movement. Its failure in the summer of 1917 was a disappointment to German socialists, especially the Independents who put forward very reasonable terms of peace. Desire for peace with Russia and indignation with the German government's delaying tactics in negotiating it at Brest Litovsk were the main motives behind a large-scale strike of munition workers which broke out in January 1918. The strikers, who numbered a million all told, also demanded Prussian franchise reform, better food, and abolition of the state of siege—all demands which were to be repeated during the early days of the revolution. The strike was the last important manifestation of large-scale discontent before the revolution. Though it did not achieve its objects, it was significant as showing the organized will of a large section of the working class despite the prevailing state of siege, which made strikes illegal in Germany, and despite the lack of enthusiasm for strike action of the S.P.D., which did not wish to embarrass the government. Moreover, the committee which led the strike remained in being, and its leader, Emil Barth, began to prepare for the revolution by collecting money and arms and training 'shock troops'. Barth and his colleague, Richard Müller, who had been conscripted for the part he had played in the strike movement, were both representatives of Left wing shop stewards or *Obleute*. These *Obleute* stood to the official Trade Unionists in much the same relation as the Independent socialists stood to the majority socialists, though they were more extreme than most of the Independents, of whose party they henceforward formed the militant Left wing. It was in the course of 1918, too, that the impact of the Bolshevik revolution in Russia became powerful in the U.S.P.D. It cannot be measured with any exactness, but it can be seen in the demand for a policy of proletarian dictatorship, which was supported by leaders of the *Obleute* and their political friends. On the other hand, the smaller Right wing of the Independents, which included the party theorist and veteran journalist Karl Kautsky, was highly critical of the Bolsheviks, whose anti-democratic example they did not wish to follow.

There was a lull in political activity in the spring and summer of 1918 while Ludendorff's great offensive was unleashed. Despite the tactical success it achieved it failed to bring a decision, and with the Allied counter-attack in August Ludendorff realized that Germany could not win the war. The retreat began. In mid-September the Austrian government asked for an armistice; by the end of September the Bulgarians had capitulated. Ludendorff told the government that the army could not wait 48 hours; armistice negotiations must be started immediately. It was decided to broaden the basis of government; this necessitated the appointment of a new Chancellor. Prince Max of Baden, a cousin of the reigning Duke of Baden, became Chancellor of a government which was based on popular support. The S.P.D. were invited, and agreed after some hesitation, to join the government on terms which included the restoration of Belgium with reparations for war damage, parliamentary government in the Reich, and equal franchise in Prussia. The overdue constitutional changes were passed by the Reichstag in October; they made the government responsible to the Reichstag, enabled members of the Reichstag to become ministers (which hitherto had been impossible, under the terms of the constitution) and subordinated the military authorities to the civilian. Germany became a parliamentary monarchy.

This was the 'revolution from above'. It came too late to have the desired effect. Abroad it was seen as a panic move, designed to avert the consequences of defeat; at home public opinion demanded stronger measures. The reality of the Reichstag's new power was not apparent, for it had followed behind events, not determined them. Prince Max was by no means ideally qualified to stand as the leader of the new democracy; constitutional reforms seemed unimportant to the man in the street, who saw that defeat was now inevitable and that the state of siege and the censorship, against which there was considerable resentment, were still being administered by generals. The S.P.D. now found themselves playing a double role: as a popular party they still wished to lead popular discontent, as a government party they had to suppress it. The S.P.D. had long been reformist not revolutionary in outlook, and this trend had been strengthened by the experience of the war years and the defection of the Left wing as the Independent socialist party. Now the party was more or less satisfied with the reforms of October and most of its leaders were prepared to keep the monarchy. The Independent socialists, on the other hand, saw events moving rapidly in their direction. They expected the majority socialists to be discredited by their last minute entry into an unpopular government, as they were already discredited in the eyes of the Independents for having so long supported the government's disastrous war policy. The Independents openly demanded a republic and socialism, there was talk in the Berlin factories in mid-October of an Independent government, and one Independent member of the Reichstag urged the outbreak of world revolution.

Prince Max had begun his armistice negotiations with President Wilson on the night of 3–4 October. He was desperately embarrassed by the Emperor William II's refusal to listen to demands for his abdication, which appeared in a thinly veiled form in Wilson's Third Note of 23 October, and openly among almost all sections of the German population. In the mood of panic which swept over the country the dismissal on 26 October of Ludendorff, the real embodiment of German militarism, made little impact; and Max's government was doomed when the S.P.D. on 7 November sent an ultimatum demanding the Emperor's abdication within 24 hours. It fell on the 9th, with the withdrawal of the S.P.D. members, Scheidemann and Bauer. With Ludendorff went the last chance of a final desperate stand, a *levée en masse*, which Max, rightly no doubt, rejected as futile; but he had not been able to achieve his two main aims of signing the armistice and holding the support of the majority socialists. The latter would now be forced to share office with the Independent socialists, and the revolution, which he knew Ebert did not want, would be inevitable.

Meanwhile the leaders of the Left had not been idle. Nor had they found agreement easy. Barth and his revolutionary committee discussed dates for a rising; the vote of the *Obleute* secured the later of the alternatives (probably 11 November). Haase, the leader of the Independent socialist party, who attended the meeting, advised caution; he preferred to wait for the revolution to mature as the culmination of an inevitable process, rather than force the issue. Barth wrote of Haase that he refused to consider what should be done on 'the morning after the revolution'. If Haase was a lukewarm revolutionary, who, like all the Right wing of the Independents, believed in parliamentary methods, the Spartacists, in Barth's view, erred in the other direction, for they wished to indulge in what he scornfully but not inaccurately described as 'revolutionary gymnastics'. Thus on the eve of the revolution the Left was divided over policy and tactics. The Spartacists knew best what they wanted; on 7 October they met and issued a demand for dictatorship of the proletariat exercised through workers' and soldiers' councils, the nationalization of all property, and the reorganization of the army so as to give power to the soldiers. They had no use for parliament, declaring:

'The struggle for real democratization is not concerned with parliament, franchise or parliamentary ministers and similar swindles; it is concerned with the real bases of all enemies of the people: ownership of land and capital, power over the armed forces and over justice.'

Unambiguous as the Spartacists' programme was, they lacked the numbers which would have enabled them to carry it out. Moreover, unlike the Bolsheviks, whose German counterpart they were, they shared with the rest of the German Left a predilection for organizational freedom and an aversion to the growing centralization and bureaucracy of the S.P.D., from which they, as party rebels, had suffered. The Independent socialists were still at loggerheads, not, as before, over war policy, but over the question of revolution; and the party's loose structure, which enabled the Right and Left wings to coexist in one party, weakened it as a revolutionary force. But while the leaders of the Left in Berlin were still deliberating, the provinces acted.

II. THE SAILORS' REVOLT AND THE REVOLUTION
IN THE PROVINCES

On 28 October the German Admiralty ordered the navy, which was assembled at Wilhelmshaven on the North Sea, to put to sea for a final battle with the British fleet. The sailors refused to obey. The order was repeated, again refused, and then withdrawn. The sailors complained of their bad food, and their overbearing officers; there had already been an abortive rising in 1917, intended as a demonstration in favour of the Stockholm formula for a compromise peace. Now, when an armistice was near, they saw no point in sacrificing themselves to satisfy the officers' desire for death with honour. When one of the squadrons arrived at Kiel sailors demonstrated in the streets, made revolutionary speeches, rioted, suffered some casualties, and elected sailors' councils. At this point the government sent Noske, a prominent Right wing S.P.D. politician, and Haussmann, a Progressive (Left wing Liberal) member of the cabinet, to Kiel to deal with the revolt. Noske, who had specialized before the war in military and naval matters, was welcomed by the sailors; shortly afterwards Haase, the U.S.P.D. leader, also arrived after a telegram of invitation. The two socialist parties were able to co-operate amicably enough, for in truth the sailors were little concerned with differences of socialist ideology. Noske was made successively chairman of the sailors' council and governor of Kiel, and found no difficulty in giving a qualified acceptance of the sailors' demand for the abdication of the Hohenzollerns, abolition of the state of siege, equal suffrage for men and women, and the liberation of political prisoners. But by now the movement had spread to other ports and inland towns. By 6 November Cuxhaven, Hamburg, and Bremen were in the hands of workers' and soldiers' councils. Whereas in Kiel the revolt had been largely non-political, in Hamburg its political aim, socialism, was in the forefront from the beginning. The factory workers joined the sailors, and both were joined by the soldiers. Unable to rely on its troops, the government was powerless. In Cologne a garrison of 45,000 men went over to the revolution almost without a shot. Soon all the towns of the West and Centre were in the hands of workers' and soldiers' councils, which sprang up everywhere with remarkable spontaneity. The leaders of these councils were certainly conscious of the part which workers', soldiers' and peasants' councils had played in the Russian revolution; but, as at first in Russia, the councils were not dominated by one party nor were they usually representative of extremist views. Everywhere they claimed full authority, but they generally allowed the old officials to carry on under their supervision. There was hardly any bloodshed, for there was no opposition.

Meanwhile, independently of the events in Kiel, the revolution had begun in Bavaria. After the Austrian armistice was signed on 2 November the Bavarians feared an Allied invasion through Austria. In Munich an Independent socialist named Kurt Eisner took the lead. Eisner, like Bernstein, the leader of the Revisionist or Right wing group on the pre-war S.P.D., had moved to the Left of the party in 1914 owing to his strong internationalist sympathies and opposition to the party's war policy. On 6 November he addressed a demonstration in Munich which was followed by a march, in the course of which the public buildings were occupied. Bavaria was declared a republic. The majority socialists, who greatly outnumbered the Independents in Bavaria, joined Eisner, who formed a new government consisting of both kinds of socialists with some 'bourgeois specialists'. Here, as elsewhere, the new government was formally approved by a workers' and soldiers' council. Eisner announced that elections would be held for a new *Landtag*, and he optimistically declared that the fratricidal struggle between the two socialist parties was at an end. Even the Bavarian peasants, usually among the most conservative elements in Germany, elected rural councils, almost the only ones to appear in the German revolution.

In Central Germany, and especially in the industrial parts of Saxony, the revolution had a more markedly Left wing character. There the Independents, followed by the majority socialists, proclaimed a republic and declared the government deposed. The elected leaders of the workers' and soldiers' councils of Dresden and Leipzig issued a manifesto on 14 November which asserted that the capitalist system and the bourgeois, monarchical form of government had collapsed, that power had been seized by the revolutionary proletariat, and that the economic system would be socialized, unearned income and bourgeois law-courts abolished, and the people armed to safeguard the gains of the revolution. Government was to be exercised by a cabinet of six, three from each socialist party. But the all-socialist coalition did not last long; a reaction against the extremists soon set in, and their programme was never carried out.

Generalizing about the revolution in the various states and cities of Germany, one can say that the Independent socialists took the lead, even where they were very much in the minority, as in Bavaria; that after the first success of the revolution a reaction set in quickly, and the hastily formed alliance of the two socialist parties, which had been at daggers drawn for nearly three years, ended with a refusal of the majority socialists to support the more extreme demands of the Left wing Independents and Spartacists; and that the latter found themselves trying to establish a dictatorship of the proletariat with only a part of the proletariat on their side. Sometimes a dyarchy existed, where the local workers' and soldiers' council functioned side by side with a pre-revolutionary elected body, such as the city parliament (*Bürgerschaft*) of Hamburg which was at first suppressed and then recalled, or with a state parliament (*Landtag*) as happened later in Bavaria. Such dual control did not prove very satisfactory, and there was friction with the permanent officials, for it was found that administration inevitably involved some exercise of political power. Tension between councils and other elected bodies was especially marked where their political composition differed widely, as it did in Bavaria, where the Independents obtained only three seats in the elections to the *Landtag* in January 1919, compared with 66 won by the S.P.D. and an even larger number won by the middle-class parties. The majority socialists feared that an attempt to carry the revolution further would result in chaos, which would cause starvation, and national disunity, which would be exploited by the victorious Allies. It was for these reasons that the all-socialist government of Prussia issued an order on 15 November that government officials should stay at their posts.

In viewing the German revolution it is as important to see what remained unchanged as to see what changed. The Hohenzollern civil service survived, where those of the Bourbons and Romanovs, in the French and Russian revolutions, did not. And significant as the revolutionary ideology was in determining the character of the policy of Left wing groups, the revolution started in areas (Schleswig-Holstein and Bavaria) where the Independent socialists were weak but where for practical reasons the desire to end the war was especially strong. All through the revolution, too, popular resentment was directed far more against the officers as a class than against capitalists or employers. Officers were stripped of their badges and epaulettes and disarmed, and throughout the Home Army (as distinct from the Field Army) power passed from the officers to the soldiers' councils.

III. THE REVOLUTION IN BERLIN

By 8 November, the day after the S.P.D. ultimatum to Prince Max of Baden, the revolution had triumphed in most parts of Germany, but Berlin remained in the hands of the government, which had concentrated forces against the revolutionary elements that it knew to be strong there. The Kiel revolt took everyone by surprise; even Haase had had no suspicion of it beforehand. It was embarrassing to everyone on the Left as well as on the Right: to the S.P.D. because

213

it was defiance of a government to which they belonged; to Barth and the leaders of the extreme Left because it broke out before they were able to direct and control it. The spontaneity of the revolution, which was traditionally favoured by the Left, and thanks to which the first breach in the citadel of authority had been made, meant, however, that leadership was in the hands of the politically un-trained sailors instead of in those of the trained and organized *Obleute*. The government learned of Barth's plans, and Däumig, one of the conspirators and a Left wing Independent socialist, was arrested on 8 November. Barth, who believed, erroneously, that Liebknecht had also been arrested, ordered his men to make their bid for power next day. When 9 November dawned, the attitude of the S.P.D. was still uncertain; *Vorwaerts*, their principal newspaper, had repeatedly urged the need for restraint and order, and the S.P.D. leaders feared 'Bolshevik chaos'. When, however, news of the Em-peror's abdication had still not come through by 8 o'clock that morning, the order to strike was given by the S.P.D., and the workers left their factories after the morning break and streamed into the middle of the city. The *Obleute* and their followers, whose decision to strike was taken the day before, were merged in the general army of strikers, which moved with impressive singleness of purpose, as though, one eye-witness reported, in response to a single master plan, though in fact no such plan existed. Prince Max, having issued a statement announcing the Emperor's abdication which slightly anti-cipated the event, offered the Chancellorship to Ebert, who accepted it. Max also announced that plans were being made for the election of a Constituent National Assembly, which would decide the future constitution of Germany. He hoped, as he wrote in his *Memoirs*, that the revolution could still be defeated and the monarchy saved, if this assembly could meet and if Ebert could be appointed Imperial Chancellor by him instead of at the hands of the mob. In this way continuity would be assured. Ebert also wanted to save the monarchy, but he abandoned this hope after Scheidemann, at about two in the afternoon, proclaimed the republic to a vast and enthusiastic crowd in front of the Reichstag. That morning one of the most reliable regiments, the 4 *Jägerbattaillon*, which had been sent to Berlin to defend the government, refused to act against the revolution. The government issued an order to the troops not to fire, and the police went home. The revolutionary crowds occupied the public buildings without difficulty, including police headquarters and the Imperial palace. Liebknecht addressed the crowd from the palace, proclaiming the socialist republic. Ebert invited the Independent socialists to join the new government, and *Vorwaerts* of 10 November urged the Independents to grasp the hand of friendship held out to them.

It was not easy for the Independent socialists to decide whether to accept this offer. Differences in policy between the parties were still wide, and were exacerbated by the personal suspicion and distrust which had grown up during the war years. The Left wing Independents saw Ebert and his friends as opportunists who, having done their best to prevent revolution and repress the Independents till the very last moment, now posed as revolutionaries: as Ledebour, a veteran Left wing socialist and leading member of the U.S.P.D. put it, Ebert had smuggled himself into the revolution. Ledebour was opposed to their party taking part in a coalition with the S.P.D. Liebknecht, who shared Ledebour's distrust of Ebert, agreed that they should join the new government for three days only, in order that Germany should have a government capable of signing the armistice, but he wanted the basis of the coalition to be recognition that all legislative, executive, and judicial power lay in the hands of workers' and soldiers' councils. This was too extreme a policy for the S.P.D., which, as we have seen, wished power to be exercised by a constituent assembly. In the end agreement between the two parties was reached, after the S.P.D. had accepted six conditions imposed by the Independents, the most important of which was that the constituent assembly should not meet until after the gains of the revolution had been consolidated. This formula was vague enough to admit of widely differing interpretations, and so it happened. Majority opinion in the U.S.P.D. was that it would be a mistake to refuse to share power at this crisis, for if they stayed out they would leave the field to their rivals. Moreover, the overwhelming wish of the population, as represented in the councils, was for a socialist coalition. In these circumstances the new government was formed; it was headed by a cabinet of six People's Commissars, three of whom were majority socialists, three Independent socialists. The majority socialists were Ebert, Scheidemann, and Landsberg; the Independents Haase, Dittmann, and Barth. The duties of the People's Commissars were allocated as follows: Home affairs and the army—Ebert; foreign affairs and the colonies—Haase; finance—Scheidemann; demobilization and health—Dittmann; press and information— Landsberg; social policy—Barth. Ebert and Haase were co-chairmen; in fact the chair was nearly always taken by Ebert, who was Chancellor as well as leader of the larger party. As late as 10 November Ebert was still thinking in terms of a broad coalition extending from the Independents to the Liberals, but the former insisted that any bourgeois members of the government should have the status of 'technical assistants' only. As the cabinet minutes show, these bourgeois ministers, who were consulted on such matters as socialization, did have considerable influence on the decisions taken.

On the afternoon of 10 November there was a meeting of about 3,000 persons, representing the workers' and soldiers' councils of Berlin, at the Circus Busch. It approved the formation of the new cabinet, but the Left wing Independents, led by Barth, who was chairman of the meeting, tried to enforce their policy on the government by proposing the election of an Executive Council which should have supreme legislative power and to which the People's Commissars should be responsible. Barth wished the Executive Council to consist entirely of Independent socialists, but his attempt to pack it was strongly opposed by the soldiers, who demanded parity between the two socialist parties in the Executive Council as in the cabinet. Finally an Executive Council was elected which consisted of 28 persons, of whom 14 were soldiers. Of the 14 civilians 7 were S.P.D., 7 U.S.P.D. The Council was later enlarged to include representatives of the parts of Germany in the East and West occupied by the Allies. Its exact relationship to the cabinet was not defined, and the powers it claimed were so wide as to make friction between itself and the cabinet inevitable.

It was on the same day (10 November) that Ebert had the first of his fateful telephone conversations with General Groener, who had succeeded Ludendorff as Quartermaster General. The agreement made between them was that in return for the support of the army Ebert promised to combat Bolshevism, by which was meant an attempt by the Spartacists and their friends to seize power. On his side Ebert undertook to recognize the officers' power of command in the Field Army, which Groener was trying to shield from the demoralization that had already undermined the army at home. One of the first decisions of the new cabinet was concerned with this problem, and on 12 November it sent a telegram to the High Command containing an assurance that the officers' power of command remained and that military discipline and order must be upheld under all circumstances. This policy was not liked by the Independents, but they agreed to it because they knew that, if the Field Army lost its discipline, it could not retreat in good order to a line east of the Rhine by 12 December, as was required by the armistice terms, and that any soldiers left behind would automatically become prisoners of war. Hindenburg and Groener recognized the formation of soldiers' councils in the Field Army as an inoculation—the word was their own—against more extreme measures, but ordered that they were not to replace the officers in giving orders but to limit their functions to matters of welfare.

Ebert was responsible for relations with the army in his capacity as one of the People's Commissars, but the generals still saw him as Chancellor of the Reich, which, technically, he had been during the thirty hours or so that had elapsed between his acceptance of the Chancellorship from Prince Max and his confirmation in the Circus Busch as chairman of the cabinet of People's Commissars. During this period Ebert had issued a number of decrees as Chancellor, and it was only because he was a more or less constitutionally appointed successor to Prince Max that the officers' corps and senior civil servants recognized him. Simons, who was one of Prince Max's most trusted civil servant advisers, wrote:

'It is quite unthinkable that the old officers and officials would have offered their services to the new government had the Prince not given it some shred of legitimacy.'

Thus by the evening of 10 November Ebert was ruling, in effect, in a double capacity. For the supporters of the old régime he was Chancellor, and there had been no organic break with the past. For the revolutionary part of the population he was chairman of a revolutionary cabinet, approved by the workers' and soldiers' councils exercising the popular will. This double commitment involved a double policy: the question was whether the various obligations which he had taken upon himself were mutually compatible. Events were shortly to show that they were not.

IV. THE REVOLUTIONARY GOVERNMENT AND THE CONGRESS OF COUNCILS

It is impossible, in the space here available, to follow the course of the German revolution in detail. It must suffice to indicate the main problems which arose and how those responsible tried to solve them. As we saw at the beginning, the revolution had three aspects or strands: democratization, socialization, and demilitarization. We have now to consider how far the revolution was successful under each of these headings.

The very fact that power was seized by workers' and soldiers' councils, and that the Reichstag was ignored, shows that the constitutional reforms of October had made no impact on the ordinary person. The régime was paying the price for its long resistance to reform, the Reichstag was paying the price for its long acquiescence in that policy. In form, at least, government by councils was a popular, and to a large extent, proletarian dictatorship, though many soldiers, of course, were not proletarians. But, as we have seen, the policy of most of the councils was moderate. Even where the Independents had a share of power—in Bavaria, for example—the

P   217

government did not confiscate the banks or interfere with the economy. Nor did the councils conceive of themselves as a permanent substitute for parliament, as soon became clear. They came into existence to fill the vacuum left by the old régime, and they gave the ordinary man for the first time experience of the practical exercise of power. The Independent socialists had never made government by councils one of their demands, and it is significant that there is no mention of them in a policy manifesto issued by them on 5 October. But now that the councils were in being the Independents seized on them as the institutional instrument of the revolution and relied on them to provide the revolutionary *élan* which alone would enable the new government to carry out its policy of socialism. There was one difficulty: the councils involved the *de facto* disfranchisement of the middle and upper classes, and were thus incompatible with the complete democracy for which socialism traditionally stood. Haase and his friends were in a dilemma: hitherto democracy and socialism had been seen as complementary, now they seemed to conflict. The escape Haase sought was to accept in principle a constituent assembly but to postpone its meeting until after the councils had had time to carry out socialization. The demand for a constituent assembly, except on the extreme Left of the U.S.P.D. and among the Spartacists, was strong and widespread, and the cabinet agreed to it, except for Barth, who on many issues found himself in a minority of one against his Independent as well as against his S.P.D. colleagues. It was agreed by Ebert that the question of a constituent assembly should be decided by a special national congress of workers' and soldiers' councils which was to meet in Berlin in the middle of December. To the dismay of the Left, this congress voted in favour of such an assembly by a large majority, and fixed the election for 19 January, a date earlier than the one originally proposed. The Right wing of the Independents accepted the decision; the Left adhered to its view that if the constituent assembly met it would kill the revolution.

Socialization was also discussed at the congress of councils and a resolution passed in favour of its being started 'forthwith'. It was evident at the congress as it had been in the cabinet that socialist opinion on this subject was divided between those who wanted to socialize rapidly and those who wanted to do so gradually. The cabinet had set up a socialization commission headed by Kautsky, who himself favoured a cautious approach, to inquire into the whole subject and make recommendations. The report was not ready till January, and in December, when the congress of councils met, Ebert was reluctant to legislate in advance of its findings. There was a widespread fear among socialists, Independents as well as majority socialists, that any property socialized by the government might be earmarked by the Allies for reparations. There was also a belief that it would be unwise to socialize industry at a time when it lacked raw materials and capital, and that the resulting dislocation would alarm the employers and make it harder for the economy to absorb the millions awaiting demobilization. As for land reform, entailing the break-up of the big estates east of the River Elbe, it was feared that such a move would dissuade the landowners and farmers from sowing next year's harvest, and thus endanger the country's food supply, especially as the amount of grain in stock was calculated to last only until 1 February. The attitude of the trade unions was affected by an agreement which had been drawn up on 18 November between them and representative employers in the Ruhr. By this, the employers recognized the unions as the sole representatives of the workers, granted an eight-hour day without loss of wages, and agreed to the formation of arbitration committees which were to exist at different levels of industry to regulate wage claims and similar matters. The trade unions saw in this agreement a substantial success. The employers, who early in October had seen the revolution coming and planned this concession in order to forestall it, considered that they had thereby averted the greater danger of socialization. The extreme Left denounced the agreement as a betrayal of socialism. It certainly blunted the edge of the revolution in its economic aspect.

The third aspect of the revolution, demilitarization, was the subject of the stormiest debate at the congress of councils, and a resolution was passed unanimously in favour of far-reaching reform of the army and its democratization. The resolution was introduced by a majority socialist from Hamburg named Lampl; hence it is usually known as the Hamburg or Lampl Points. The main provisions of the Points were that power of command in the army was to be exercised by the People's Commissars under the supervision of the Executive Council, that all badges of rank were to be abolished, that officers should be elected by the men, and that the standing army should be replaced by a popular militia. Ebert knew that the High Command would never accept these Points, and Hindenburg soon declared his rejection of them; but Ebert did not think it politic to oppose them at the congress. The generals considered them a breach of his promise to them on 10 November. On the other hand, the great bulk of socialist opinion, majority as well as Independent, supported the Points. A showdown between the socialists and the generals could no longer be avoided. At a cabinet meeting which was attended by Groener, Ebert temporized, telling Groener that the Points did not apply to the Field Army in the East (which was still deployed in what had been the Russian Empire) and that, as regards the Home Army, implementation instructions would be issued shortly. Every day's delay favoured the generals, for it brought nearer the date on which the constituent assembly would meet. (Hindenburg had written to Ebert on 8 December urging, among other things, that the assembly be convened in December.) The wish of the majority of socialists of both parties had been to rely, not on the Imperial Army, which was in process of demobilization anyway, but on republican forces which had been brought into existence by the revolution. Berlin had a *Sicherheitswehr* or police force commanded by an Independent socialist named Eichhorn, a *Republikanische Soldatenwehr* or civic guard commanded by a majority socialist named Wels, who was the commandant of Berlin, and a *Volksmarinedivision* of revolutionary sailors who had come from Kiel to defend the government. The cabinet also decided to form a *Volkswehr* or national guard to consist of 11,000 men. These various forces were of little or no military value, however, partly because they were divided among themselves (Eichhorn *versus* Wels), partly because they lacked the will to fight, and partly because their officers, who were elected, lacked authority. A proposal made early on in the revolution by Däumig for the establishment of a Red Guard was rejected by the soldiers' councils, which considered that they could give adequate protection to the government. On the Left there was a strong tradition of anti-militarism and a long-cherished belief that force was a weapon worthy only of reactionaries; socialists, it was held, could reach their aims without recourse to it, by appealing to men's reason and conscience. This aversion to force was reinforced by the war-weariness that resulted from long years of irksome discipline and harsh conditions. It is not surprising that the German working class was unwilling to continue to bear arms, even for the sake of the socialist republic; but it was, nevertheless, disastrous, as was very soon evident.

The congress of workers' and soldiers' councils, at which a decision was made on these three main themes of democracy, socialism, and army reform, has been called the revolutionary parliament. It was the climax of the revolution, the forum in which the hopes and fears unleashed by the revolution found expression, and its debates were the most important which the period produced. It made two things very clear. One was that the bulk of the German working class wished to live in a parliamentary state; the other was that in regard to socialization and demilitarization it wished to carry the revolution very much further than the leaders of the S.P.D. were willing to go. The congress ignored the warnings of those on the Left who argued that these policies could never be carried out through parliament, but only through the proletarian dictatorship of workers' and soldiers' councils. It also ignored the warnings of those on the Right who pointed out the dangers of over-hasty socialization. The congress almost certainly believed, as did many people at the time, that the constituent assembly would have a socialist majority; by-election results at the time justified this expectation. Considerable attention was paid to the view of Cohen, one of the majority socialist speakers at the congress, that an attempt to govern Germany permanently by means of councils would lead to a civil war. Within a month of the congress's dispersal two things had happened which upset their calculations: the election of the constituent assembly took place and failed to produce a socialist majority; and the unleashing of an armed rising by the extreme Left in Berlin brought into play counterrevolutionary forces in the shape of the newly created Freikorps. Thus the congress resolutions proved incompatible.

V. THE RESIGNATION OF THE INDEPENDENT SOCIALISTS AND THE JANUARY RISING

On 23 December there began in Berlin the episode known as the sailors' revolt, of which it is impossible to do more than give the barest summary. The quarrel started when the sailors, who were truculent as they feared disbandment, refused to obey a government order to evacuate the royal palace in which they were quartered. Their reaction was to march to the Chancellery, declare Ebert and his startled colleagues arrested, and to arrest Wels, the commandant, against whom they had a grudge, and imprison him. Ebert thereupon telephoned the army, telling them to act against the sailors to secure Wels's release. Next morning the army appeared in force and shelled the palace. When the sailors surrendered an hour later, Wels was released, but about thirty people had been killed. Meanwhile an attempt at mediation between the government and the sailors had been made on the initiative of the Independent socialists. There exist various accounts of this tangled and deplorable episode; they conflict with one another, and the truth is difficult to establish. The main significance of the affair is that it led directly to the resignation of the Independents from the government. They refused to believe Ebert when he said that he had told the army to save Wels's life, claiming that his intention had been to crush the sailors, not to save Wels. Moreover, the Independents were justifiably indignant with Ebert for consulting his S.P.D. colleagues, but ignoring his Independent colleagues before speaking to the army. They accused Ebert of bad faith. The dispute was referred to the Central Council.

This was the successor body, on the national level, to the Executive Council, which now was concerned only with Berlin. The Central Council had been elected by the congress of councils, and consisted solely of majority socialists, the Independents having decided to boycott it at the insistence of their Left wing, who considered the powers assigned to it by the congress inadequate. The folly of this boycott was now apparent, for in a dispute between the two socialist parties the all-majority socialist Central Council could hardly side with the Independents. It gave a conciliatory answer to a number of questions put to it by the Independent members of the cabinet, but the latter were bitterly aggrieved, and resigned (28 December).

The final breach between the Independents and their S.P.D. colleagues was but the culminating point of a series of disagreements ranging, as the cabinet minutes and Barth's memoirs testify, over all the major subjects of home and foreign policy. Distrust between them had been greatly increased by a combination of episodes that had occurred on 6 December, when soldiers acting under government orders had fired on a crowd of demonstrating Spartacists, killing 16 and seriously wounding 12. Ebert was suspected of collusion with Right wing elements, and in consequence the extreme Left became more aggressive. Liebknecht's followers marched armed, almost daily, through the streets of Berlin, and the Spartacist press denounced Ebert as a counter-revolutionary. A manifesto issued by the Spartacists at this time proclaimed that the rule of the working class could be established only through armed revolution of the workers, of which the Communists were the forerunners, and that the constituent assembly would be counter-revolutionary. To this the S.P.D. in *Vorwaerts* of 22 December replied that Liebknecht was inciting to civil war but that the workers of Berlin would not support him. The more provocative Spartacus was, the more dependent on the army Ebert became. Yet the sailors' revolt made plain the limitations of this help, for the soldiers who were sent to suppress it showed that they sympathized with the rebels. Like most of the troops of the old army who had been sent to Berlin by agreement between Ebert and the generals, they quickly succumbed to the revolutionary atmosphere of the capital and to the desire to spend Christmas with their families. The lesson drawn from the sailors' revolt by Groener was that the old army must be written off and reliance placed only on the Freikorps which were then being formed, in the first place to protect the Eastern frontier from the Poles and the Russians, and in the second place to combat the Spartacists, in both cases under the slogan of anti-Bolshevism.

The resignation of the Independent socialists removed the last safeguard against the outbreak of a civil war that had been threatening for some time. The extreme Left optimistically believed that the government could not prevent it from seizing power. It was not appeased by the resignation of Haase and his colleagues, which had come too late to heal the breach (if such a thing was ever possible) between the Right and Left wings of the Independent party. The Spartacists had at last decided to part company with the Independents, whom they blamed for co-responsibility for, or connivance at, the policy of the hated Ebert government. At the end of December the Spartacists and other tiny Left wing groups founded the German Communist party. In its first programme the new party declared that it would 'never take over the power of government except by the clear, unambiguous will of the majority of the proletarian masses in Germany'. At the same time it decided, against the advice of its best leaders, including Rosa Luxemburg and Karl Liebknecht, not to take part in the elections to the constituent assembly. Though small, it was not a united party, and, as a comparison between the policy urged by its chief organ, *Die rote Fahne*, and its day to day activities shows, its practice did not match its theory. There was a strong likelihood that the revolutionary *Obleute* would join the Communists, but negotiations between them broke down. At the same time the *Obleute* and Left wing leaders of the U.S.P.D. were on very bad terms with Haase, for political not personal reasons. Haase, despite these difficulties, was optimistic about the future; he wrote on 1 January that the first phase of the revolution was over, but the revolution itself would go on. This was also Rosa Luxemburg's belief; the second phase, she declared, would see the social and economic revolution which would complete the political one.

Berlin at the end of December and beginning of January was the scene of gigantic demonstrations by hostile crowds, one S.P.D., one Spartacist, both claiming to represent 'the people', both denouncing the other for terrorism. Many of the demonstrators were armed. The government could hardly carry on, being almost a prisoner in its own capital. The cabinet was now united, two majority socialists having been co-opted to replace the Independents. One of the new men was Noske, who became responsible for army matters. At this crisis he was made commander-in-chief of Berlin and given the task of suppressing the Spartacists, who controlled a large part of the city. The rising, which began at this time (6 January), was touched off by an attempt of the Prussian government, which, following the example of the Reich government, now consisted entirely of majority socialists, to dismiss the police chief, Eichhorn, whose Left wing sympathies were well known. Eichhorn defied the dismissal order, and the Left treated it as a *casus belli*. A revolutionary committee consisting of *Obleute* and Spartacists met and declared the government deposed. The declaration was signed by Liebknecht, Ledebour, and an *Obmann* named Scholze. The rising was badly organized and much of the armed help on which the rebels counted did not materialize. The Spartacists seized newspaper offices and other buildings, but by the end of the week (11 January) the government had begun its reconquest of the city. Noske had collected the Freikorps, which proved more than a match for the Spartacists. The rebel leaders, Rosa Luxemburg and Liebknecht, who had refused to leave Berlin despite the danger, were arrested, taken to the headquarters of the *Garde-Kavallerie-Schuetzendivision* in the Eden Hotel, and murdered in cold blood while on the way to prison at Moabit. Ledebour had already been arrested. The first atrocities, which were to be a tragic but characteristic feature of the latter stages of the German revolution, now took place, and included the shooting and mishandling of prisoners.

Within a few days of the Spartacist rising in Berlin the constituent assembly was elected. The results gave 38 per cent of votes cast to the S.P.D. and 7 per cent to the Independents. The S.P.D. invited the latter to join them in a coalition which would necessarily have included at least one non-socialist party; the offer was brusquely rejected, for the murder of Luxemburg and Liebknecht had widened the breach between them. The majority socialists, desiring a broadly based coalition, formed a government with the Progressives and Centre. On 6 February the constituent assembly met at Weimar and passed a provisional constitution. Ebert became President, Scheidemann Prime Minister.

VI. THE CONSEQUENCES OF REVOLUTIONARY FAILURE

The establishment of parliamentary government with the meeting of the constituent assembly at Weimar and the formation of a bourgeois-socialist coalition government in February 1919 marked, in a formal sense, the end of the German revolution. The régime of workers' and soldiers' councils was over, though many Independents in them put up stiff rearguard opposition to their loss of power. The council idea was retained in the Weimar constitution to the extent that specific economic functions, and even limited political ones, were assigned to workers' councils in industry (*Betriebsräte*). In the new, provisional Reichswehr which replaced the old, Imperial Army, there was no place for soldiers' councils, and all hope of putting the Hamburg Points into effect vanished after the January rising. The Spartacist attempt to seize power flared up in other places besides Berlin. In Bremen the Spartacists and Left wing Independents declared a dictatorship of the proletariat which lasted only a few days and was supported only by a minority; then Bremen was occupied by Noske's forces, who reinstalled the majority socialists in power. Similar outbreaks occurred elsewhere and were similarly suppressed. The Left wing Independents, who had been disillusioned by their failure at the polls in January, were embittered by Noske's use of reactionary Freikorps to crush revolutionary movements. Many individual majority socialists regretted this dependence on the Frei-korps, but saw no other way of meeting the Spartacist challenge. The industrial workers felt cheated because they had not got socialism, and in the Ruhr took steps to seize the coal mines. The government passed a framework socialization act, but this was not followed by socialization as the Left understood it. General strikes broke out in many districts, including Berlin, where street fighting followed, in the course of which 1,200 people lost their lives.

The political consequence of these events was that the Independent socialist party abandoned its belief in parliamentary methods of achieving socialism, and at its conference in Berlin in March adopted a programme which included for the first time a demand for proletarian dictatorship to be exercised by workers' councils, adding the qualifying phrase 'as representatives of the great majority of the nation'. Significantly, this qualification was dropped at the party's next conference at Leipzig in December 1919. In Bavaria the ex-treme Left declared a council dictatorship in April; this tragi-comic régime was suppressed by the army with bloodshed. The final consequence of the shift to the Left inside the U.S.P.D. was the party's split in October 1920 and the absorption of a considerable part of it into the Communist party. Their experience of the Weimar régime made many socialists reject parliamentary democracy. On the Left many people still believed that a revolutionary situation like that of November 1918, of which they felt so little use had been made, would recur, and next time they were determined not to bungle it through democratic inhibitions. As to the S.P.D., it had a thankless task, having to shoulder most of the unpopularity acquired by the government that signed the Versailles treaty, and to make the compromises which its situation as a partner in coalition governments demanded. These compromises brought it the scorn of the Left, without winning it respect from the nationalist Right. The general election of June 1920 placed the Weimar coalition in a minority. Socialization and demilitarization had not been put into effect; now it appeared that even democracy was in danger, less than three months after the failure of the Kapp Putsch, both from the Right and from the Left. The republic had become, in Scheidemann's vivid phrase, a candle burning at both ends.

VII. CONCLUSION

The German revolution suffered from a threefold handicap, which, it may be said, doomed it from the start, and which was inherent in the historical circumstances that gave it birth.

First, the revolution, like the Weimar Republic which followed it, was the product of defeat. This meant that for a large section of the population the revolutionaries were traitors, and democracy and socialism were associated with national humiliation. The stab in the back legend, which cast its baneful shadow over the Weimar Republic, had its origin during the days of revolution and defeat; in its crudest form it implied that the Left wanted Germany to lose the war in order to impose its reforms. For this reason opposition to the men of November 1918 was much greater than it would otherwise have been, especially among the middle classes.

Secondly, there was the fact that the socialists were divided. This division was beginning to appear before the war, but the war brought it to a head, and the gulf between the two wings of German socialism was widened by the Russian revolution. How could a revolution succeed when the leaders of one party were satisfied with the reforms of October 1918 and considered the revolution over on 9 November, while those of the other (especially its Left wing) saw in the events of that day only the beginning of the changes they desired?

Thirdly, the German revolution did not conform to the type German socialists had been trained to expect. They thought in terms of Marxist revolution, in which the capitalist economic system would collapse. What happened in Germany in November 1918 was not a collapse of capitalism, but a weakening of state power owing to military defeat. If the capitalists were without capital and raw materials at the time, that was due to the blockade and the lost war, not to any inherent weakness of the system. The revolution began in mess-rooms and barracks, not in factories and workshops, and the enemy was the officer not the employer. That the revolution was a rejection of militarism rather than of capitalism was recognized even by Liebknecht, who wrote in *Die rote Fahne* of 19 November 1918:

'The bulk of the soldiers are revolutionary against militarism, against war and the open representatives of imperialism: in relation to socialism they are still divided, hesitant and immature.'

Liebknecht also admitted that by then many of the proletarian soldiers and workers 'fondly imagined' the revolution to be over, and wanted nothing but rest and demobilization. But neither in Marxist theory nor in S.P.D. tactics had it ever been expected that the revolution would start as a trial of strength between soldiers or sailors and officers. When the army High Command through its pact with Ebert became a factor in the political struggle the Left had no comparable force to use against it. As we have seen, the Left expected to win political power by weight of numbers and rejected the idea of forming a Red Guard. Its failure to win the election of January 1919 outright was a disappointment, and a blow to the party theorists, who expected the socialist vote to be commensurate with the working class share of the population, which was over half. When, in January 1919, the small group of Spartacists and *Obleute* resorted to force, they were overthrown by the Freikorps. Scheidemann, writing later of the Kapp Putsch of March 1920, saw it as a consequence of the rôle which the Spartacists had provoked the Freikorps to play: 'without Ledebour', he put it, 'there would have been no Lüttwitz'. (Lüttwitz was the Reichswehr general who was Kapp's accomplice.) Thus the Left should either have refrained from using force altogether, or built up a republican force that could have played the part of a Red Army. Had it chosen the second alternative, civil war would have been inevitable. It is unlikely that the Left could have won such a war, nor could the Allies have been counted on to refrain from intervening, as the example of Hungary was to show. By using force, even though inadequately and inefficiently, the Left provoked the nationalist Right, and thus endangered nearly all the gains of October and November 1918.

In themselves, the gains of the November revolution did little more than complete the formal democratization of Germany's political structure which Prince Max of Baden's constitutional reforms had begun. The dynasties were deposed, class franchise in the states was abolished, the secret ballot was guaranteed, votes were given to women, and proportional representation was introduced. Psychologically, the November revolution was important for the sense which it gave to the ordinary man that he was free, that he could exercise some degree of political power, that at last reform could come from below, not only, as so often in Germany, from above. It is difficult to assess the effect of the revolution on the country's social life, but it certainly existed. On the other hand, the republic's failure to infuse a new spirit into the civil service and the judicial system was a mistake for which it was to pay dearly. That the revolution had failed in so far as it was socialist was evident by the spring of 1919; and it was a realization of this which caused the Independent socialists to abandon democratic socialism and brought about their estrangement from the Weimar régime. That the revolution was a partial failure in so far as it was liberal and democratic became clear soon afterwards, as (among other things) the success of the Right- and Left-wing extremists in the general election of June 1920 showed. Thus the weaknesses and incompatibilities which resulted from the half-completed revolution were inherited by the republic to which the revolution gave birth, and were reproduced in that republic's troubled history.

NOTE ON BOOKS

There is no definitive history of the German revolution in English. The causes of the revolution are well analysed in Arthur Rosenberg's *Birth of the German Republic* (London, 1931) and its main features are described in the first few chapters of the same author's *History of the German Republic* (London, 1936). A useful selection from the findings of the Reichstag Committee of Inquiry into the causes of the German collapse in 1918 is contained in R. H. Lutz's *Documents of the German Revolution* (Stanford University, California, 1932). This Committee's official Report in 12 volumes (Berlin, 1925–28) is a mine of information for those who read German. Several books of memoirs by those who took part in the revolution have been translated. Among them are Prince Max of Baden's *Memoirs* (2 volumes, London, 1928) and Philipp Scheidemann's *Memoirs of a Social Democrat* (2 volumes, London, 1929). An Independent socialist account is Heinrich Stroebel's *The German Revolution and after* (London, 1928), while Paul Froelich's *Rosa Luxemburg* (London, 1940) gives the Spartacist point of view. Light on the revolution in the provinces is thrown by Albert Grzesinski's *Inside Germany* (New York, 1939) and Toni Sender's *Autobiography of a German Rebel* (London, 1940). Autobiographical material on the revolution is contained in the early part of Ruth Fischer's *Stalin and German Communism* (London and Oxford, 1945). A general study of the S.P.D. during the war and the revolution is A. J. Berlau's *The German Social Democratic Party*, 1914–21 (Columbia U.P., 1949). Rudolf Coper's *The Revolution which failed: Germany in 1918–19* (Cambridge U.P., 1955) is an unbalanced book and must be used with caution.

The following is a short list of recommended books in German:

Barth, Emil, *Aus der Werkstatt der deutschen Revolution* (Berlin, 1919).
Bernstein, Eduard, *Die deutsche Revolution* (Berlin, 1921).
Ebert, Friedrich, *Schriften, Aufzeichnungen, Reden* (2 volumes, Dresden, 1926).
Froelich, Paul, *10 Jahre Kreig und Bürgerkrieg* (Berlin, 1924).
Haase, Ernst, *Hugo Haase, sein Leben und Wirken* (Berlin, n.d.).
Ledebour, Georg (ed.), *Der Ledebour Prozess* (Berlin, 1919).
Liebknecht, Karl, *Ausgewählte Reden, Briefe und Aufsätze* (East Berlin, 1952).
Meyer, Ernst (ed.), *Spartakus im Kriege* (Berlin, 1927).

Meyer, Ernst (ed.), *Spartakusbriefe* (2 volumes, Berlin, 1922–6).

Müller, Hermann, *Die November Revolution* (Berlin, 1928).

Müller, Richard, *Vom Kaiserreich zur Republik* (2 volumes, Vienna, 1925).

Müller, Richard, *Der Bürgerkrieg in Deutschland* (Berlin, 1925).

Noske, Gustav, *Von Kiel bis Kapp* (Berlin, 1920).

Prager, Eugen, *Geschichte der U.S.P.D.* (Berlin, 1921).

Schüddekopf, Ernst (ed.), *Heer und Republik: Quellen zur Politik der Reichswehrführung*, 1918–33 (Hanover and Frankfurt, 1955).

Tormin, Walter, *Zwischen Rätediktatur und sozialer Demokratie* (Düsseldorf, 1954).

W. N. MEDLICOTT

The Coming of War in 1939

I. THE LEGACY OF VERSAILLES

THE outbreak of a second world war on 1 September 1939 might have been expected to produce in due course a great controversy on 'war guilt'. But there has been nothing comparable with the debate which took place during the nineteen-twenties on the 1914 issues. The angel of peace, in the words of Dr. Walther Hofer, was murdered, killed consciously and deliberately, in 1939.[1] The assassin, by general agreement, was Adolf Hitler. Even in Germany, political trends in the post-Nazi era have made a break with the past expedient, and it has been nobody's business to defend the fallen superman. In so far as there has been any serious controversy among historians it has concerned the relative delinquencies of those powers which failed to stop him.

How did it come about that Germany, the conquered power in 1918, was able to regain her strength and to make war so successfully in 1939 and 1940? There are a number of answers to this question and they all arise, directly or indirectly, from the peace settlement which followed the First World War.

In the moment of defeat Germany was prepared to make large concessions to the demands of the victorious Allies, but she retained both a sense of grievance and the basic resources of a powerful state. The peace of Versailles was sufficient to confirm the one without permanently destroying the other. Deepest of all German assumptions was that the war had been fought in self-defence and that the

[1] W. Hofer, *War Premeditated 1939* (1955), p. 11.

231

defeat was both a humiliation and an accident. There remained a grudge against the world, an inner consciousness of unfairness, which confirmed pre-war beliefs that Germany was surrounded by jealous neighbours who were determined to deny her her rightful place in the sun. The terms of the peace treaty strengthened but did not create this feeling. It is not easy for apprehensive neighbours to judge whether severe or prolonged defeat has killed the desire of a defeated power for revenge. It had certainly not done so in the case of Germany after 1918.

But the victorious powers had differing views as to what precautions they should take. The British and Americans believed that militarism had been fostered by the German imperial régime before the war and that a change of constitution might mean a change of heart; it was therefore hoped that the majority socialists who dominated the new Weimar Republic would repudiate war. But their alliance with the Reichswehr made this difficult. Lloyd George believed that the trial of the Kaiser would be a warning against aggression, but he was uneasy at the prospect of excessive demands for indemnities which would alienate the German people. The French, conscious of the superior economic potential and manpower of Germany, wanted something more than a parliamentary régime. They wanted, but failed to secure, the permanent reduction of the German base of aggression in the Rhineland.

The peace treaty accordingly embodied compromises, which to the Germans emphasized in the vividest possible manner the humiliation of defeat, without giving France the sense of security that she sought so desperately. The Allies were certainly insulting in tone and manner, although this was a product of war feeling which had its counterpart on the German side. The drastic reduction of Germany's armed forces, and even the taking of her colonies, were governed by fear of leaving her with the material resources and strategical positions suitable for a future war. It was difficult to deny the existence of a case for reparations to repair damage done to Belgium and northern France, and the Allies recognized in Article 232 that the amount should be based on Germany's ability to pay. Germany's chief territorial losses in Europe were to France and Poland; in both cases she restored territory which she had taken by force of arms at earlier periods. Her chief grievance between 1920 and 1924 was the excessive size of the reparations demands, and the apparent determination of France to make this an excuse for permanently crippling her.

But France did not succeed in doing this, and after 1924 she had to accept the alternative British policy of conciliating Germany by restoring her position as a great power. So between 1925 and 1932 'unarmed' Germany was able to secure a number of considerable diplomatic successes. The Locarno agreement of 1925 was followed by Germany's admission to the League of Nations in 1926; the Dawes scheme of 1924 gave Germany reparations figures that she could meet; there was a further scaling down of the figures by the Young Plan of 1929, and reparations were virtually abolished in 1932. Allied troops evacuated the Rhineland ahead of time in 1930, and Germany's right to rearm was recognized in principle at the end of 1932. Vast foreign loans were secured which produced a period of considerable prosperity between 1925 and 1929. But the policy of fulfilment, in spite of its advantages, failed to popularize the republican régime, partly because of the inexperience of its leaders; although several men of considerable ability emerged, no politician of outstanding popularity was associated with it. When the world economic crisis hit Germany the promise of Hitler and the National Socialists to relieve this distress led to their rapid increase in importance after the summer of 1930.

Thus the story of the nineteen-twenties is one of failure to solve, although not perhaps to understand, the German problem. Many French leaders and politicians remained convinced that there were powerful militaristic forces in Germany which might launch a war of revenge if their political representatives were allowed to seize power. But the Ruhr occupation of 1923 discredited direct action, and the decisive victory of the Left in the elections of May 1924 was in effect a demand from the French people for tranquillity in terms too powerful to be ignored. In Great Britain the conviction that Germany was a reformed character, and that the best hope of keeping her in the path of virtue was to trust her, strongly reinforced the policy which Briand, the French foreign minister, labelled *apaisement*; but it has to be remembered that no French government was prepared to compromise its security by sacrificing its military superiority. Thus the earlier policy of 'appeasement' was one of limited concessions made in the hope that the Weimar régime would stay in office and accept the peace settlement; when the world economic crisis made the government of Heinrich Brüning increasingly shaky between 1930 and 1932 the French faced the insoluble dilemma of having to choose between substantial political and financial concessions in order to keep Brüning in office, and a refusal of such help with the consequent risks of the accession to office of one of the extremist parties. The acquisition of power by the Nazi régime in 1933 simplified the problem to the extent of confirming French views as to the unwisdom of military concessions, but the bad odour which the new German government speedily created through its domestic policies did nothing to increase the willingness of the

French people for foreign adventures. In Great Britain too the government was watchful, apprehensive, but inactive. As France had been disillusioned by the Ruhr occupation, so the non-success of intervention in Russia in 1919 and Turkey in 1922 had discredited in England attempts to overthrow the Nazi or any other post-war régime by force. The disarmament movement was at its height in 1933 and 1934, and while the Labour party in opposition deplored Hitler's domestic policy it also blamed its own government for luke-warmness towards disarmament and a lack of sympathy towards Germany's legitimate aspirations.

From 1933 until the spring of 1938 Germany's conduct was at times alarming, but never sufficiently so to produce any forceful reaction from her neighbours. Indeed, concessions continued. She had already recovered her status as a great power, and rid herself of reparations; by the spring of 1936 she had commenced to rearm, reoccupied the Rhineland, and recovered the Saar territory. In spite of much apprehension abroad, Great Britain and France were still prepared to accept repeated modifications of the peace treaties; the strong anti-war feeling in both countries, and the widespread acceptance of the view that the Versailles treaty was morally and politically untenable, meant that, as Rauschning and some of Hitler's more conservative advisers told him, Germany could have secured almost any reasonable demands put forward in conciliatory language. He was prepared on occasion to talk for hours about his desire for peace, or, as he said in a speech in January 1937, 'to collaborate loyally in getting rid of those problems that are a cause of anxiety to ourselves and also to the nations'. But his ultimate aim was no less than the hegemony of Europe and he had no taste for the real but limited advances that could be secured through the accommodating tactics of the later Weimar era.

The policies of the two western powers were hampered however by other causes than their popular pacifism and their uncertainty as to Hitler's aims. In the years before 1914 Russia had been acceptable to both powers as an ally in a future war with Germany; but the Bolshevik seizure of power in November 1917 ended the wartime association and added new fears to older suspicions. Soviet foreign policy after 1917 passed through various stages in its relations with other European states; but there seemed to be no adequate ground for the belief that the ultimate objective of world revolution, to be achieved through the setting-up of workers' republics in the existing capitalistic states, had been consciously or permanently abandoned. Expediency merely dictated from time to time a postponement of this objective. The treaty of Rapallo in 1922 established close relations, both military and political-economic, between Germany and

Russia and enabled von Seeckt to continue his secret rearmament plans and to re-create the *Luftwaffe* on Russian soil. But Stresemann, and still more, Brüning, found collaboration with the west more profitable. Stalin's success in the struggle that followed Lenin's death was followed by the inauguration of the first Five Year Plan in 1928. During the period of the first Plan, Soviet foreign policy was primarily defensive: it consisted in the opening up of normal economic and diplomatic relations with foreign powers and the signature of pacts of non-aggression with Russia's neighbours, but there was no pretence of any acceptance of their political outlook. These were rather obvious precautionary moves resulting from the cooling of Russo-German relations. The violence of the Nazi propaganda campaign against Communism and Russia in and after 1933 made it obvious that the Soviet Union could no longer regard Germany as a shield or buffer against the west, and as a reinsurance Soviet foreign policy now entered a phase of more active co-operation with the League powers. The Soviet Union welcomed the French scheme for an eastern Locarno, joined the League in September 1934, and in May 1935 signed a pact with France by which each of the two powers undertook to come to the other's assistance if attacked by a third great power. At the same time Stalin continued from 1935 to 1937 to put out feelers for an agreement with Hitler.

Russia played her part in the sanctions policy against Italy in 1935–6, although she did not display any desire to do more than the other member states; she protested against their attitude towards Fascist aggression in Spain in 1937, and in Austria and Czechoslovakia in 1938. On the other hand, the tone of the Moscow press remained, from 1935 onwards, consistently hostile to England, and to a lesser degree to France; the three great purges of high officers and officials (the last in March 1938) produced voluminous and explicit denunciations of British, French, German, and Japanese intrigue; Stalin's desire for a long period of peace in order to secure the success of his industrial programme was repeatedly proclaimed; it was, in fact, easy to draw the conclusion that the Communist in his heart of hearts still saw little difference between one 'capitalistic' state and another, and that, while he was willing to bluff Germany into good behaviour by protestations of League solidarity, he had no serious intention of being drawn into a major war in defence of other states.

This at least was the belief of many French and British politicians. France's dilemma was that she distrusted both the Soviet and the German governments. Yet she was not strong enough to dominate a Europe in which both were hostile to her. She did not wish to ensure the triumph of Communism in central Europe, but she desired even less to join Germany in an anti-Communist crusade. She would have preferred to rely on a strong and well-armed Britain, but British governments were one stage further away from the continent; they were slow to rearm, more ready than France to take the risk of conciliating the Germans, less ready to bring themselves to the point of formal defensive commitments to Moscow. France however did not add a military convention to the Soviet-French mutual aid pact of 1935. A further complication was the opportunism of Italy and Japan.

After a sly and not unskilful playing off of the Anglo-French against the German theses in the rearmament negotiations in 1933 and 1934, Mussolini attempted to profit from the ensuing deadlock by seizing Abyssinia in 1935. This is the classic Italian policy which was to fail in the Second World War as it failed in the First: Italy did not have the skill or the restraint to maintain a genuine neutrality, to balance indefinitely between the two sides. Even although Laval, the French foreign minister, was prepared throughout 1935 to facilitate Italian aims in Africa and frustrate the attempt of the League to impose sanctions, Mussolini found his dramatic rôle so much to his taste that he ended in 1937 with an open quarrel with France and Great Britain and with an open threat to their Mediterranean interests. His entanglement in the Spanish Civil War forced him to reassure himself by drawing closer to Germany; on 6 November 1937 Italy joined the anti-Comintern pact (concluded by Germany and Japan on 25 November 1936), and on 12 December Italy announced her decision to leave the League of Nations. The quarrel with France and demands in due course for the cession of Tunis, Corsica, Nice, and Savoy were deliberately enflamed by Mussolini and Ciano in 1938 and 1939. Neville Chamberlain's attempts from the autumn of 1937 onward to remove Anglo-Italian differences led to somewhat easier relations with England, although Mussolini enjoyed himself on occasion by shouting insults at the 'bleating democracies', and many Englishmen regarded him as the one implacable enemy of the British Empire.

While Italy was thus providing a serious diversion of French attention from the rising menace of Germany, Great Britain was uneasy as to her Mediterranean communications with the Far East and her defences there against Japan. If Russia was Japan's Public Enemy Number One the Japanese threat to British possessions in China was sufficiently real to constitute a greater and more direct challenge to the British Empire than any that had emerged in Europe before 1939. The British government could not undertake a major war in the Far East so long as its forces might be needed in Europe; but it offered in November 1937 to support the United

States government with substantial naval forces if it would take the lead in employing sanctions against Japan. This President Roosevelt was unable to do, and the Japanese advance into China continued. These events had a major influence on the course of European diplomacy, for they enabled Hitler to distract his potential European opponents by parading the anti-Comintern pact, which although ostensibly directed against the Communist International was important mainly as a threat of future German-Japanese co-operation in all fields.

Among German's potential opponents there was little doubt by this stage as to the likelihood of some German offensive in the near future. There was still, however, a basic difference of opinion as to the nature of Hitler's ambitions and the best way to meet them. In Russia, while Litvinov was the exponent of the policy of collective action against totalitarian aggression, there were continuing hints of an interest, mainly voiced by Molotov, in Russo-German rapprochement; they show that Stalin was prepared in certain circumstances to believe that Hitler's ambitions could be diverted elsewhere.[1] In England Neville Chamberlain, after taking office as Prime Minister at the end of May 1937, sought 'appeasement' by the elimination of grievances, but only in cases in which the grievance was the real obstacle to peace; with regard to Germany he believed that her territorial demands in central Europe and the colonies had some basis in genuine feeling against the peace treaties. He seems to have had a thorough dislike of Germans and of the Nazi leaders in particular; he believed that Hitler was a domestic and international bully, but probably a shrewd man subject to brainstorms rather than a megalomaniac with 'Napoleonic' ambitions. He believed that Russia was military weak and politically untrustworthy. He was prepared in the last resort to acquiesce in the Nazi assimilation of Austria and even of the Sudetan German regions of Czechoslovakia if this came about by some 'peaceful process' and was to be the prelude to a genuine détente. At the same time he held what seems to be the partly contradictory view that Britain could not speak with real weight until her rearmament had reached a point, sometime in 1939, when it would be safe for her to threaten war.

While France maintained what was still believed to be the strongest army in Europe her air defences were deplorably weak. There was a strong disinclination in right-wing circles to embark on any active policy in defence of the central and east European allies

[1] The Soviet Trade Delegation in Berlin also served at times as an avenue for these soundings. J. Erickson, *The Soviet High Command* (1962), gives full details against the background of the purges (Chaps. 12–14). Cf. G. Hilger and A. G. Meyer, *The Incompatible Allies* (1953), pp. 277–80.

whose place in the French security system had been increasingly in doubt since France retired spiritually behind the steel and concrete defences devised by André Maginot in 1930. On 29 and 30 November 1937 Chautemps, the French Prime Minister, and Delbos, the foreign minister, visited London and agreed that the two powers could not act if Germany seized Austria; Delbos, however, insisted that France must fight, in view of her alliance, if Hitler attacked the Czechs. In the United States, Roosevelt, while maintaining an extreme isolationism which excluded all promise of help, even economic, to the western powers, still aspired to lead Europe morally, and was playing in the winter of 1937–8 with plans for a disarmament crusade which could not but have encouraged pacifist sentiment in western Europe. Somewhat incongruously he was also promoting secret staff talks with the British. Thus in spite of wide differences of opinion as to the best tactics to employ, Russia, France, Britain, and the United States were alike in their anticipation of fresh Hitlerite offensives and in their varying degrees of reluctance to oppose him. Each felt that the initiative lay elsewhere.

II. HITLER'S PREPARATIONS

For Hitler the problem by this stage was essentially one of ways and means, the co-ordination of his political schemes with a tight programme of rearmament. There seems no reason to doubt that he deliberately accepted the risks of a major war in 1939, and the fact that he hesitated over some of his tactical moves does not mean that he had no broad or long-term aims. It can be said of him as of Bismarck that with certain precise ends of national interests ahead, he had always several ways in view by which to reach them, and never hesitated to change from one to another if circumstances rendered it advisable.[1]

There was no serious plan for world domination, although the British and other empires would be divided up as an incidental result of victory. He distrusted the water; even a short sea voyage seemed to him to involve major problems of organization, as he once revealed when planning the holidays of post-war Germans. 'Cyprus would be lovely, but we can reach the Crimea by road.' It seems tolerably clear that the return of the colonies was demanded merely as a means of emphasizing the Versailles grievances and not because their possession played any part in his plans for achieving hegemony

[1] This has long been recognized in Bismarck's case and indeed Anglo-Saxon scholars have tended to show unnecessary surprise at what is a universal formula for political success. *Cf.* J. V. Fuller, *Bismarck's Diplomacy at its Zenith* (1922), p. 75; C. G. Robertson, *Bismarck* (1918), pp. 220–1.

in Europe. The United States, to judge from his relatively few direct references to it, was remote, politically distasteful, impossible to fit into his plans, but probably ineffectual. Throughout, from the days of *Mein Kampf* until 1944, the objective was the black-soil region of Russia and east Europe generally, as living space for German colonists. In this he was simply following plans and precedents going back to the First World War.[1] Only here could Germany make conquests that were within her reach and power, and establish the great land empire, approximately double the size of the existing Reich, which would make Germany a world power comparable with the United States. The references to this objective in *Mein Kampf* are repeated in the sequel, *Hitlers zweites Buch*, which was written in 1928 but not published during his lifetime.[2] They form the basis of the programme for conquest which he outlined at the 'Hossbach' meeting on 5 November 1937; they are repeated during the similar planning discussions in 1939, and in July 1940, a few days after the French collapse, he gave instructions for the crowning campaign against Russia.

With this general objective clearly defined in his mind Hitler could persuade himself that he had a rare gift of farsightedness, and he dismissed with some contempt the circumscribed revisionism of his predecessors. He did not share their preoccupation with the 1914 frontiers, the details of which he cared little about except as propaganda material. The problem of ways and means was, however, at once emotional, diplomatic, and strategical. We can detect a conflict, mainly unconscious perhaps, between his lust for great military victories and his canny desire to gain the hegemony of Europe as economically as possible; in this latter aim he was strengthened by pride in his own political flair but also by his memory of the exhausting length of the First World War, by the technical arguments of his military advisers, and by the strong pressure from the lower echelons of the Nazi party to avoid the popular discontent which would follow war privations and losses. To win over or alternatively to unnerve possible opponents was an essential problem from the start, and here too the governing ideas are already present in *Mein Kampf*; he hoped for Italian and English friendship, a free hand against France, and later a free hand against Russia. From 1935 onwards there were vast public exaggerations of Germany's land and air strength and of her invulnerability to blockade, and while he courted Mussolini himself he sent Ribbentrop to London to charm the Englishmen. It was

[1] Cf. Fritz Fischer, *Griff nach der Weltmacht. Die Kriegszielpolitik des kaiserlichen Deutschland, 1914–1918* (1961); Hilger and Meyer, pp. 191–2.

[2] It was published under the title *Hitler's Secret Book* in an English translation in 1962.

already clear to many foreign observers by this stage that Hitler was ready to follow extremely opportunistic tactics—to profess belief in peace, to renounce or parade territorial ambitions, to drop or take up friendships and enmities, even to put aside the anti-Communist creed—if they suited his immediate purpose. But could one conclude that *nothing* was vital to his programme—that self-glorification, the enjoyment of power for its own sake, was his only end? The present writer took somewhat this view in an earlier essay on this subject, published in 1940. He argued that for Hitler the ultimate objective had probably never been more than some half-mystical, ill-defined stroke of politics or war which would produce tremendous glory for Germany and her Führer—an objective quite distinct from the more immediate purpose of destroying various points in the Versailles settlement by a series of risky local triumphs. The defeat of 1918 continued to rankle, and the primary reason why Germany started a new war in 1939 was that she happened to have lost the last one.[1] These views have to be modified in the light of the explicit information as to Hitler's careful planning of the war which has become available since 1945.

There was nothing haphazard in the crucial decision as to the point at which Germany's relative strength could be most profitably deployed against potentially stronger opponents. All the powers were increasing their armaments from 1936 onwards, and Germany's rearmament had not gone very far at that point. One of the decisive limiting factors was the demilitarization of the Rhineland, for this was her main industrial region, with 80 per cent of her coal production, and she could not build up a great armaments industry until this vital industrial base was secure. But the Rhineland was reoccupied without French intervention on 8 March 1936, and the Four Year Plan quickly followed. It was designed on the military side to defeat a future blockade by making Germany self-supporting in essential raw materials, and Hitler's instructions contemplated the preparation of the German Army for a large scale war within four years.

So early a plunge into war had no attractions for the service chiefs, who had a professional preference for overwhelming strength. Hitler took a year to think the matter over, and we find his verdict in one of the most curious documents which has emerged from the war, namely the so-called Hossbach memorandum. This shows Hitler expounding his programme in a big speech to a small gathering of the army, navy, and air force heads (Blomberg, Fritsch, Raeder, and

[1] A. J. P. Taylor in *The Origins of the Second World War* (1961) also argues that Hitler had no long-term plans, and spent the first years of power 'dreaming in his old feckless way' (pp. 68–72).

Goering) and the foreign minister von Neurath, on 5 November 1937. Germany must have more land in Europe, and must take it by force since autarky and other peaceful expedients were useless. What would be the best time to fight? There were arguments in favour of a later date, 1943–5, but he favoured the earliest possible: 1938 or 1939. He agreed that Germany would be much stronger by the later dates, but argued that her opponents would by then have completed their rearmament, and would be stronger still. It was a deliberate choice, against the normal inclination of the professional military men, for 'armaments in width' instead of 'armaments in depth'; it meant building up quickly, from the existing armaments industry, a superiority in aircraft, ammunition, and weapons sufficient to win a series of rapid victories before Germany's opponents were fully rearmed. The choice was between, for example, the use of the existing supplies of steel to put out large numbers of tanks and weapons instead of using them to construct factories and munition works which would insure a bigger ultimate output but would only become fully productive at a later date.

Germany did in fact go to war in 1939, and we know now that her margin of strength was—on paper at any rate—very much less than seemed to be the case at the time. This was partly because of tremendous propagandist boastings about her power, partly because Hitler's violent diplomacy suggested confidence based on strength, partly because the brilliant German victories in 1939 and 1940 were so overwhelming in the field. Her limitations and deficiencies only became public knowledge in the official survey conducted by British and American economists immediately after the war, in 1945. Thus it was discovered that her aircraft production in the autumn of 1939 had been about 675 a month, no more than that of Great Britain; her tank production was less; she had started the war with only three months' supply of aviation petrol, and so on. She had to treble her output of armaments and munitions after February 1942 to meet the demands of war with Russia and America. But all these facts merely prove that in 1939 and 1940 Hitler took a calculated risk which brilliantly succeeded, even if he miscalculated the risks later.

Thus early war, deliberately courted, might be the most economical way to success, and he proceeded to hurry things along in central Europe. The direct line of events leading to the outbreak of war in 1939 commenced with the German annexation of Austria in March and of the Sudeten district of Czechoslovakia in October 1938. Chamberlain condemned German action against Austria in parliament on 14 March, and denied that the British government had given its assent or encouragement to the annexation. 'Nothing could have arrested this action by Germany unless we and others with us had been prepared to use force to prevent it.' In France Chautemps and his cabinet had resigned on 10 March, and a new Socialist-Radical government under Blum was not formed until the 13th, when the German invasion of Austria was an accomplished fact. Blum was succeeded on 10 April by Daladier, with Georges Bonnet as foreign minister. The French and Russian governments both accepted the *Anschluss*. The Moscow press attempted to lay the chief blame on Great Britain, which was stated to have known of, and authorized, the German action.

On 24 April Konrad Henlein, the leader of the Sudeten German party in Czechoslovakia, opened the Sudeten campaign by presenting to the congress of the party at Karlsbad an eight-point programme, which included full self-government for the German areas, and full liberty to profess German nationality and a German *Weltanschauung*; Czechoslovakia should cease to associate herself with the enemies of the Reich, and completely revise her foreign policy. France had an obligation, under the treaties of 25 January 1924 and 16 October 1925, to defend Czechoslovakia against German attack; Russia, by the Czech-Soviet pact of mutual assistance of 16 May 1935, had undertaken to defend Czechoslovakia against aggression if France did the same. The French government on 14 March 1938 and the Soviet government on the 15th informed the Czechs that they would honour their engagements. The British government had always refused to guarantee the frontiers of Germany's eastern neighbours, and its aim was now to discover a 'peaceful solution', although there was never any doubt that a direct German attack on France would be resisted.

Although the evidence is somewhat conflicting it seems on balance to show that in 1938 Hitler wanted the emotional satisfaction of a fight with the Czechs, but not with the western powers, France and England. During May, June, and July, while the Sudeten leaders found repeated excuses for not accepting the increasing offers of the Czechs, the French government's aim was to find, with British assistance, any solution which would spare it the need to honour its formal commitment to fight. But during August it was becoming clear that Germany would probably demand the cession of the Sudeten territory, and would back up her demand by the threat of force; on 12 September, in a speech at Nuremberg, Hitler demanded 'the free right of self-determination' of the Sudeten Germans with such vituperation against President Beneš, and such violent denunciation of Czech atrocities, as to rule out all apparent hope of the 'peaceful procedure' that Chamberlain was still so patiently advocating. When at the Berchtesgaden meeting (15–16 September) Chamberlain agreed to the principle of self-determination for the Sudetens,

Hitler was momentarily pleased at his own economy of effort. But he had said in a directive to the *Wehrmacht* of 30 May 1938 that it was his unalterable intention to smash Czechoslovakia by military action in the near future, and by arranging for a peaceful handing over of the Sudeten-German areas under international auspices Chamberlain would be cheating him of his prey. At the Godesberg meeting (22–24 September) his taste for violence asserted itself, and he insisted on the *appearance* of a violent solution; he demanded the prompt occupation of the disputed areas by German troops, boundary and other matters to be worked out later. Only the forcible procedure, he told Chamberlain, 'corresponds to the dignity of a great power'. Such an advance the Czechs would resist, and France, under the terms of her military alliance, would then be forced to go to war.

The British and French were thus brought to the point of threatening war unless the British requirement of peaceful procedure for future German expansion were accepted. The turning-point in the pre-Munich discussions was Chamberlain's warning to Hitler, given by Sir Horace Wilson at dictation speed on the early afternoon of 27 September, that if France were drawn into war against Germany, the British government would feel obliged to support her. Hitler's angry reaction shows that he understood the message. The first hint of the change of front which led to the Munich agreement is contained in his letter to Chamberlain in reply on the same evening. In his memoirs Duff Cooper supports Churchill in arguing that Hitler's change of tactics was due to the mobilization of the British fleet, but this was not announced until 11.38 p.m., three hours after the receipt by the Foreign Office of Hitler's letter. Although the modifications introduced into the German programme at the Munich conference (29–30 September) were just sufficient to satisfy the uneasy consciences of the French ministers that their formal obligation under the Franco-Czech alliance was not involved, it was certain that the two western powers could not again tolerate a campaign of violence with preliminary vilification against one of Hitler's neighbours.

It seems consistent with these events to argue that Hitler had nearly allowed passion to defeat calculation in his moves in September; he intended to fight France and England in due course (as he told Mussolini on 29 September) but realized that the margin of superiority was insufficient to guarantee victory at the moment. He handled himself rather more cautiously during the Polish crisis a year later. He was clearly in an extremely bad mood for some weeks after the Munich conference, and appears to have drawn two conclusions from the crisis; first, that he had been cheated out of his war with the Czechs, secondly that although the British and French were hostile and unsympathetic they might be unnerved and out-manœuvred in future crises if they were thoroughly convinced of the strength and determination of German policy. He continued to think of *Lebensraum* in 'the east' as his ultimate objective, but was determined to dominate or neutralize the western powers first, and as quickly as possible, either by a successful lightning war or by a war of nerves which would sap their will to resist. Whatever his views in 1938, he felt that he could take the military risk involved in forcing matters in 1939. In a speech to the *Wehrmacht* leaders on 22 August 1939, looking back over recent events, he said that his original plan, which had appealed to him most, had been to start by fighting the western powers, and that he had intended after Munich to establish a 'tolerable relationship' with Poland in order to have his hands free for war with France and England. Ribbentrop did, in fact, make proposals to Beck, the Polish foreign mininster, on 24 October 1938, and Poland was invited to join the anti-Comintern pact. On 26 November Keitel, on Hitler's detailed instructions, drew up plans for an all-out attack on France and England with land, sea, and air forces, in concert with Italy. The document incidentally contains the comment that a break-through of the Maginot line was considered perfectly possible.[1] The aim was above all to knock out France speedily; it was evidently assumed that after this England, deprived of bases on the continent, would be ineffectual, and could be brought to defeat by a sea-blockade and air attack.

However, this plan had to be modified for two reasons. In the first place it was rather too virile for the Italians, who had shied nervously away from an earlier German alliance proposal in May 1938. After Munich the Italian general staff had been pressing Germany for staff talks, and Mussolini gave his consent to alliance negotiations in January 1939, but although the military alliance, the 'Pact of Steel', was finally made with Germany on 22 May 1939 it was with a stipulation by Mussolini (on 30 May) that Italy should not be expected to fight for three or four years. In any case the German-Italian pact was a *pis aller*, for Ribbentrop had failed completely to persuade Japan to enter a tripartite military alliance. In the second place the Poles were not prepared to be accommodating. Hitler had therefore to find means of neutralizing Poland before dealing with France and England.

Poland was a considerable military power, although her strength was over-estimated in some western circles. On the theory that a war on two fronts must be avoided it was unwise—or so the German generals thought—to get involved with both the Poles and the western powers. But although Hitler may have preferred to avoid

[1] *Documents on German Foreign Policy, 1918–1945* (Series D, vol. iv, no. 411). This document has been curiously ignored by historians.

this he was satisfied that the military situation would allow him to risk it, although he intended to avoid simultaneous war with all three of the great powers—France, England, or Russia—either in 1939 or later. Ribbentrop had proposed in October 1938 the return of Danzig (technically a free city, although the Nazis had already a majority there), and an extra-territorial road and railway line through the Polish corridor, thus linking Germany and East Prussia. The Poles had been unresponsive, assuming, no doubt rightly, that acquiescence in the German demands would mean their moral collapse and further demands, although they still hoped for gains, with German connivance, in the final carving up of Czechoslovakia. But Poland reaffirmed her non-aggression pact with Russia on 26 November 1938 and refused to join the anti-Comintern pact in January 1939. Beck seems, however, to have given the impression in talks with the Germans in January 1939 that a bargain was possible, on a basis of some compensation for Poland, and it was for this reason that, after the seizure of the remainder of Czechoslovakia on 15 March and of Memel on the 22nd, there was still hope of Polish acquiescence. Ribbentrop again asked for Danzig and the extra-territorial strip on 21 March, and hinted to Lipski, the Polish ambassador, that Poland might receive some compensation, perhaps in Slovakia. Two days later, Ribbentrop even drew up a draft treaty for a German-Polish agreement, definitely offering part of Slovakia and a 25-year guarantee. This, however, was cancelled on Hitler's orders, perhaps because it would have been too embarrassing if Poland had rejected the offer and then published the details.

It soon became probable that Poland would indeed behave in this defiant way. Hitler's course henceforth was largely defined for him by the British and French governments, which gave guarantees to Poland at the end of March and Rumania on 13 April. The guarantees did not lead him to modify his plans for war in 1939. On 25 March he stated that he hoped for a peaceful surrender of Danzig, but was prepared to annihilate Poland if this were refused; on 3 April, after the Polish guarantee, he instructed the *Wehrmacht* to be ready for war with Poland at any time after 31 August. Thus the guarantees, if they influenced his plans at all, did so by producing a tough reaction. His views on a two-front war are conveniently defined in the document known as the Schmundt minutes of 23 May, the record of another long talk to senior officers. Here he says quite clearly that while his aim would be to avoid simultaneous fighting with Poland and the West, Germany must, if necessary, be ready 'to fall upon the West and finish off Poland at the same time'. He reaffirmed this in his address on 22 August.[1] After the Polish rejection

[1] *Ibid*. Series D., vol. vi, no. 433; vol. vii, no. 192.

of his 'offer' his diplomatic technique was very much that of the war of nerves; direct approaches to Poland were ominously suspended, even to the point of keeping the German ambassador away from Warsaw. In the same way it had been hoped that the conclusion of a German-Japanese-Italian military pact would deter the western powers from intervention in eastern Europe; but the Japanese refused to involve themselves in war with any power except Russia, and England and France were bound to seek Russian aid. An agreement with Soviet Russia was accordingly essential to Hitler's plans and the able German ambassador in Moscow drew from Molotov on 20 May the admission that a satisfactory political base for an agreement might be found. But Molotov made it clear that the Germans would have to propose this, and it was again in all probability the fear of a rebuff which led them to delay doing so until August.

III. ANGLO-FRENCH REACTIONS

It is when we turn to the Allied side that the more complex problems of historical evidence appear, and although a consistent interpretation of British and French policy seems to be possible it must be subject to reservations at some points in view of the paucity of Russian and French documents. The Czechoslovak crisis in 1938 had shown the British government to be tactically somewhat inept, but to be driven by the Prime Minister's stubborn sense of his duty into some unexpected commitments. When Anthony Eden, the British foreign secretary, had offered to stand shoulder to shoulder with the United States in the Far East in November 1937 Norman Davis, the American delegate to the Brussels conference, had said without much beating about the bush that his country was unwilling to pull chestnuts out of the fire for Britain. As Britain had no treaty obligation to defend Czechoslovakia, Chamberlain and Halifax might have used similar language to France when pressed for support in a possible war over Czechoslovakia in 1938. But there was never any doubt that the security and survival of France was of vital importance to Britain, although if it became necessary to fight Germany a better cause than the continuance of Czech rule over the obstreperous Sudeten Germans seemed necessary. There was no question that help to France against German attack would be, in the eyes of the Chamberlain government, such a cause. The result was that as the Sudeten crisis became acute in 1938 Chamberlain, while steadily resisting any commitment to Prague, tightened his links with Paris. He did not want war, he did not think that militarily this was the best time to undertake it, he thought Germany had a case over the Sudetens, he was not convinced that Hitler had Napoleonic ambitions. Nevertheless, if France fought, Britain must fight too. She could not afford a French defeat.

The all-sufficiency of this Anglo-French link in the eyes of both governments seems to be the clue to their conduct not only in the Sudeten crisis but during the twelve following months. The French had begun to lose interest in military collaboration with Russia as soon as British rearmament was undertaken in 1936. From the time of the Chautemps visit to London in November 1937 through the summer of 1938 the French government's sole solution of its problems appeared to be unqualified British support in a war; pressure to this end was of equal importance to Daladier, who thought that France might have to fight, and to Bonnet, who found in British reservations some excuse for not doing so. On the British side it is interesting to note the circumstances of the British promise of a guarantee to Czechoslovakia. In the Anglo-French discussions in London on 18 September 1938 after the Berchtesgaden meeting Chamberlain at first demurred on the ground that a guarantee would help Czechoslovakia rather than France; Daladier replied with a lengthy exposition of French military plans, which still depended (in spite of his acceptance of the Berchtesgaden terms) on the use by French air squadrons of Czech airfields to attack Berlin and the industrial regions of Saxony. 'A British guarantee for Czechoslovakia,' he said, 'would therefore help France in the sense that it would help to stop the German march to the East.' Chamberlain then said that the matter was now quite clear to him (one wonders if it was), and the guarantee was accepted on these terms. Again, when war seemed imminent, Chamberlain gave Daladier at midnight on 25–26 September a firm promise of a British expeditionary force if France went to war with Germany.

The two powers had already reached agreement to act together some weeks before Hitler extinguished the remainder of the Czech state on 15 March 1939, an event which seems to have caused the minimum of surprise to the French and British cabinets. Probably nothing is further from the truth than that Chamberlain lost his innocence, his ingenuous faith in Hitler's good word, overnight. Persistent warnings from both Nazi and non-Nazi circles in Germany as to Hitler's intention to expand beyond the German-speaking territories, together with circumstantial reports as to the imminence of an attack on London from Dutch air bases, had led the British and French governments to reaffirm in February 1939 their intention to support one another in all circumstances. It is interesting to compare the uncomplicated negotiations in this case with the exhaustive and fruitless bargaining forced on the two powers by Molotov in the following summer. Indirect aggression was to be met, following a

French suggestion, by British assurances to the French and Belgian governments that a German attack on Switzerland or Holland would be regarded as a *casus belli*. It was also agreed that Anglo-French staff discussions should deal with the possibility of war with Germany and Italy in combination.

As it happened—and by something of a coincidence—the safety point in rearmament seemed to Chamberlain and his cabinet to have been reached just at the point at which Hitler's occupation of Prague had finally revealed to the world the speciousness of his claim that his only object was to re-unite German minorities. Namier and other writers profess to be puzzled by the fact that the cabinet were willing to guarantee Poland (to whom they knew they could not give direct military support) in March 1939 while they had been unwilling to guarantee Czechoslovakia (whom they also believed they could not directly aid) in September 1938. This is a mystery only to those who ignore the extent to which the British government had been preoccupied with the armaments position since 1937. It is true that in 1938 Chamberlain believed his course to be right in itself, and he still hoped that Hitler would know when to stop. On the other hand Boris Celovsky and other writers are certainly at fault in denying that the state of British armaments played any part in Chamberlain's policy in 1938.[1] He had no doubt as to the deterrent value of powerful French and British forces and arms, and believed that his policy of appeasement would be more likely to succeed if it were based on strength. There are numerous records of anxious Anglo-French discussions on the military position in the summer of 1938. But the cabinet had been warned by the Chiefs of Staff that war was inadvisable before the spring of 1939 (there were other estimates later), and we find Chamberlain writing to a correspondent in March 1938: 'in the absence of a powerful ally, and until our armaments are completed, we must adjust our foreign policy to our circumstances, and even bear with patience and good humour actions which we should like to treat in very different fashion'. On the other hand the diplomatic correspondence shows signs, incidental though they are, of greater confidence in March 1939. On the 23rd Mr. R. S. Hudson spoke to Litvinov of 'the remarkable progress of British rearmament which had completely reversed the previous situation' (of 1938), and Chamberlain on the previous day had told Bonnet that Britain had successfully overcome her air rearmament problems and was now producing about 600 planes a month (as compared with 250 in September 1938).

But we may go further and ask whether military considerations were not also the decisive factor in the abortive Anglo-French-

---

[1] Boris Celovsky, *Das Münchener Abkommen von 1938* (1958), p. 171, fn. 5.

Russian alliance discussions. It is certain that each side assessed un-
favourably the military prospects as well as the political reliability of
the other. The fact that England and France went to war in September 1939 while the U.S.S.R. did not do so is proof of their seriousness
of purpose, but their moves were probably genuinely puzzling from
the Soviet point of view. If we agree, as indeed we must, that in
January and February 1939 they were anticipating a German offensive and drawing together to meet it, we can ask why they did not at
once seek to bring Russia into the combination. Sir William Seeds,
the British ambassador in Moscow, spoke on 28 March of the
'aloofness which had poisoned relations since Munich'. If the
answer is that they did not trust the Russians we must ask why they
sought the Soviet alliance so persistently a few weeks later.

Were they trying to embroil Russia and Germany in war? This is
the most familiar Soviet explanation. It has been argued that
Chamberlain's hesitation to declare himself between 15 and 17
March was due to the situation in Carpatho-Ukraine or Ruthenia,
the easternmost tip of the Czechoslovak state. If Hitler occupied it
the assumption could be that he was about to launch a Ukranian
liberation movement as a preliminary to an invasion of Russia, and
it was only when it became clear that Hitler had assigned Ruthenia
to Hungary and was turning against Poland, France's capitalistic
friend, that Chamberlain, so it is argued, decided to join France in a
guarantee. But in fact it was Rumania, and not Poland, which
appeared on 17 March to be Hitler's next victim. It was in Rumania's
defence that Halifax on the 17th asked Russia, France, and Poland
to join Britain in offering help. A German attack on Rumania could
have been a preliminary to an attack on Russia, and there is no sign
that the British were holding back. As it happened Rumania hastily
denied that she was threatened, and the British guarantee of Poland
was announced on 31 March, because a German attack seemed
imminent; an Anglo-French guarantee was also given to Greece on
13 April, because an Italian attack seemed possible. This procedure
was adopted because Poland had refused on 20 March to be associated with Russia in a four-power guarantee; that there was no
desire in Paris or London to exclude Russia may be assumed from
some uneasy questions in the Anglo-French discussions as to
whether Russia would take a guarantee of Poland ill.

And yet this almost casual elimination of the Soviet government
from the first stage of the guarantee system seems very odd to us
today. The oddness is lessened if we assume a failure to take Russia
seriously in a military or political sense; if she were considered a
useful, but rather minor, factor in the European situation. This, at
least, seems to have been the British approach; the French showed

greater urgency. Even so the French position, as Bonnet put it on 21 March, was that while France must have assistance from eastern Europe in a war against Germany, Polish help was more important than Russian, if a choice had to be made. 'It was absolutely essential to get Poland in,' he said. 'Russian help would only be effective if Poland were collaborating.' We must remember that the British embassy in Moscow, including the service attachés, was steadily and invariably pessimistic as to Russian strength and willingness to co-operate with the west. This had been the case throughout the Sudeten crisis in 1938. On 20 February 1939 the embassy said that in the event of a European war there was every reason to suppose that the Soviet government's attitude would be one of 'nervous neutrality', its main preoccupation being to avoid any course of action, economic or otherwise, that would antagonize Germany. Seeds said much the same on 21 March. Chamberlain's remark on 26 March, that he had 'no belief in her ability to maintain an effective offensive, even if she wanted to', has been much quoted, but it merely expresses the normal doubts of many British service men and diplomats at the time. On 6 March Colonel Firebrace, the military attaché in Moscow, had given it as his opinion that the Red Army considered a war to be inevitable; it would prove a formidable obstacle to an invader, but would have much less value in an offensive war; it had suffered severely from the purge, and it was doubtful whether the country could stand the strain of war. The air attaché thought that the Soviet Air Force was capable of developing little offensive power against Germany.

It might be thought that the long drawn out alliance negotiations with the Soviets in the following summer prove that the western powers, however offhand in March, had woken up in June and July to the desperate need for Soviet military help. But as late as 22 May there is a British Foreign Office memorandum which shows that there had been no change of views as to Russia's limited usefulness.

'It has to be considered that the actual material assistance to be expected from the Soviet Union is not very great. It is true that the Soviet fleet might contain a proportion of German naval forces in the Baltic, and that the Soviet air forces might be able to render some assistance. It is, however, unlikely that on land their military effort could be of very much effect, and even in the matter of furnishing munitions and war materials [i.e. to Poland] their assistance would be limited by the fact that the Russian transportation system is in an extremely backward state.'

When we add to this the fact that at the end of the year the British and French governments thought so little of the Soviet armed forces as to be ready to involve themselves in war with Russia over Finland as a by-product of their plan to secure control of the Narvik iron-ore route, we can hardly doubt that Soviet military power continued to have little value in their eyes. In these circumstances the course of the Anglo-French-Soviet alliance discussions in June and July 1939 takes on a different appearance: it does not suggest desperation on Britain's part so much as a determination to strike a good bargain. Halifax (very much in accord it would seem with Chamberlain on this point) had been unwilling to enter into full alliance negotiations before 20 May, fearing apparently that these would finally drive Hitler over the edge; but he was quite willing to make Soviet participation in the guarantee system dependent on the prior involvement of Britain and France in war. There seems little doubt that but for French, parliamentary, and perhaps cabinet pressure he would not have agreed to the full negotiations even at this point. And again in August, although the Soviet-German non-aggression pact of 23 August was a great shock, the British and French governments showed themselves—much to Hitler's suprise— to be as ready to act without Russia as they had been in March.

But it may also be true that the Soviet government, although no doubt genuinely concerned not to be double-crossed, was moved primarily by consideration of its military position. Although Stalin could see the theoretical advantages of a common front against Germany (instead of allowing Hitler to destroy his opponents one by one) he was probably unconvinced of its military value and also of his own strength. Seeds found Litvinov in the spring of 1939 arguing that France 'was practically done for' and the two British divisions that were to be sent to France did not make much impression. Stalin's frankest explanation of his decision was made in the mellow atmosphere of the supper party on the night of 15–16 August 1942, when Churchill asked him why he 'had double-crossed us at the beginning of the war'.

'Stalin replied that he thought England must be bluffing; he knew we had only two divisions we could mobilize at once, and he thought we must know how bad the French Army was and what little reliance could be placed on it. He could not imagine that we should enter the war with such weakness. On the other hand, he said he knew Germany was certain ultimately to attack Russia. He was not ready to withstand that attack. . . .'

Of course, any discussion of Russian motives is continually frustrated by the absence of Soviet documentation; there are few of the frank and damaging admissions that crop up (so conveniently for the historian) in the British and American diplomatic papers. Nevertheless, when we remember how anxious Stalin was to postpone war against Russia even in 1941 we can well question whether he would have fought in any circumstances in 1938 or 1939 unless directly attacked. He told Churchill in November 1943 among the incidental talk at Teheran that he personally had never believed in 1938 that the Czechs meant to fight. On the same occasion, he said that:

'In the winter war against Finland, the Soviet Army had shown itself to be very poorly organized and had done very badly; that as a result of the Finnish War, the entire Soviet Army had been reorganized; but even so, when the Germans attacked in 1941, it could not be said that the Red Army was a first-class fighting force.'

But after that it had become steadily better. All he criticized in foreign views was the failure to believe that the Soviet Army was capable of reorganization and improvement under the strain of war. He did not deny its weakness when war began.[1] It may also be noted that the recently published Soviet official history of the war gives the routine view that Anglo-French military weakness in 1939 proves that they wanted Russia to do the fighting, but it treats the Soviet-German pact as something distasteful, forced on Russia by her own military weakness.

All that need be added here with regard to the actual course of the negotiations is that they did not, as is still very generally believed, break down because of an Anglo-French refusal to guarantee certain states against their will. The two powers were genuinely unwilling to have on their consciences the charge that they had condoned a Soviet annexation of the Baltic states, and sought to meet the situation in mid-June by providing for future discussion when the need arose in the cases of those states which refused to be guaranteed. But Molotov would have none of this, and early in July they agreed that certain states were to be 'assisted' whether they liked it or not; Molotov's only concession was that the names of such states should be recorded but not published. He refused to include Holland and Switzerland, which stood in the same relations to the western powers as Latvia, Estonia, and Finland did to Russia. The negotiations came to a standstill in July over two different questions. The first was a Soviet demand for the inclusion in the treaty of a definition of indirect aggression which would allow the three powers to intervene in

---

[1] *Foreign Relations of the United States: The Conferences at Cairo and Teheran, 1943* (1961), pp. 553, 836–7; A. Bryant, *The Turn of the Tide* (1957), p. 472; *The White House Papers of Harry Hopkins* (1949), ii, 784.

neighbouring states even where these were under no threat of force; this the British government could not swallow. The other was the Soviet demand for a satisfactory military agreement before the main treaty could be signed. The western powers, who had regarded the pooling of resources as the sequel to a political agreement, found in the military discussions which commenced in August that the process had been reversed: they had first to satisfy the Soviet experts that their own military strength and preparations made them viable allies. What was already becoming a highly embarrassing discussion on this theme was cut short by the announcement of the Soviet-German pact of 23 August.

IV. THE LAST DAYS OF PEACE

This, however, was not the decisive event, although August was the decisive month. For climatic reasons the fighting against Poland must begin by 1 September, and Stalin was able to drive a fairly hard bargain as his price for non-intervention. But what made war certain was the British government's reply in the form of the signature at long last of the Anglo-Polish agreement on 25 August. Poland's unwillingness to accept either the British Treasury's terms for a cash loan or Russian military help had remained unsolved problems throughout the period of the Anglo-French negotiations in Moscow, but now the signature gave Hitler the unwelcome news that the Soviet-German pact would not be followed by a more or less awkward Anglo-French withdrawal. At almost the same time he heard that Italy would not join him in a war with Poland and the western powers, owing to deficiencies in armaments. Ribbentrop claims in his memoirs that at this point he urged Hitler to cancel the attack on Poland. He did postpone the attack for a week.

The resulting manœuvres had sometimes been taken as evidence that he had no desire for a major war in 1939. This however confuses military strategy with diplomatic tactics. The Soviet-German pact certainly makes it clear that he had no intention of fighting Russia at this stage, and his approaches to the British government through Nevile Henderson during the last week in August can be taken to mean that he was seeking to avoid simultaneous fighting against both the Anglo-French forces and those of Poland. But it is also evident that he was attracted by the plan to defeat France as quickly as possible after disposing of Poland, and then to use his U-boats and air attack from French bases for a blockade of England. By the beginning of August he had satisfied himself (this is clear from Halder's diary and other German sources) that the British government's many well-meant efforts to maintain peace were proof that it had lost its nerve, and that he had overrated its resolution in May (as in the 'Schmundt' meeting). Others encouraged him in this view. Dr. Wohlthat's discussions in London with Sir Horace Wilson and R. S. Hudson (18–21 July) had taken place on the initiative of the Englishmen; and although Wilson insisted on Germany's abandonment of aggression as the prerequisite of a comprehensive economic and colonial agreement the mere fact that such an offer was made at all evidently convinced Ribbentrop that the British were desperately seeking to escape from their Polish entanglement. Goering's semi-independent peace feelers through Wenner-Gren, Birger Dahlerus, and other Swedish intermediaries were based on the same assumption; there was never any suggestion that Germany would modify substantially her demands on Poland. Ribbentrop told Attolico, the Italian ambassador, on 25 July that it was a war of nerves, and that Germany would get her way if she made no concessions. As the ambassador in London, Dirksen, took a different view, Ribbentrop ignored him, and relied on an unreliable agent, Rudolf Likus, who reported as late as 28 August that Britain did not intend to engage in a life-and-death struggle. But although Hitler evidently thought it worthwhile to fob off the western powers with some vague offers in order to give himself a free hand for a few weeks while he disposed of Poland, he could not leave the problem of his relations with the western powers in the air; they must either bind themselves to him by some voluntary surrender, or be crushed. As the former was unlikely, war in the west must be waged as soon as practicable, although a few months' delay for stocking-up his oil supplies and other preparations would be useful.

Early on the afternoon of 25 August he had given Henderson what he called a large comprehensive offer, which included a guarantee of the British Empire and of Germany's frontiers in the west, but on the understanding that he must be left to settle as he saw fit the problem of Danzig and the Corridor. He was now prepared to see whether anything would come of this. The British reply, given by Henderson to Hitler late on 28 August, was to the effect that while an Anglo-German agreement would be welcomed, the British could not desert Poland. It suggested direct German-Polish negotiations. Hitler seemed to like this proposal, and believing that it might indicate an Anglo-French desire to find a plausible excuse for leaving Poland in the lurch, put to the British ambassador on the 29th a promise 'to agree to accept the British government's offer of their good offices in securing the despatch to Berlin of a Polish emissary with full powers', who must, however, arrive by the following day. The position was that if the emissary did arrive, negotiations could be broken off on the 31st; if he did not, Poland would have put herself in the wrong. This fatuous plan received its first rebuff when even the accommodating ambassador was led to remark that it sounded very much like an ultimatum; this disconcerted Hitler and Ribbentrop, who replied heatedly. The plan came to nothing. Although Henderson and Coulondre, the French ambassador, thought that a Polish emissary ought to be sent as a last effort at peace, Beck was not prepared to accept any such peremptory German summons, and the British government was not prepared to press him. The time limit expired; the German armies attacked and after an embarrassing delay occasioned by the French hopes of a post-last minute settlement through Italian intervention, Britain and France declared themselves at war with Germany on 3 September.

Could it all have worked out differently? Up to a point everyone could see after Prague where Hitler's ambition was leading, and misunderstanding or negligence was not a major factor as it may have been in 1914. The German problem was the product of a paradox: Germany's achievements before 1914 had created a sense of potentialities which could be satisfied only by greater achievements, and while the sense of potentiality remained after 1920 her place in the world had to be re-won. 'The world is against us; it is always against us,' said Goebbels in October 1938. 'The only question is whether the world can do anything against us.' Hitler was not interested in restoring the 1914 position; from the mid-1920s he had his vision of the well-rounded greater Reich which would satisfy the unfulfilled dreams of the pre-1914 expansionists. But the aim was tolerably well concealed, and it was fear of the Nazi Reich as a destructive force indulging an uninhibited taste for violence which drove Poland, France, and Britain to war.

SHORT BIBLIOGRAPHY

M. Baumont, *La faillite de la paix* (2 volumes, 1951).
A. Bullock, *Hitler* (1952).
E. H. Carr, *International Relations between the Two World Wars* (1947); *German-Soviet Relations between the Two World Wars* (1952).
B. Celovsky, *Das Münchener Abkommen von 1938* (1958).
G. Hilger and A. G. Meyer, *The Incompatible Allies* (1953).
W. Hofer, *War Premeditated, 1939* (1955). The best account of the immediate origins.
W. N. Medlicott, *British Foreign Policy since Versailles* (1940).

L. B. Namier, *Diplomatic Prelude* (1948). Must now be regarded as a pioneering effort. The criticisms by Professor Desmond Williams (see below), and by Mr. D. C. Watt, in 'Sir Lewis Namier and Contemporary European History' (*The Cambridge Journal*, July 1954) are important.

Europe in Decay, a Study in Disintegration (1950) and *In the Nazi Era* (1952), are essays supplementing the above work.

P. Renouvin, *Histoire des relations internationales*, vol. VIII (1958).

A. J. P. Taylor, *The Origins of the Second World War* (1961).

M. Toscano, *Le Origini del Patto d'Acciaio* (1956).

A. and V. M. Toynbee, *The Eve of the War, 1939* (1958); a work of composite authorship in the Chatham House *Survey of International Affairs, 1939–1946*. The fullest and perhaps the best account of 1939 developments.

T. Desmond Williams, 'Negotiations leading to the Anglo-Polish agreement of 31 March 1939' (*Irish Historical Studies*, vol. X (1957), 59–93, 156–92); and 'The Historiography of World War II' (*Historical Studies*, 1958).

Index

257

85559